SEE TIME FLY®

Visualizing and Verbalizing® HISTORY STORIES

VOLUME TWO

A Timeline of History for The Renaissance: 1454 to 1610

Nanci Bell

Gander Publishing
412 Higuera Street, Suite 200
San Luis Obispo, California 93401
(800) 554-1819 • (805) 541-5523

 Printed in Canada. ISBN: 0-945856-28-8

Acknowledgements

This book was written with the help of many people. Thank you to Ben Earl, Katelyn Mirolla, Ariana Spaulding, and Michael Sweeney for their writing assistance and their professional editing; to Jane Miller and Fred Schiller for their earlier work in the trenches; to Valarie Jones for writing and making a beautiful book out of all of this, and Henry Santos for his talented illustrations of our Ivan.

Special Thanks

As we begin visualizing the Renaissance, my special thanks extend, as usual, to the children and adults I have been privileged to teach. As I watched and interacted with them, I realized that not only did they have difficulty visualizing and comprehending language, but they also had enormous information gaps. Many of those gaps were in history. I remember their faces. They weren't sure if the American Civil War was before or after the American Revolution or even Egyptian civilization. History seemed to be an array of random parts, unconnected and unrelated.

Out of my desire to help these individuals came the idea for a Visualizing and Verbalizing® history book with the purpose of creating an imaged timeline of history. Little did I know what a long journey it would be. Thank you.

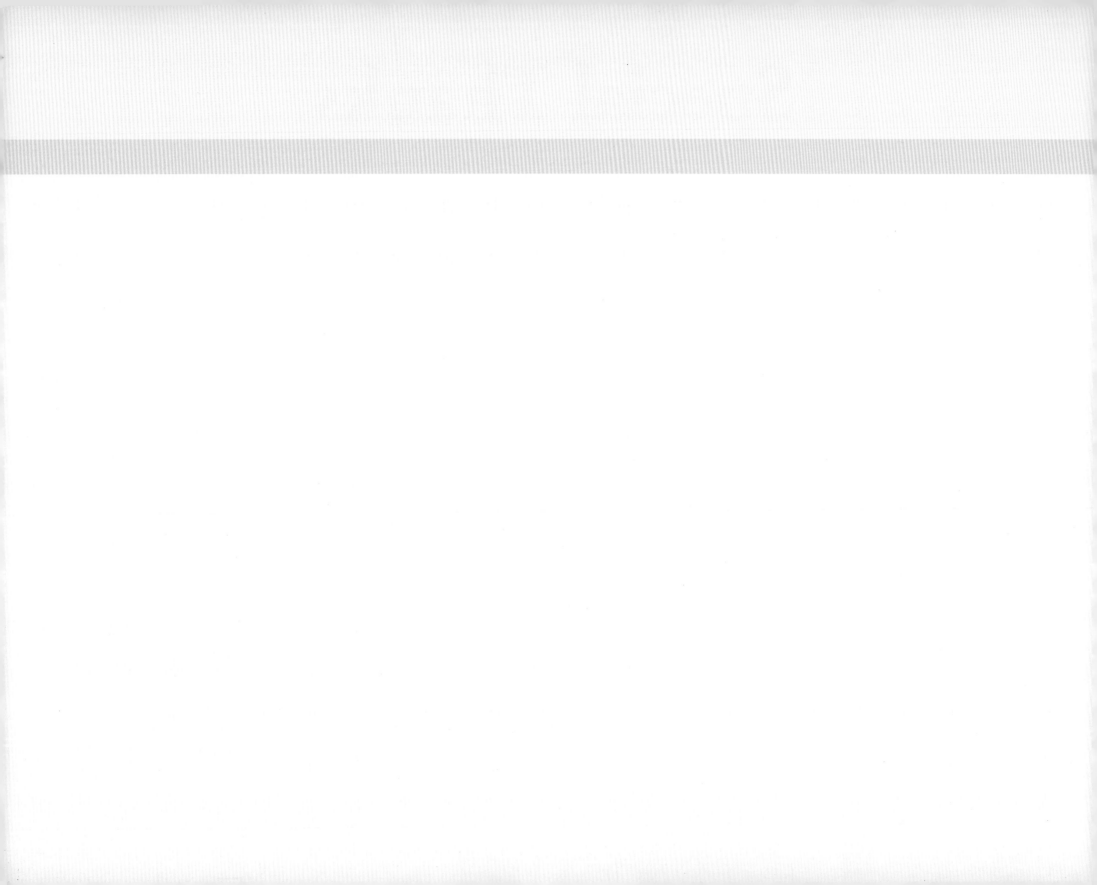

To Rhett

You are with me always.

I love you.

Introduction

The *See Time Fly®* books are a timeline of history, primarily Western Civilization. The purpose is twofold: 1) develop gestalt imagery for language comprehension and critical thinking, and 2) teach an imaged timeline of history.

The paragraphs are written to support the *Visualizing and Verbalizing® for Language Comprehension and Thinking* (V/V®) Program. Each Flight-section has five paragraphs and five higher order thinking skills (HOTS) questions per paragraph. The first question is generally a factual recall question. The remaining four questions address main idea, inference, conclusion, and prediction.

The paragraphs in each Flight create a gestalt for that historical event, place, or person. However, the paragraphs are also self-contained so that an imaged gestalt can be stimulated from just one paragraph. This means students don't have to complete a whole Flight in one lesson, they can instead do one or two paragraphs one day and the rest the next day.

The paragraphs sometimes consist of five sentences so that a V/V® Sentence-by-Sentence lesson can be easily accomplished. However, in writing this it soon became clear that it would be difficult to teach some areas of history within the confines of five sentences per paragraph; hence, some paragraphs have many sentences. Those paragraphs can either be split in half for Sentence-by-Sentence lessons, or they can be used for Multiple Sentence or Whole Paragraph lessons.

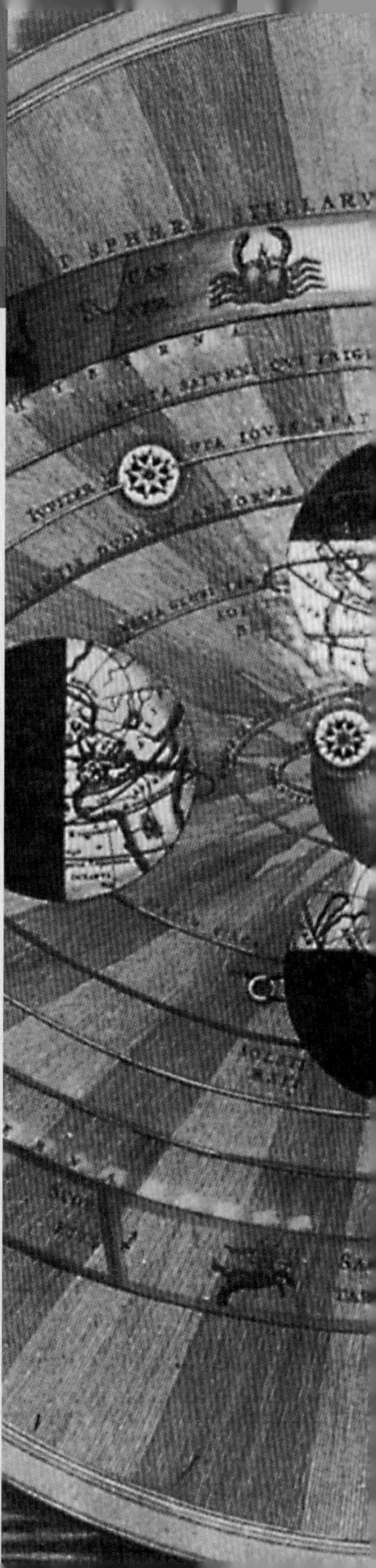

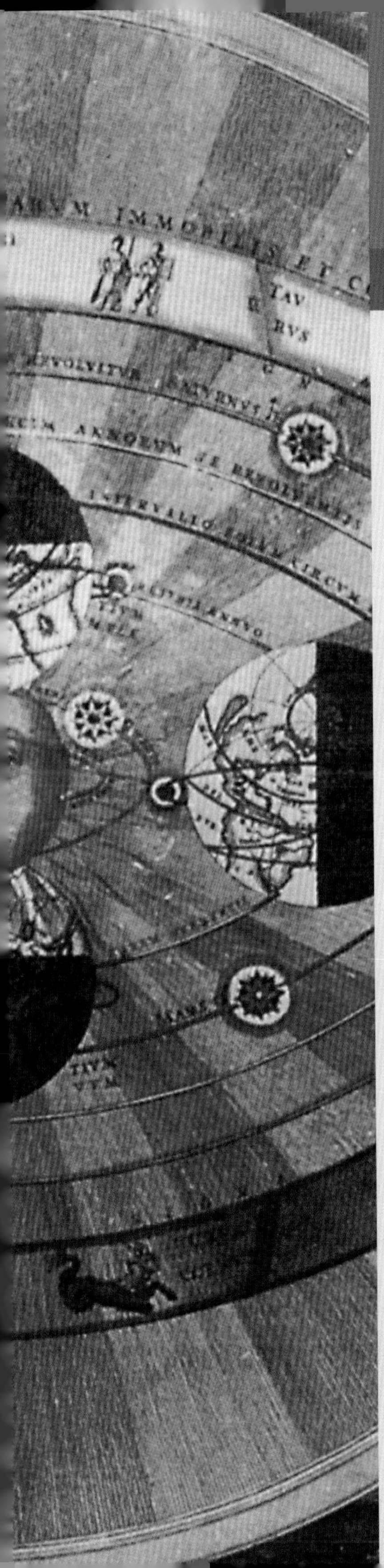

The readability of *See Time Fly*® ranges from approximately fourth to eighth grade. The readability was often affected by names and places, but the paragraphs are appropriate for middle school through college. All ages of students should have access to a visualized history timeline.

The Flights were chosen for their significance in history, but not all historical events could be included. The purpose is to create a visualized timeline on which students can then add more information. An internal visualized timeline allows students to accurately place new information. Historians don't always agree on a specific date or even some specific information. In fact, some Renaissance references had three different pairs of dates for this period in history. We have done our best to settle on the dates, based on extensive research. Our primary sources included World Book Encyclopedia®, Encyclopedia Britannica® and National Geographic®, among dozens of other books and websites.

Ivan the Cat guides the Flights. For many people, a great history teacher made history come alive—made it interesting. Ivan does that. He is the history professor we all wanted. His goal is to give the student a "set" at the beginning of the Flight, and a "close" at the end of the Flight. He often sets the next Flight with imagery. He teaches history and entertains with his silly humor of wanting to eat, sleep, and trick.

And now, we begin the imagery of the Renaissance, from approximately 1454 to 1610. Remember, you can teach this—you can do anything.

Nanci Bell
November, 2004

Meet Ivan

a.k.a. *Ivan the Great*

Hello again. Right. It's Ivan the Cat here—often known as Ivan the Great, King Ivan, or just plain King of the Neighborhood.

I'm your history professor. Remember? We met on our trip from early human life through the Middle Ages, in *See Time Fly, Volume One*. Oh, yes. We had some great imagery flights from one startling event to another.

As the most interesting history professor, my goal is to take you on an imagery-journey to help you create an imaged timeline of history. Your flight schedule takes you into the Renaissance to meet some famous artists, explorers, rulers, and writers. Sometimes history just floats around in random bits and pieces, but not with me. I'm going to help you see a big picture of history, so that when you learn more history you can place it on your own visualized timeline.

Let's get started, because this is one of the most colorful and important periods in history—THE RENAISSANCE. I've got my paintbrushes and books and I'm ready to fly you on "IMAGINE AIR" through Europe and the New World for a grrrrreat time with history.

First things first. Renaissance means rebirth. In this case, it means a rebirth of interest in the classic art, philosophy, and literature of ancient Greece and Rome. Because of the Renaissance, people created many masterpieces that we still *oooohh* and *aaaahh* over today. And there were discoveries in science and medicine, too.

Let's back up a bit and get the big picture going here. You see, the Dark Ages was right before the Renaissance. It was a time of superstition. Even education was viewed with suspicion, and many people actually thought books were evil, maybe because most people couldn't read them. Books were burned and, sadly, much knowledge was lost. The Renaissance, which began in Florence, Italy, brought culture out of the Dark Ages and into the light. Knowledge was king again...although no threat to King Ivan, of course!

Before we begin our first Flight, I want to be sure you have a good picture of me. I'm smarter than the average cat. I have two main things I love to do, and I do them very well. I EAT and SLEEP. I have a third thing I love to do, and that is play tricks on my human, but I'll try to behave while we're on our journey together.

It's just you and me. You're special. Remember, you can do this. You can do anything.

Let's fly!

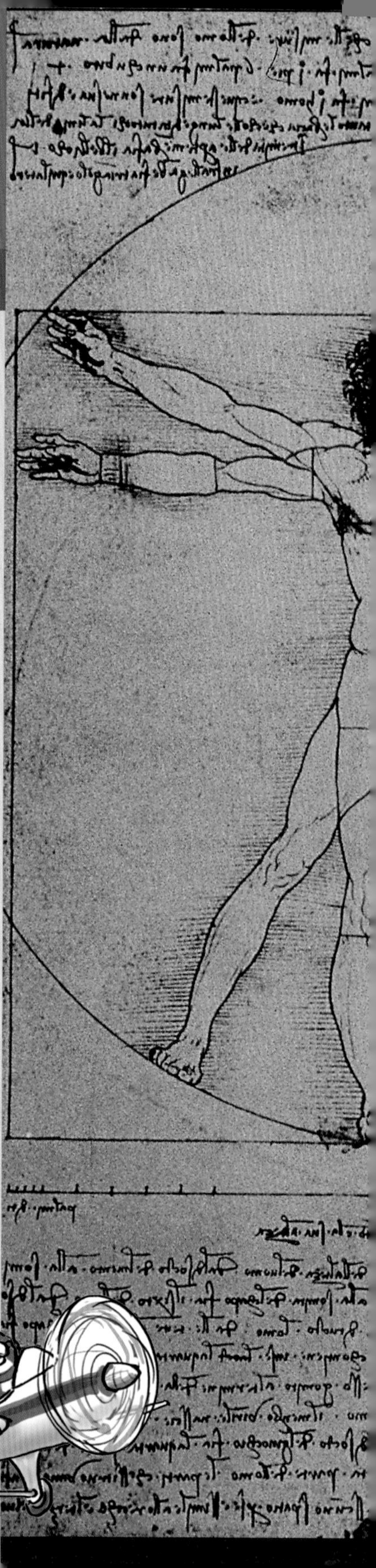

Imagine Air

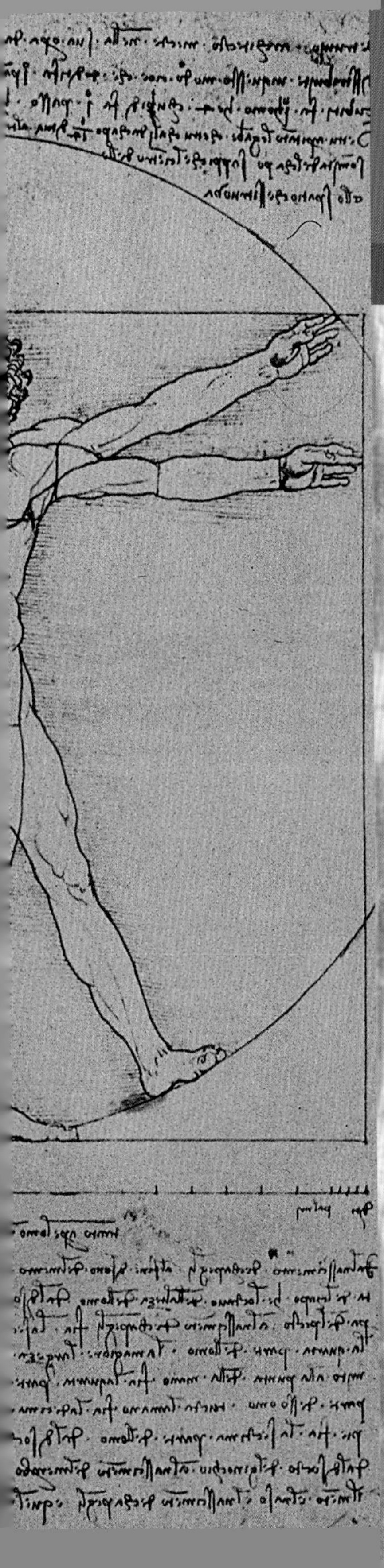

Flight Information

Early Renaissance

Flight Information

High Renaissance

Flight Information

Late Renaissance

EARLY RENAISSANCE

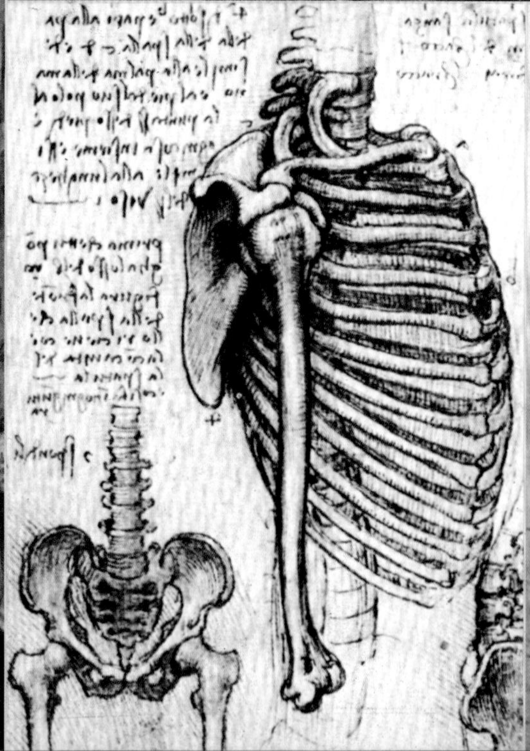

TINA
PVLCH
NVLLA TA

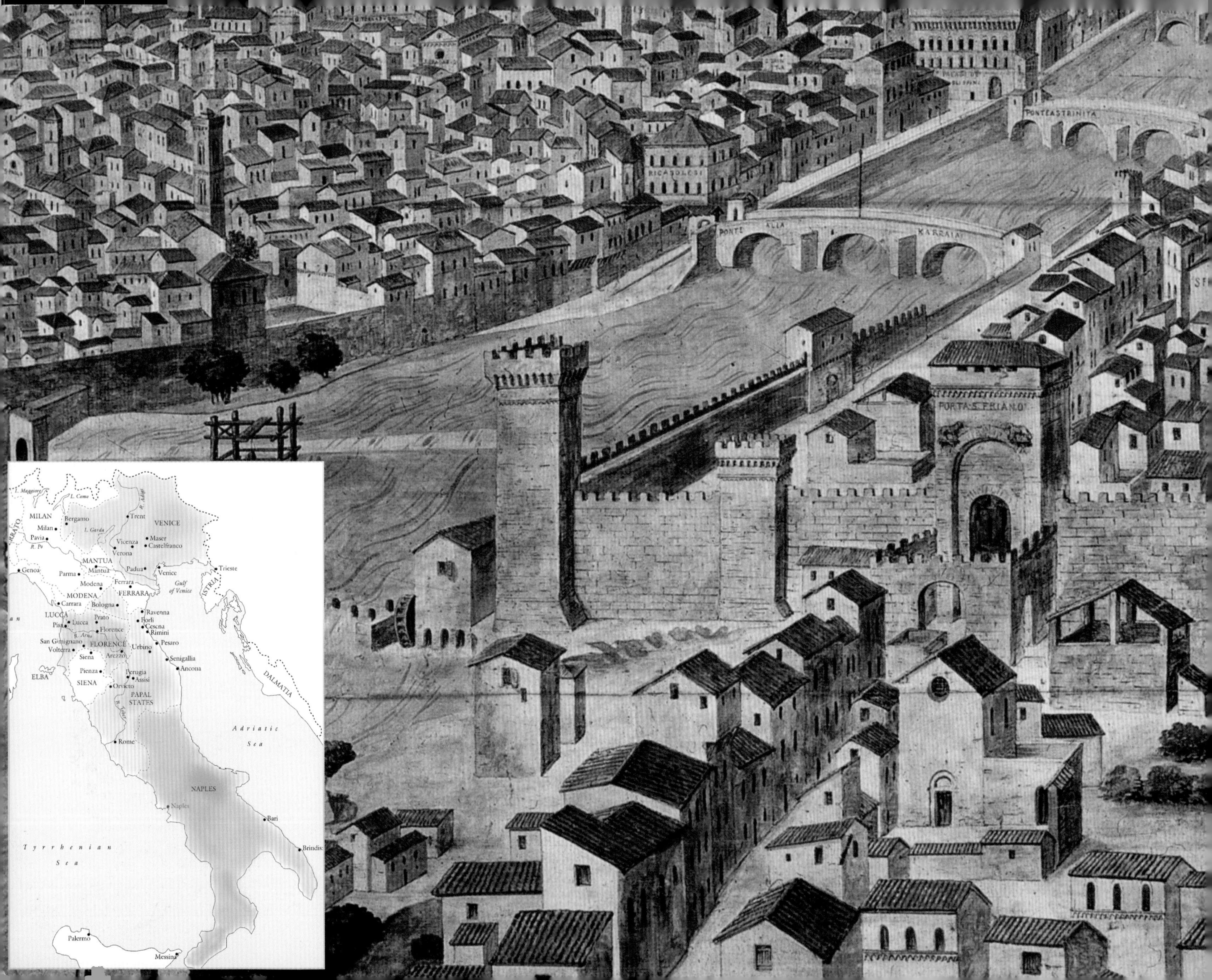

RICASOLESI
PONTE ALLA CARRAIA
PONTE A S TRINITA
PORTA S. FRIANO
L. Maggiore
L. Como
R. Adige
MILAN
Bergamo
Trent
VENICE
Milan
L. Garda
Pavia
R. Po
Vicenza
Maser
Castelfranco
Verona
MANTUA
Mantua
Padua
Venice
Trieste
Genoa
Parma
Modena
Ferrara
Gulf of Venice
ISTRIA
MODENA
FERRARA
Carrara
Bologna
LUCCA
Ravenna
Prato
Forlì
Pisa
Lucca
Cesena
Florence
Rimini
R. Arno
San Gimignano
FLORENCE
Pesaro
Volterra
Urbino
Siena
Arezzo
Senigallia
Ancona
Pienza
Perugia
ELBA
Assisi
SIENA
Orvieto
PAPAL STATES
R. Tiber
DALMATIA
Adriatic Sea
Rome
NAPLES
Naples
Bari
Tyrrhenian Sea
Brindisi
Palermo
Messina

Flight 1

S. SPRITO

Florence, Italy, detail from *Carta della Cartera*, ca. 1496; map of Italy, ca. 15th c. *(inset)*

Florence, Italy

1400's

Let's begin our Flight. Make sure you're buckled in and your tray tables are up. We're going to fly to one of the most beautiful and historic cities in the world, Florence, Italy. I must say, I've wanted to come here for a long time, but then I hate to fly. So the way you and I fly is pretty handy—we imagine! Much better. No turbulence.

Your first Flight for the Renaissance (*REN-uh-zons*) takes you to the place where most people believe the Renaissance was born: Florence. The rebirth (Renaissance) pretty much all started with the Medici (*MEH-di-chee*) family wanting to improve their lives and those of the people around them. Boy, I wish my family would try to improve itself. I have an uncle who is so lazy that he has someone scratch his fleas for him. Since he's too lazy to lick himself, he has to buy hairballs. Hmmm.

This Flight shows how education and art came back into style and changed from being for just a few snobby people, to being for all people. The city of Florence was the center of this rebirth. Picture sweet breezes and green hills. Nestled on the banks of a calm river are whitewashed buildings with red clay roofs. Imagine sculptures and fountains created by some of the most famous artists who have ever lived. We've landed in Florence, Italy. *Arrivederci*. That's goodbye in Italian. You head for the cobblestone streets and I'll head for the pasta. See you in a bite—er, bit.

1

During the Middle Ages, the *plague* (a deadly disease) spread quickly, killing more than a third of the people in Europe. With the deaths of so many people, farm fields lay barren and towns lost their blacksmith, baker, or other tradesmen. Most merchants lost lots of money because there were few people alive to buy products. Finally, the numbers of healthy people started to rise, and there was a need for goods and work. Better and swifter ships sailed to distant lands and brought new rich cargo to busy ports on the shores of Italy. A new middle class of merchants and bankers appeared, towns grew into cities, and people grew rich and powerful. They began to spend their money and free time on education and the arts.

1. **What caused merchants to lose money during the Middle Ages?**
2. **How do you think ships helped improve the economy of Europe?**
3. **Why might it have been important for a ship to be swift?**
4. **Why do you think a new middle class of merchants and bankers appeared?**
5. **Why do you think the merchants and bankers began to spend their money on education and the arts?**

2

In the 1400's, Italy was a major trading center, lying at the crossroads for most sea trade routes. Goods from *Muslim* countries and the Far East came into Europe through cities like Florence. Merchants and bankers grew rich on the new products. They wanted their children to learn to read and do math so they could help in family businesses. They began to hire private tutors to teach their children, who were freed from labor in the fields by the new economy. In Florence, one of the most powerful and rich banking families, the Medici, improved not just their own lives, but also their neighbors' lives by building great public places like a library and an academy for learning.

1. **What country was a major trading center in the 1400's?**
2. **Goods for all of Europe came through Italy. How might that have helped the Italians to grow wealthy?**
3. **Why was it important to be able to read and do math?**
4. **Why might children have time to learn from tutors now and not before?**
5. **Do you think the Medici's were kind? Explain.**

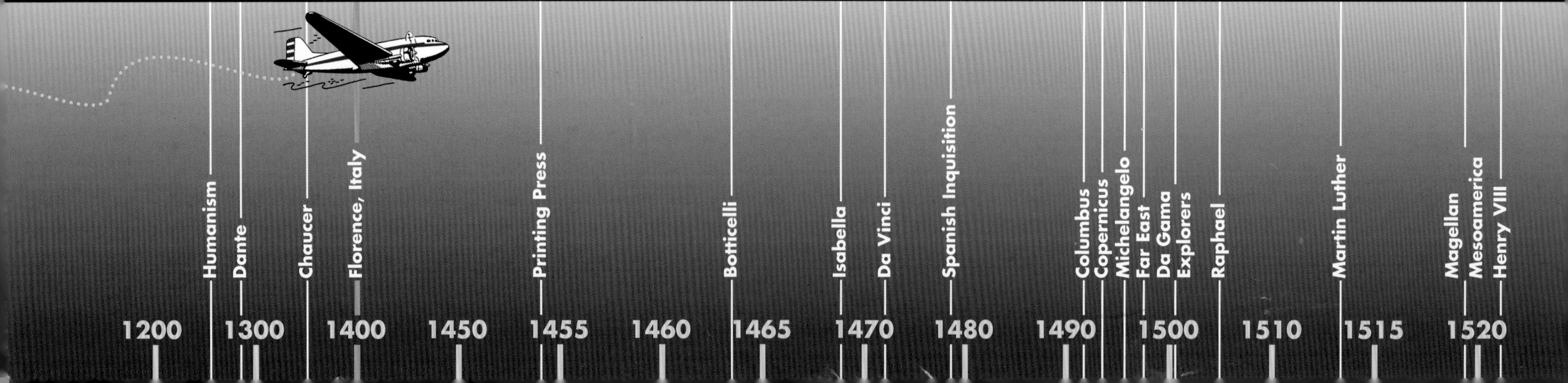
Humanism
Dante
Chaucer
Florence, Italy
Printing Press
Botticelli
Isabella
Da Vinci
Spanish Inquisition
Columbus
Copernicus
Michelangelo
Far East
Da Gama
Explorers
Raphael
Martin Luther
Magellan
Mesoamerica
Henry VIII
1200
1300
1400
1450
1455
1460
1465
1470
1480
1490
1500
1510
1515
1520

3

The Medici family was very rich, involved in banking and trade throughout Florence. They used much of their wealth to help the people of Florence and soon they ruled the city. They built churches and commissioned (paid for) great works of art to be put up all over the city for everyone to enjoy. Cosimo de'Medici, the head of the family, enjoyed the arts and used his riches to support many painters and sculptors so they could create artwork full time. As a result, during his rule from 1434 to 1464, there was a surge in the amount of art produced in Florence.

1. **Who did you visualize as the leader of the Medici family?**
2. **How do you think the Medici became powerful?**
3. **Why do you think the Medici's put great art in the city for everyone to enjoy?**
4. **Do you think Cosimo's love of the arts helped start the Renaissance? Explain.**
5. **Why do you think there was a surge in the amount of art produced in Florence?**

4

The most powerful and famous member of the Medici family was Cosimo's grandson, Lorenzo de'Medici. He took over Florence in 1469, at the age of 20, and ruled for 23 years. He held exciting free horse races and musical concerts that drew huge crowds of people, even from other countries. Lorenzo also supported some of the best musicians, writers, and artists of all time. To the people of his city, who adored him, he was known as Lorenzo the Magnificent. Under his rule, Florence became the most famous city in Europe, known as the center of the arts.

1. **How was Lorenzo related to Cosimo?**
2. **How do you think free horse races and concerts may have helped Florence?**
3. **Why do you think Florence became the most famous city in Europe?**
4. **Do you think the people of Florence liked having Lorenzo as a ruler? Explain.**
5. **Why do you think Lorenzo became known as Lorenzo the Magnificent?**

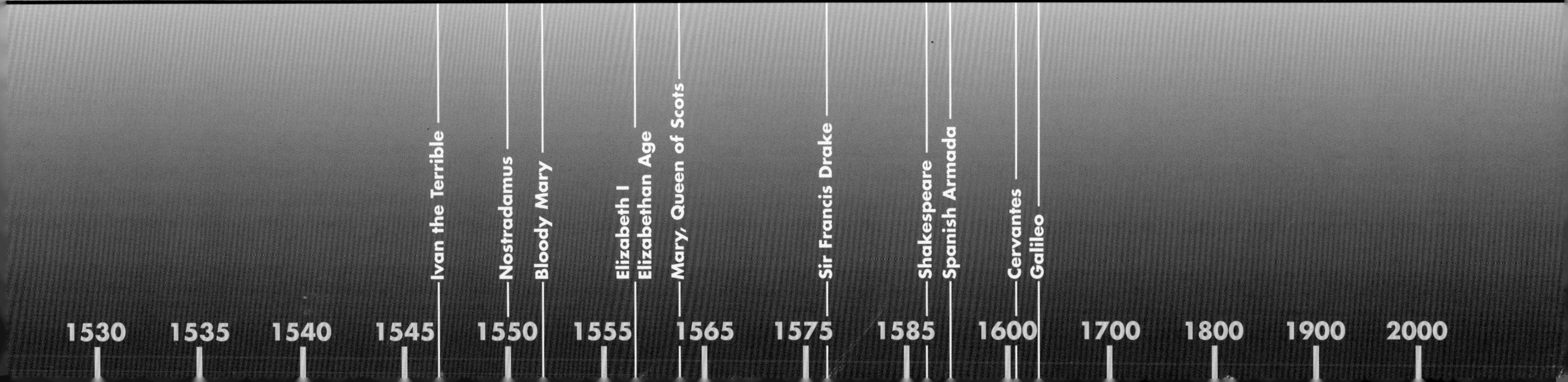

Ivan the Terrible
Nostradamus
Bloody Mary
Elizabeth I
Elizabethan Age
Mary, Queen of Scots
Sir Francis Drake
Shakespeare
Spanish Armada
Cervantes
Galileo
1530
1535
1540
1545
1550
1555
1565
1575
1585
1600
1700
1800
1900
2000

5

The rebirth of art, music, and literature that started in Florence began to spread across Italy and into other parts of Europe. People who visited Florence were impressed, and wanted to improve their own lives and cities. Art and education began to touch every part of life for the rich upper classes. At the same time, some of the rich people finally began to notice the terrible starvation and poverty the peasants suffered. They saw that the poor had to work or beg from dawn to dusk just to survive, much less enjoy art. Some began to think that all people, not just the rich, should have the same access to education and the arts. What had started with one family had blossomed into the Renaissance, a rebirth, that forever changed the world.

1. **What did some of the wealthy people finally notice?**
2. **Why do you think the rebirth of art, music, and literature spread to the rest of Europe?**
3. **How do you think art and education touched every part of life for the upper classes?**
4. **Do you think this rebirth touched the lives of the poor as much as the upper classes?**
5. **How do you think the Renaissance forever changed the world?**

A view of Florence *(left)*; Lorenzo de'Medici on a bronze medal, ca. 1490 *(above)*, and in a portrait, ca. 1534 *(right)*

Ivan says—

Wow, it seems like a single human family helped change the world. Can you imagine that? Me? I'm lucky if someone changes my litter box once a month.

By the way, to give you an idea of how widespread the Renaissance became, all around the world there were Muslim, Jewish, and Christian scholars hard at work translating all the books of the ancient Greeks and Romans into Latin and Arabic so they could be read by a new generation of people.

Read? Right. Let's read on and learn about something called Humanism. Human-what? Cat-ism, I say. Humans. Humbug. Like all great cats, I can take or leave humans, really. Let's get back on IMAGINE AIR and start visualizing Cat-ism...oops, I mean Humanism (I can't really get that out of my mouth easily, you know).

I'm ready if you are. Let's go.

6

Flight 2

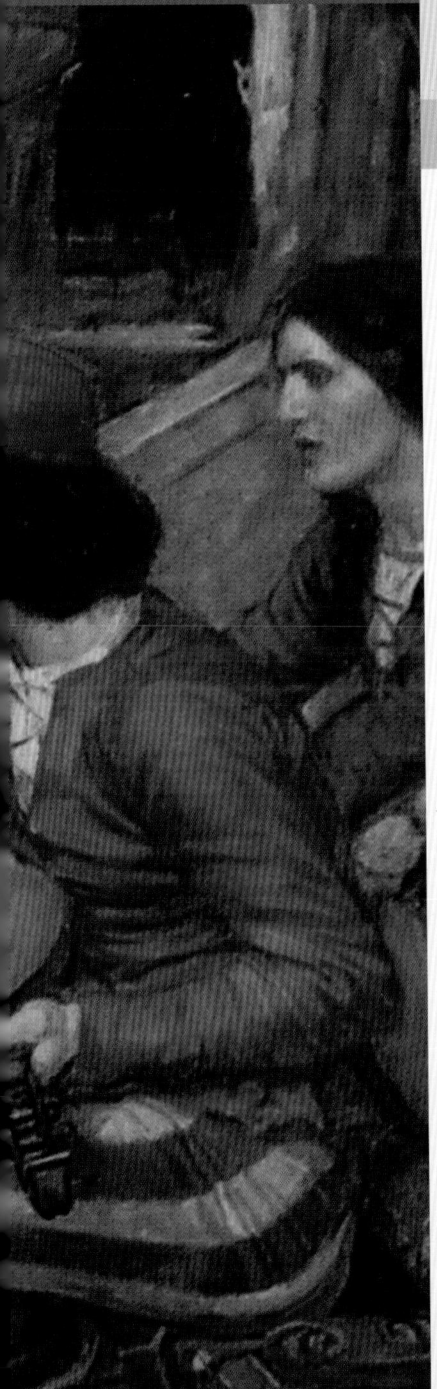

A group listens to *A Tale from the Decameron*, as imagined by John William Waterhouse, 1916.

Humanism

1300's-1500's

Your next Flight is on Humanism—which is a way of thinking that is based on the values, characteristics, and behaviors that are believed to be the best in human beings.

Humanism. It wasn't easy for me to take you to this Flight. Just the name creeps me. I looked up the synonyms for Humanism and here is what I found: caring, kind, gentle, compassionate, charitable, and civilized. Humanism started a more caring, kind, gentle, compassionate, charitable, and civilized period of history. Here is an official definition of Humanism: *an intellectual movement of the Renaissance that spread through Europe as a result of the rediscovery of the arts and philosophy of the ancient Greeks and Romans*. Hmmmm. That was a mouthful.

Well, personally, I like the idea of Cat-ism more. I excel in a philosophy based on catnaps and catnip. Myself, I like a little catsup on my mound of catnip. Then I'll have a little catnap. Say, Cat-ism could be a whole new movement in history based on being aloof, arrogant, intelligent, and furry.

Anyhow, get your imagery tuned up. While you're learning about Humanism, I'm going to practice a little Cat-ism. Let's see. When my human calls me...I turn my back and stare at something very interesting in the other direction...Next, I stre-eetch...

1

Humanism is the way of thinking that says that there is more to life than just survival. Until this time, people had few choices about their lives and jobs. They had worked from dawn to dusk just to survive, without time to improve their minds. Humanism said that since God created people, then people must be worthy and each person deserved the best life he or she could make. Many people now had more food and money than before, so they also had more free time to spend learning. Humanistic thought said that people, not just God, could create beautiful things. So people began to learn and create which was the driving force behind the Renaissance. As people tried to improve their lives and minds, every new idea someone thought up led to more new ideas.

1. What did you visualize for Humanism?

2. Why do you think people didn't have the time to learn before the Renaissance?

3. Why might having free time be important to learning?

4. How do you think having more money and food helped people learn?

5. How do you think one idea lead to new ideas?

2

During the Renaissance, schools began to open in every major city. Not everyone could afford private tutors, and some educated people decided to become teachers instead of private tutors. The discovery of great *Roman* and *Greek* writings, both artistic and scientific, forgotten for hundreds of years, gave the new schools plenty to teach. Not since ancient times had thinking and learning been so important. Now, the more people learned, the more they wanted to know. New subjects like science, anatomy, math, and logic were being studied. Curiosity had been dangerous in the past, as it was often mistaken for rebellion. Now the curious were being praised and even paid for learning new ideas and coming up with new ways of doing things.

1. What opened in every major city during the Renaissance?

2. Why might there have not been a lot of schools or tutors prior to the Renaissance?

3. Why might Roman and Greek writings have been forgotten until the Renaissance?

4. Why might reading books and studying art be seen as dangerous?

5. Why might people have wanted to pursue learning during the Renaissance?

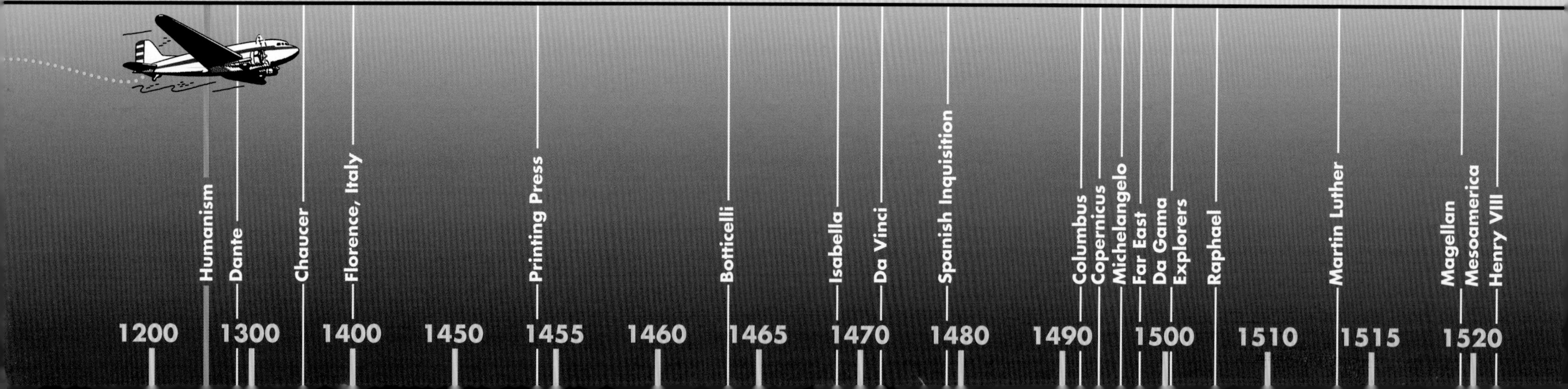
Humanism
Dante
Chaucer
Florence, Italy
Printing Press
Botticelli
Isabella
Da Vinci
Spanish Inquisition
Columbus
Copernicus
Michelangelo
Far East
Da Gama
Explorers
Raphael
Martin Luther
Magellan
Mesoamerica
Henry VIII
1200
1300
1400
1450
1455
1460
1465
1470
1480
1490
1500
1510
1515
1520

3

One of the leaders of Humanist thought was Petrarch, an Italian poet who lived from 1304 to 1374. The curious and opinionated monk traveled all over Italy. He loved Laura, a girl he met when he was young. Though she married another, she inspired him to create the sonnet (a poem with 14 lines) as a way of expressing his love. He was later named *poet laureate* (official poet) of Rome for his poetry. He believed that people could learn more about solving their problems by reading about history. He translated great literature from Greek into the more commonly used *Latin*. Petrarch, often feeling alone and without someone to talk to, wrote letters about his thoughts to Cicero, a Roman poet he admired who had died over 1,200 years before.

1. **Besides being a poet, what else did you visualize for Petrarch?**
2. **Why do you think it was important that Petrarch traveled?**
3. **Why might studying history help people solve their problems?**
4. **Why do you think Petrarch translated great literature from Greek into Latin? How is this important?**
5. **Why do you think Petrarch wrote letters to a man he had never met?**

4

Petrarch did make some like-minded friends on his journeys. He shared his ideas about Humanism with one friend, the Italian writer Boccaccio (*Bo-CAH-chee-o*). Boccaccio (1313?-1375) had written popular medieval romances before he met the monk in 1350. After talking with Petrarch, he wrote *The Decameron*, a witty book of 100 tales that describes a group of regular people during the terrible years of the plague. The stories were unusual because they were about real people, told in a down-to-earth, realistic manner. Readers could identify with the people in *The Decameron* more than they could to the mythical knights and heroes written about in the Middle Ages. This book helped bring medieval society to the changing world of the Renaissance.

1. **How many tales were in Boccaccio's *The Decameron*?**
2. **How might Petrarch have influenced Boccaccio?**
3. **How might a book about real people be different from Boccaccio's other books at that time?**
4. **Why might the plague years have been an unusual time to write about regular people?**
5. **Why might being able to identify with people in a book be important?**

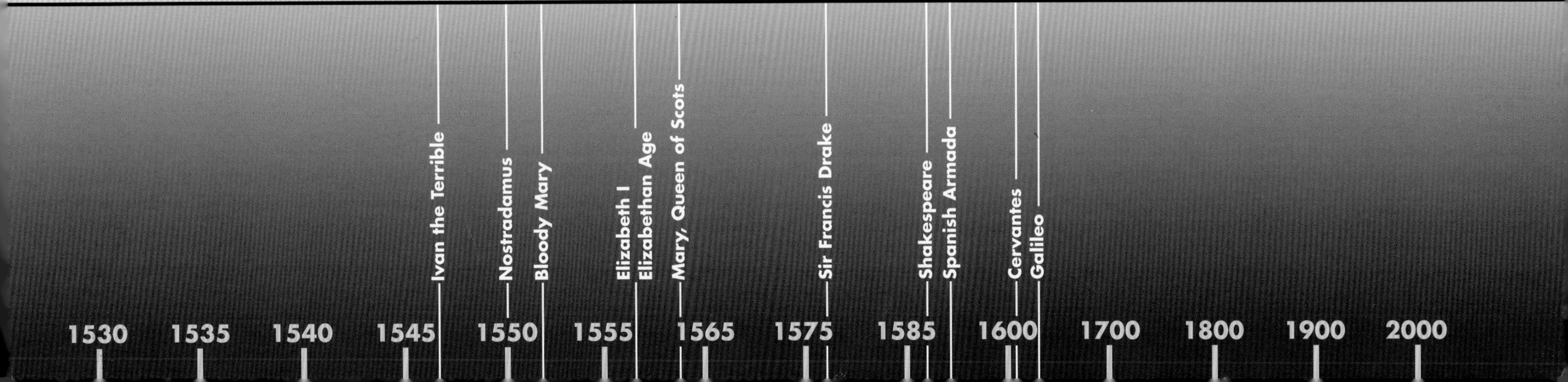
Ivan the Terrible
Nostradamus
Bloody Mary
Elizabeth I
Elizabethan Age
Mary, Queen of Scots
Sir Francis Drake
Shakespeare
Spanish Armada
Cervantes
Galileo
1530
1535
1540
1545
1550
1555
1565
1575
1585
1600
1700
1800
1900
2000

Portrait of Federico da Montefeltro shows a typical man of the period, dressed in armor to show strength and holding a book to show off his good education

Portrait of Giovanna Tornabuoni, 1488, by Ghirlandaio, features a graceful young woman of the Renaissance

Humanism helped usher in a rebirth of education and the arts that affected all classes of people. More importantly, it led to many scientific discoveries and a widespread love for art and literature. For the first time since the fall of Rome in 476 A.D. and the deadly epidemic of the plague, children and adults were studying math, grammar, poetry, and ethics. They were examining nature and the human body, finding out how the body worked. They went to see great works of art or collected books. Many would never go back to just being farmers again.

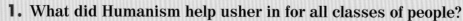

1. **What did Humanism help usher in for all classes of people?**
2. **Why might there have been many scientific discoveries during this time?**
3. **How might studying how nature and how the human body works be helpful?**
4. **Why hadn't people been making scientific discoveries before the Renaissance?**
5. **Why might some people never go back to being just farmers again?**

Lucrezia Borgia, a humanist who sponsored artists and writers in Rome and Ferrara, Italy

St. Jerome, patron saint of Humanists, displays his books and scientific tools, showing how a Renaissance man spent time reading

Ivan says—

Here's some news. Visualize this. Petrarch, the poet and monk, enjoyed new experiences. He was the first recorded person to climb Mont Ventoux, a 6,000-foot high mountain in France. He climbed all the way to the top just so he could look around.

Hmmmm. I must say I can think of a lot of reasons to climb, but just to look at the view probably isn't one of them. Know what I mean? Oh, yes. Birds.

Speaking of climbing, climb back into your seat. IMAGINE AIR is ready to take you to meet one of those writers that helped usher in Humanism and the Renaissance.

Let's meet the famous Dante—say it after me, *DON-tay*. Don't worry, I'll help you with this Italian as we fly along. Nothing to it. If I can say these names with my little pink tongue, you can too.

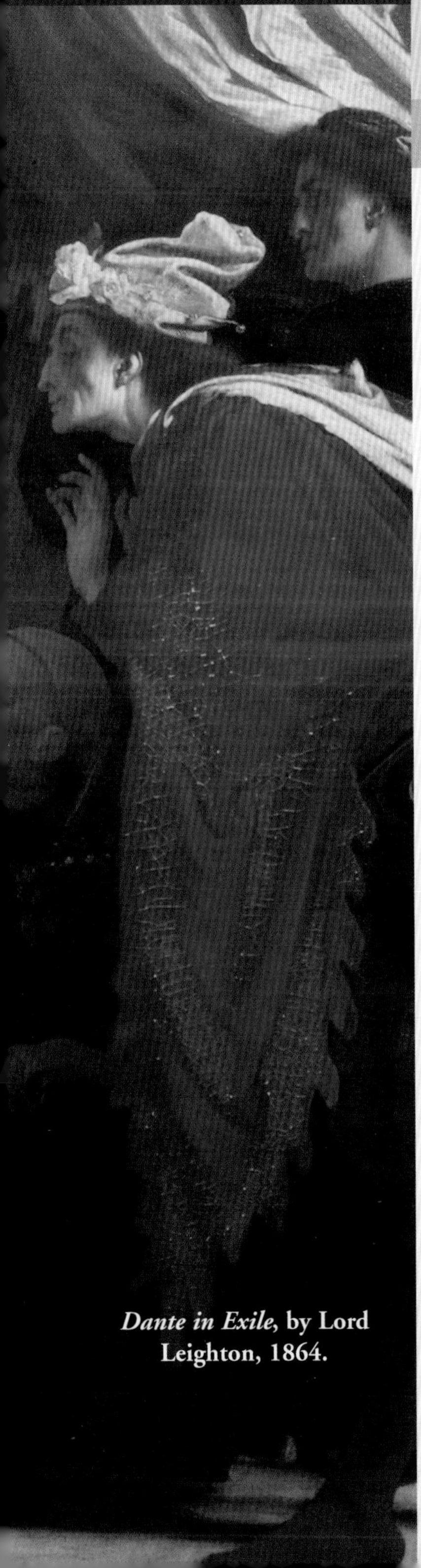

Dante in Exile, by Lord Leighton, 1864.

Dante

1265-1321

Unbuckle but eat some extra peanuts before we disembark in Italy, because you're going to need it to read about Dante. He wrote a celebrated and very long poem, really more like a book, called *The Divine Comedy*, although I don't think it was particularly funny, as you'll see.

Dante wrote about his imagined journey through a place Down Under, and I don't mean Australia! I mean Hell, a place where some believe that, after death, people's souls remain until they have made amends for their sins and can go on to Heaven, or stay to be punished. Frankly, I only believe in Heaven. Just Heaven, and I find it in so many simple ways, you know. Let's see, there's eating and there's sleeping, and sleeping and eating.

Here's something you'll love. Part of the reason that Dante's long poem is so famous is that it is full of imagery.

Well, while you visit with Dante, I'll be in cat Heaven enjoying heavenly fish pie with my friend, the Dish. Catch you later.

1

Prior to the Renaissance, the few artists and writers around mainly created works that glorified (showed the beauty of) the Church. One of these writers was the poet Dante. What makes his work amazing is that he focused on what he felt about such human feelings as love, hate, good, and sin. He wrote his most famous work, the epic poem *The Divine Comedy*, nearly 700 years ago, but its combination of Humanist values and imagery made it an instant classic. Dante wrote himself as a character who travels through *Heaven*, *Hell*, and *Purgatory*, the three places he thought people went after death, to learn about mankind's flaws and virtues.

1. Prior to the Renaissance, what did people write or paint about?

2. How do you think Dante's work was different than other works of his time?

3. Why do you think it might be different for a writer to write about human feelings?

4. Do you think Dante had questions about mankind's flaws and virtues? Explain.

5. Why might Dante's *The Divine Comedy* have become an instant classic?

2

Dante was born to a wealthy family in Florence, Italy, in 1265. He was well educated, had a position in the politics of Florence, and married his wife, Gemma, when he was 20. But his heart still belonged to a childhood sweetheart, Beatrice. He had loved the beautiful girl at his first sight of her, when he was nine, but they both married others. Dante had never acted on his love for Beatrice, except to write poetry about her. She died when she was only 26. Dante wrote about his love for Beatrice, his life, his political troubles, and his desire to do things to his enemies that he couldn't do in real life.

1. Where did you visualize Dante was born?

2. Why do you think Dante was well educated?

3. Why might Dante have chosen to write poems to express his love for Beatrice?

4. How do you think Dante felt about Beatrice's death?

5. Why might Dante have written about his own life and his enemies?

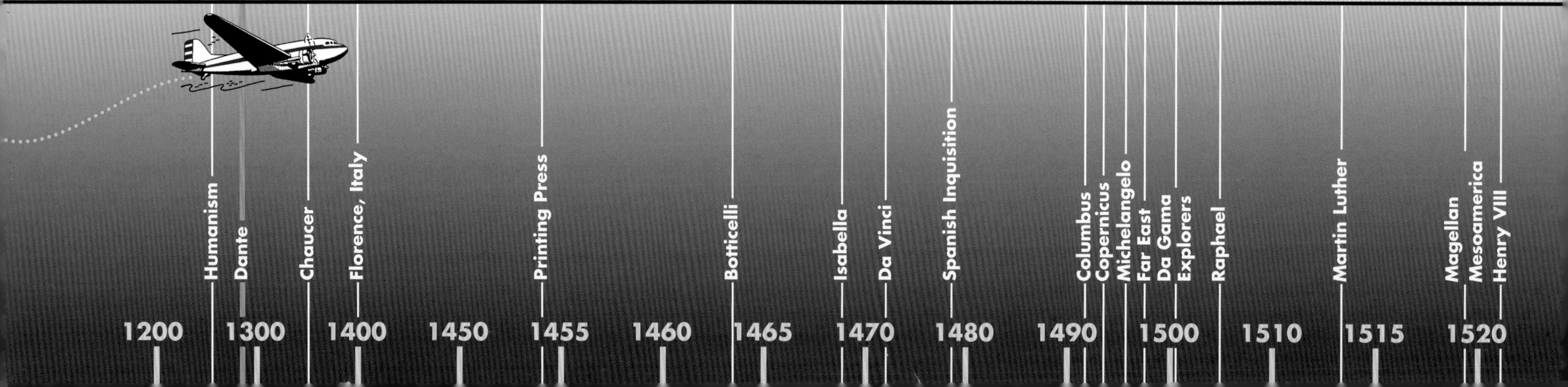
Humanism
Dante
Chaucer
Florence, Italy
Printing Press
Botticelli
Isabella
Da Vinci
Spanish Inquisition
Columbus
Copernicus
Michelangelo
Far East
Da Gama
Explorers
Raphael
Martin Luther
Magellan
Mesoamerica
Henry VIII
1200
1300
1400
1450
1455
1460
1465
1470
1480
1490
1500
1510
1515
1520

3

The Divine Comedy tells the story of Dante's personal journey through Hell, Purgatory, and Heaven. These were places that Catholics like Dante believed the soul went to after the death of the body. Bad people went to Hell, good people went to Heaven, and people who still had a chance of repenting (asking for God's forgiveness) went to Purgatory. In the poem, Dante finds a cave and is met and then led on the first part of his journey by the ghost of *Virgil*. Dante sees the spirits of many people on his trip, all of whom are symbols for the good and bad things in human nature. Virgil is pure logic and thought, while Beatrice, whose ghost leads Dante through Heaven, is pure love.

1. What is the name of Dante's poem?

2. Why do you think Dante writes that he is led on his journey by a ghost?

3. How do you think Dante being a Catholic influenced his poem?

4. Why might Dante write of meeting spirits that were symbols of both good and bad things in human nature?

5. Why might Dante have written about a personal journey instead of someone else's journey?

4

The Divine Comedy has inspired poets through the ages with its vivid imagery. Dante describes sinners suffering in Hell, being stung by hordes of bees, and seeing great demons with spears, lakes of blood, headless men, and more. He wrote of the host of angels singing in the glory of Heaven and the lost souls trapped in Purgatory. The realistic way Dante wrote about the things he imagined in Heaven or Hell was different and exciting to read at the time. Dante wrote as if he was seeing the real thing, not just imagining it in his mind. His images were so good that the readers could also imagine them. Many of the images he created and described, like angels singing in the clouds of Heaven, are the ones people still use today.

1. What made *The Divine Comedy* different from other written works of its time?

2. Why do you think Dante described sinners as suffering?

3. Why might Dante's writing have been exciting to read back then?

4. What do you think the paragraph meant by, "many of the images he created...?"

5. Why might vivid imagery make a poem easier to understand?

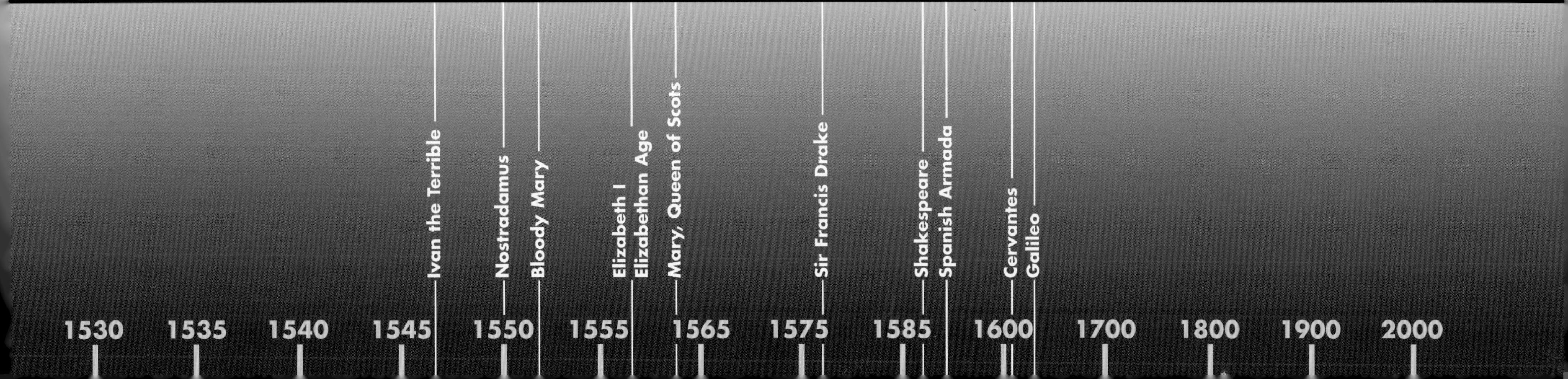
Ivan the Terrible
Nostradamus
Bloody Mary
Elizabeth I
Elizabethan Age
Mary, Queen of Scots
Sir Francis Drake
Shakespeare
Spanish Armada
Cervantes
Galileo
1530
1535
1540
1545
1550
1555
1565
1575
1585
1600
1700
1800
1900
2000

A detail from *Parnassus*, showing Dante, Homer, and Virgil, by Raphael *(left)*; a portrait of Dante *(right)*

5

The Divine Comedy was written with images of scary monsters and demons as well as beautiful angels in Heaven. Dante's poem was very popular. The scary stories brought poetry to many people who hadn't read it before, and sparked their imaginations to read more. It also gave other writers thc courage to write stories in his style, with their own imagery. Using imagination and pictures to tell a story, his epic poem became the norm for all writing.

1. **What was scary in *The Divine Comedy*?**
2. **Why might the scary stories have made people want to read more?**
3. **Why do you think Dante's poem was very popular?**
4. **How might Dante's work have improved the writing style of other writers? Explain.**
5. **What do you think about the power of imagery?**

Scenes from *The Divine Comedy*, engravings by Gustave Doré, ca. 1861 *(left)*; another view of Dante and Virgil traveling through Hell *(right)*

Ivan says—

Now, that was some poem. Here was a sad and lonely man, filled with grief, who wrote with enough imagery to influence a whole movement in literature. Good grief—what a little grief can do. Hey, I wrote a poem once. Try this for imagery:

Fish, fish, they look rather funny.
They flip, flop, all the way to my tummy.
I look in my empty Dish
And scream, "I want more fish!"
I scratch and plead,
I beg with greed,
But in the end I know
It is to the fish tank I must go.

That was just the first verse. I've got more, but just thinking about it makes me hungry. Come here, little fish. It is time to meet my Dish.

We're boarding again, for a trip to meet another writer...the famous Chaucer. I took a class and read some of Chaucer, wrote a paper on him, and finally taught a class. And if you believe that, I'll sell you some fish in the desert.

Flight 4

Everyday life for the poor and for the nobles in Chaucer's time.

Chaucer

1340?-1400

Pilgrim, we've left Florence and landed in England to learn about *The Canterbury Tales*. Get ready to tell me a tale about your life. Er, guess not. Anyhow, this Flight is all about another great writer named Geoffrey Chaucer.

Chaucer is considered the Father of English literature. The first thing you should know is that Chaucer survived the plague, which was a pretty big accomplishment all by itself. The second thing to know about Chaucer is that he wrote the famous *Canterbury Tales*. He wrote about knights and a rooster, housewives, and lots of other ordinary people telling stories on their way to Canterbury, a cathedral in merry old England.

Speaking of roosters, I knew a rooster once that drove me crazy. He lived across the street and crowed every morning so loudly I had to stick cotton in my furry little ears. Finally, I dressed as a fox and grabbed him right out of the tree. Learned that trick from Chaucer. You believe me, don't you?

Read on, my friend. Read on.

1

Geoffrey Chaucer is considered the greatest poet and writer of the late Middle Ages, and he influenced later writers of the Renaissance. Unlike most medieval writers, Chaucer didn't write about gods or kings. He thought most people couldn't relate to them. Instead he wrote about normal people putting food on the table or running an inn. Chaucer was a short, chubby man full of energy whose exciting stories helped many people to start reading. His work was more fun than most, because he used humor and drama in his stories. Chaucer became known as the Father of English literature because of his influence on later writers.

1. **What did Chaucer write about?**
2. **Why might stories of the Middle Ages have been about kings instead of people?**
3. **How might Chaucer's writing have been something people could identify with?**
4. **Do you think writing about everyday things helped make Chaucer popular? Why?**
5. **Why do you think Chaucer's writing helped people to start reading?**

2

The Canterbury Tales are a set of stories told by a group of pilgrims, or travelers, on their journey to Canterbury, a city in England. To entertain each other in the evenings as they rested by a fire or at an inn, the weary pilgrims took turns telling stories. Each story is then about that person, or an ordinary, everyday person they knew. The storytellers included a Knight, a Cook, a Friar, a Wife, and a Shipman. Every person in the story was normal, with flaws and problems, rather than perfect and heroic. One story was even about a rooster named Chanticleer, who was known far and wide for his ability to crow.

1. **What did you visualize for *The Canterbury Tales*?**
2. **Why might Chaucer have chosen a group of pilgrims to tell the stories?**
3. **Why do you think telling stories was used as entertainment back then?**
4. **Why might the stories have been about everyday people?**
5. **Why might it have been important that the people in the stories aren't perfect?**

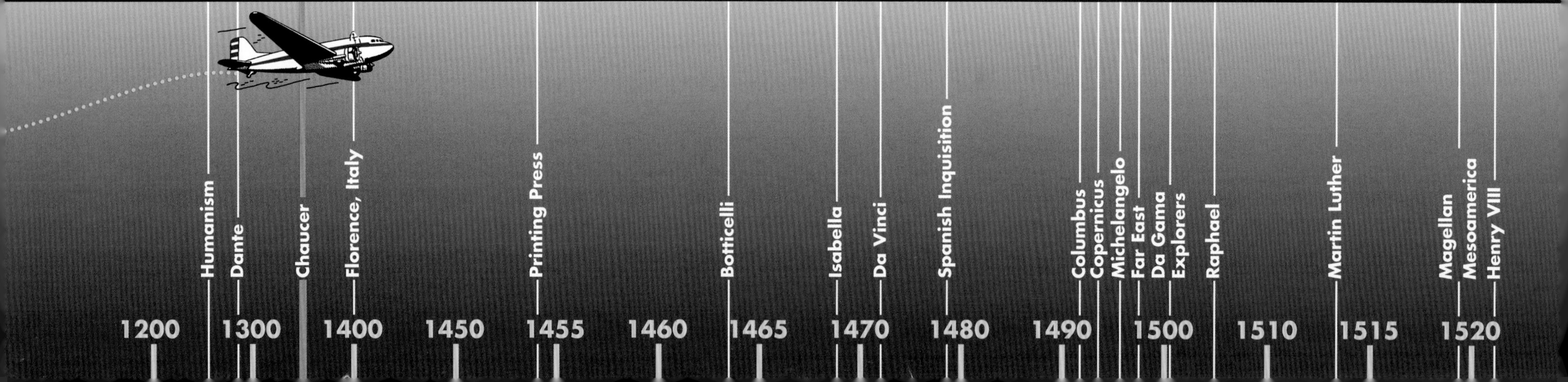

Humanism
Dante
Chaucer
Florence, Italy
Printing Press
Botticelli
Isabella
Da Vinci
Spanish Inquisition
Columbus
Copernicus
Michelangelo
Far East
Da Gama
Explorers
Raphael
Martin Luther
Magellan
Mesoamerica
Henry VIII
1200
1300
1400
1450
1455
1460
1465
1470
1480
1490
1500
1510
1515
1520

3

The famous rooster story in *The Canterbury Tales* starts with Chanticleer the rooster picking herbs one day. Suddenly, a fox comes out of the woods. The rooster is afraid until the fox says that he only wants to hear the famous rooster crow. Chanticleer is very happy to hear the compliment and begins to sing. The fox then grabs the poor rooster and starts to take him away for supper. As a crowd appears, eager to catch the fox, Chanticleer convinces the fox to stop and talk to the crowd. When the fox opens his mouth to speak, the rooster escapes. The moral (lesson) of the story is to avoid being too proud, and to learn from your mistakes.

1. **What is the moral of the rooster story?**
2. **Do you think the fox is being sly by asking the famous Chanticleer to crow? Explain.**
3. **How does Chanticleer's ego cause him to get caught by the fox?**
4. **How does the fox's pride cause him to lose the rooster?**
5. **What happens in the story to help you learn the moral?**

4

In a different tale, a proud young knight goes on a quest to find out what women want most in life. His answer, given to the Queen, has to be right, or he will lose his head. As time passes, the knight in shining armor grows sad and tired. Each woman he asks gives a different answer. But on the road, he meets a gray old woman. She promises him the right answer if he will marry her. He agrees, and brings her with him to see the Queen. When he says that women just want to be in charge of their husbands, it pleases the Queen. Then the woman says she will magically change herself to a young, pretty, and disloyal girl, or stay an old, wrinkled, and loyal woman, to make him happy. Unable to decide, he asks her to choose for him. The woman sees the knight has learned his lesson and changes herself into a young pretty girl who stays loyal to him.

1. **What is the knight asked to find out about women?**
2. **Why is the knight worried about finding the right answer?**
3. **Why do you think that the Queen and her maids are pleased with the knight's answer?**
4. **Why do you think the old woman gives him the choice of a young pretty disloyal girl?**
5. **What is the moral of the story?**

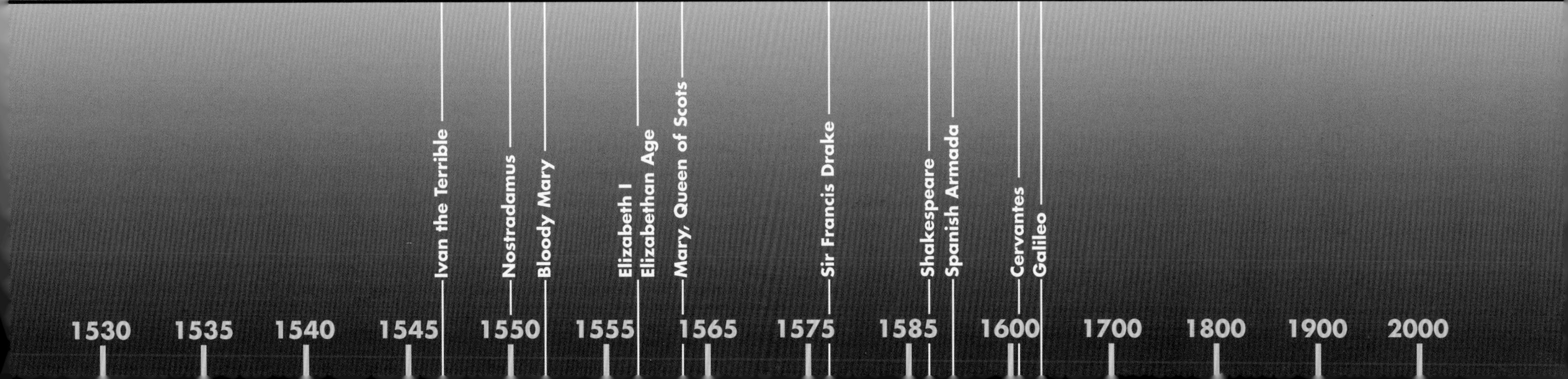
Ivan the Terrible
Nostradamus
Bloody Mary
Elizabeth I
Elizabethan Age
Mary, Queen of Scots
Sir Francis Drake
Shakespeare
Spanish Armada
Cervantes
Galileo
1530
1535
1540
1545
1550
1555
1565
1575
1585
1600
1700
1800
1900
2000

15th c. Arras tapestry depicting courtly love *(left)*; a painting that features Chaucer reciting, ca. 1300's *(right)*

5

Chaucer's writings became extremely popular in England. However, he did not make much money. Chaucer never sought out fame, money, or power. His first love, more than his wife and children, was writing. His stories were often read aloud in public for peasants and merchants who could no read, and Chaucer lived to become one of the most well-known writers during his lifetime. Over 50 years after h death at age 60, his books found their way into everyday people's hands through printing and his work became eve more popular. Finally, one hundred and fifty years after his death, Queen Mary I had a monument placed near his tomb in Westminster Abbey to honor him and his huge influence on English literature.

1. **What was Chaucer's first love?**
2. **Why do you think Chaucer did not make much money?**
3. **Why do you think Chaucer's writing became more popular over time?**
4. **Why might it have taken 150 years after his death for there to be a monument placed near his tomb?**
5. **What do you think of Chaucer?**

A portrait of Chaucer *(left)*

Ivan says—

Picture this. A man strides through an English village square ringing a brass bell. Quickly, people gather and crowd together, facing a large tree stump. There are wealthy merchants in fine clothes, farmers, soldiers, and peasants in rags. Another man holding a large book climbs up onto the stump, clears his throat, and begins to read aloud. He reads from *The Canterbury Tales* and the crowd listens raptly, as stories of knights, plowmen, and monks fill their minds with pictures. The year is 1390, and that is how people, most of whom can't read or write, are entertained.

While these are famous tales, they are not about the best tails. Not nearly enough stories in the *Tales* about that most wondrous of tails, the feline...the cat...ME!

Oh, well. Hold on tight as we fly across the English Channel! We're off to Germany, where a clever man made it possible for you and me to have this book. Let's meet Gutenberg and his printing press.

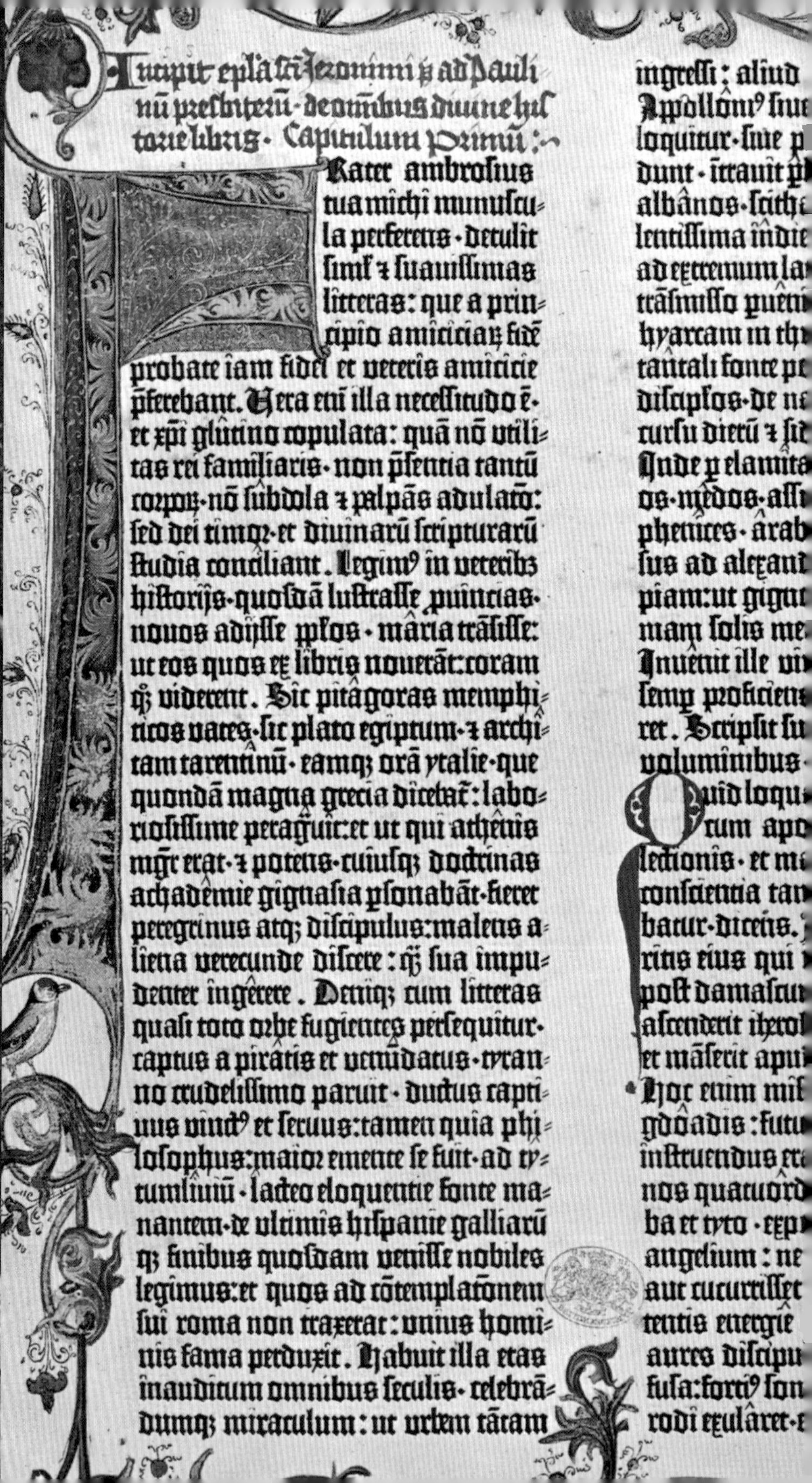
Incipit epistola sancti Ieronimi ad Paulinum presbiterum de omnibus divine historie libris. Capitulum primum.

Frater ambrosius tua michi munuscula perferens detulit simul et suavissimas litteras: que a principio amiciciarum fidem probate iam fidei et veteris amicicie preferebant. Vera enim illa necessitudo est et Christi glutino copulata: quam non utilitas rei familiaris, non presentia tantum corporum, non subdola et palpans adulatio: sed dei timor et divinarum scripturarum studia conciliant. Legimus in veteribus historiis quosdam lustrasse provincias, novos adisse populos, maria transisse: ut eos quos ex libris noverant: coram quoque viderent. Sic pitagoras memphiticos vates, sic plato egiptum et architam tarentinum, eamque oram ytalie que quondam magna grecia dicebatur: laboriosissime peragravit: et ut qui athenis magister erat et potens, cuiusque doctrinas achademie gignasia personabant, fieret peregrinus atque discipulus: malens aliena verecunde discere: quam sua impudenter ingerere. Denique cum litteras quasi toto orbe fugientes persequitur, captus a piratis et venundatus, tyranno crudelissimo paruit, ductus captivus vinctus et servus: tamen quia philosophus: maior ementem se fuit. Ad tytum livium lacteo eloquentie fonte manantem, de ultimis hispanie galliarumque finibus quosdam venisse nobiles legimus: et quos ad contemplationem sui roma non traxerat: unius hominis fama perduxit. Habuit illa etas inauditum omnibus seculis celebrandumque miraculum: ut urbem tantam

Gutenberg holding his 42-line Bible *(left)*; a Gutenberg-printed page with illumination added by hand *(right)*

The Printing Press

1454

You're about to meet a man named Gutenberg (*GOO-ten-berg*) who developed something that enabled me to write this book for you—the printing press. Without this invention, I'd have to write each page by paw.

Seriously, a lot of people don't realize that before the printing press came along, each book had to be copied by hand. Imagine the cramps in those fingers. I mean each word, each sentence, each page in a book had to be copied and then copied again, and again, and again, and again. Imagine spending your entire life just copying words on page after page. My paw is shriveled up just thinking about it.

Printing on a press meant that books were reproduced without the need for copying each word by hand. That made producing books a whole lot faster and cheaper than before. This helped improve the flow of information and ideas during the Renaissance. Can you imagine walking into a school that has no books? That's what it used to be like. Being able to print books meant being able to educate more people.

You read these printed words and I'll go for some sardines and peanut butter. Have to cure that ache in my paw, you know.

1

Before the Renaissance, books were hard to find and were very costly because each book had to be handmade. Booksellers hired religious *clerics* (people who worked for the Church but were not priests) who could read and write to do the work. Churches were the only places that trained clerics to keep records and copy books. The men had to sit for long hours and carefully write each word on every page, using inks of black, red, blue, and green. The pages had detailed drawings, called illuminations, as well. This work took a very long time, and if a mistake was made, the whole page had to be thrown out and a new one started. In addition, there were often mistakes that didn't get spotted, which meant that a book might not be accurate.

1. How did books before the Renaissance have to be copied?

2. Why do you think only religious clerics copied the books?

3. Why might it be better if someone who could read and write did the copying?

4. Why do you think a whole page had to be thrown out if a mistake was made?

5. Do you think it was a problem if books were inaccurate? Explain.

2

A way to print, rather than copying by hand, was invented at different times around the world. In the year 700, the Chinese were printing scrolls by using wooden blocks they could easily carve symbols into. These were dipped in ink and pressed onto paper. They later went from wood, which wears out easily, to bronze (a type of metal) plates. However, Europeans didn't know about printing because China was very isolated from the rest of the civilized world. The secret of printing was undiscovered in Europe for years, until Marco Polo, an Italian traveler, began to explore and trade with China in the late 1200's. From that point onward, many people tried to perfect a printing method that would make books easily available and inexpensive to make.

1. What did you visualize for how the Chinese printed in the year 700?

2. Why was it helpful to the Chinese to be able to carve symbols on wooden blocks?

3. Why do you think it was a problem that wood wore out easily?

4. What do you think the "secret of printing" meant in the paragraph?

5. Why might people have wanted to perfect a printing method that would make books easily available?

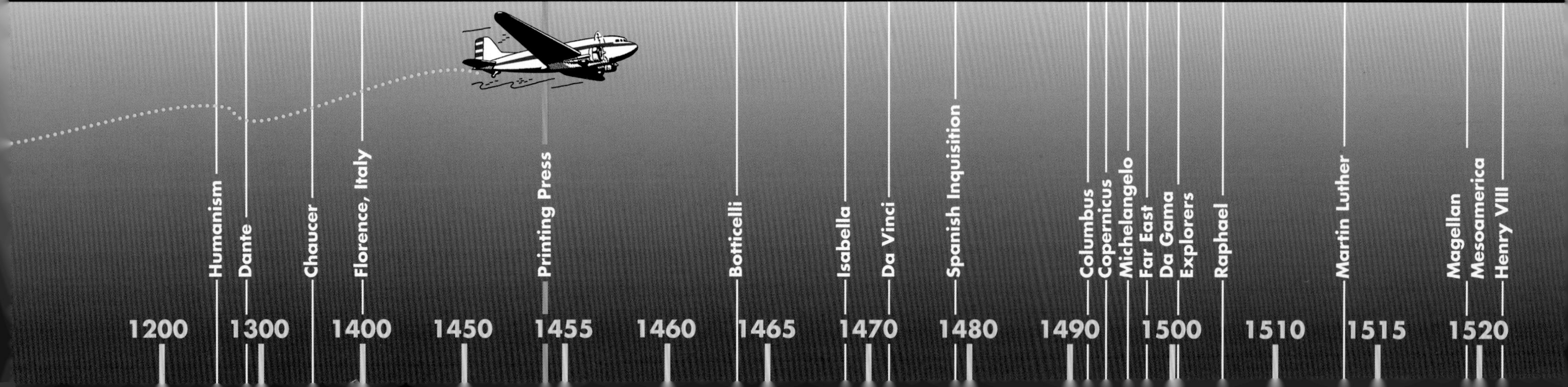
Humanism
Dante
Chaucer
Florence, Italy
Printing Press
Botticelli
Isabella
Da Vinci
Spanish Inquisition
Columbus
Copernicus
Michelangelo
Far East
Da Gama
Explorers
Raphael
Martin Luther
Magellan
Mesoamerica
Henry VIII
1200
1300
1400
1450
1455
1460
1465
1470
1480
1490
1500
1510
1515
1520

3

In 1454, Johannes Gutenberg, a German goldsmith (a craftsman who shapes gold), perfected a way to print with movable letters made of metal. Gutenberg made a tiny copper mold for each letter of the alphabet. Then he poured molten lead into the letter molds to make a solid block with the letter poking up out of it. These metal letters were then put in a wooden frame called a form, building words and sentences one letter at a time. Then they were coated with ink, and pressed onto paper. Words could be made and remade using the individual metal letters and the wooden forms, instead of carving a block of wood for each page that would be useless after a few printings. The printed-paper sheets were then bound into books for a fraction of the cost of copying them by hand.

1. Who invented movable metal letters?

2. Why was it important to have movable letters?

3. Why was it important to have a letter be able to be changed?

4. Why might a wooden block with a whole page carved on it become useless after a few printings?

5. Why might it be better to print many copies of a book at once?

4

The first book that Gutenberg printed with his new press was the *Bible*, the most popular book at the time. He was able to print thousands of Bibles in less time than it would have taken to copy one by hand. Printing shops quickly sprang up throughout Europe. These printing presses were used to print books, but they were also used to produce papers and posters. Anyone who had a story or an opinion to share could get it printed. Notices were posted on church doors and papers were made daily with the latest news on them. Now there could be a lasting record of the stories that had once been passed on through the generations by word of mouth.

1. What was the first book that Gutenberg printed on his press?

2. Why might Gutenberg have chosen the Bible as his first book?

3. Why might printing shops have sprung up all over Europe?

4. Why was it important to be able to print news daily?

5. What might happen to a story that is only passed on by word of mouth?

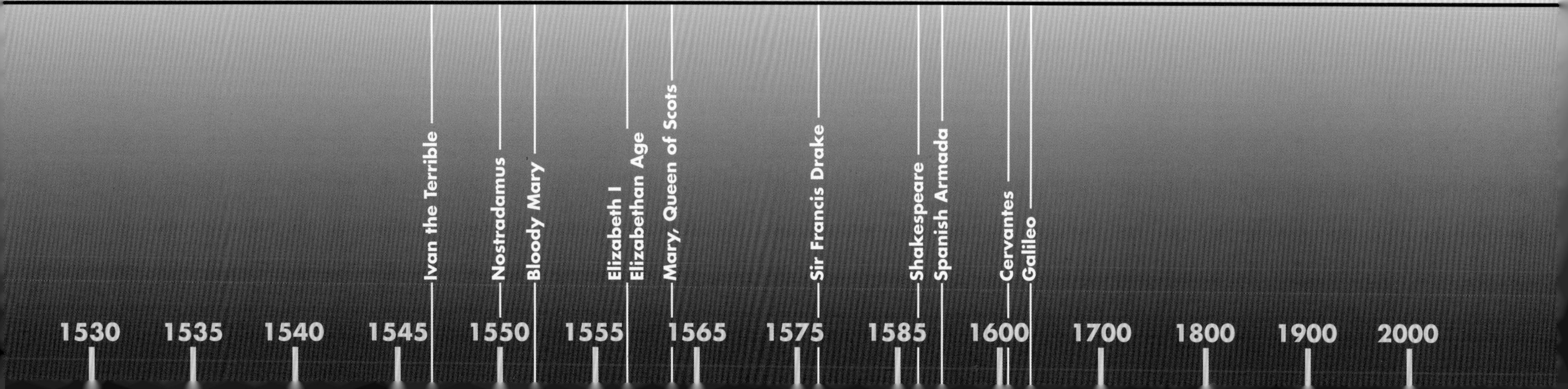
Ivan the Terrible
Nostradamus
Bloody Mary
Elizabeth I
Elizabethan Age
Mary, Queen of Scots
Sir Francis Drake
Shakespeare
Spanish Armada
Cervantes
Galileo
1530
1535
1540
1545
1550
1555
1565
1575
1585
1600
1700
1800
1900
2000

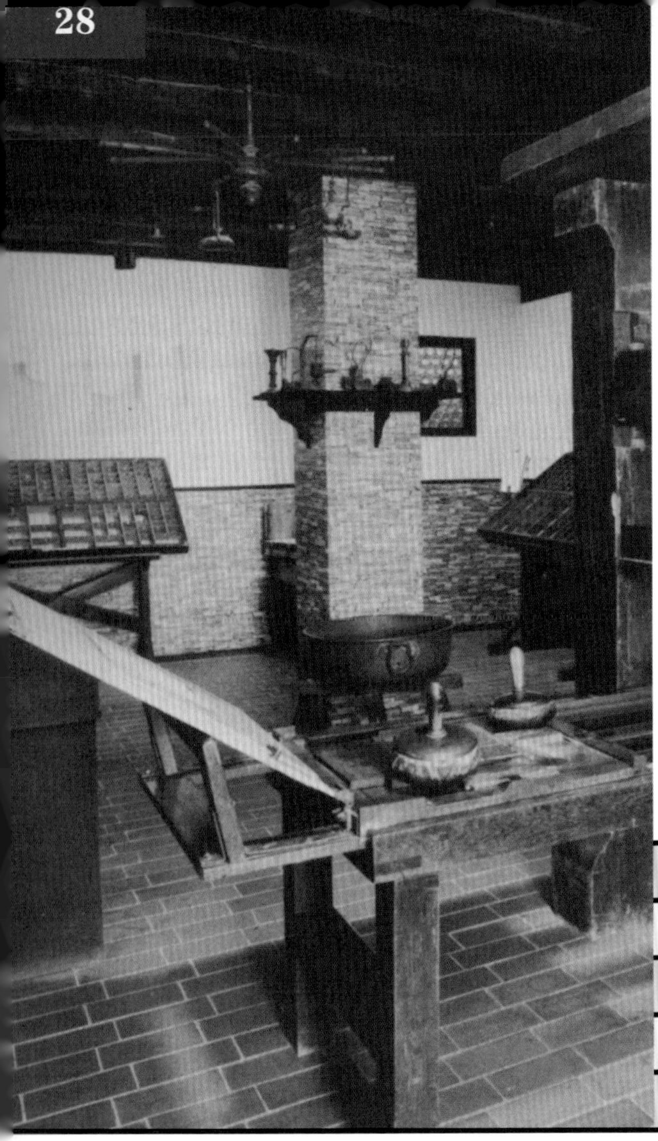

A reconstruction of Gutenberg's workshop *(left)*; metal letters for type, which are placed backwards, in a form to await inking, ca. 16th c. France *(right)*

1
2
3

5 Not all Church leaders and kings were pleased with the printing press. Church leaders had controlled the scribes (people who wrote books) and monks who made books by hand, thus controlling what everyone else knew or learned. The kings and lords preferred that their people stay on the farms, working their lands, instead of reading and getting new ideas about how to live their lives. But books were showing up everywhere now that anyone could write and print what they wanted. Religious texts were still in high demand, but stories, new ideas, and political opinions were now available on paper. Everyone had an opinion to share. This encouraged more reading and led to more writing.

1. Who did the Church leaders control before the printing press?

2. Why might the Church leaders be unhappy with printing presses?

3. Why do you think the people in power didn't like the printing press?

4. Why might the printing press be important to people who had opinions to share?

5. Do you think the sharing of new ideas was important to the growth of civilization? Expla

A 16th c. printing house in England. In the foreground, one printer inks the type while next to him another removes a freshly printed folio. In the background, others place type into forms *(right)*

Ivan says—

The printing press was pretty important, huh? Without books, where would we be? Everything passed on by word of mouth—have you ever tried to remember a story word for word? Not good. No, not good at all.

Here's more for you to visualize. Even though Asia had the basics of printing first, it didn't take off like it did in Europe because of the complexity of Asian languages. The Chinese language has thousands of characters, each one representing a word or idea, while English has just 26 letters that make all the words. It is a much smaller bite.

Mmmm...bite. Excuse me for a moment or two, I hear a can opening. I think it's time for a little clam chowder. And speaking of clams, you're not going to believe it, but in the next Flight we're going to read about a GIANT CLAM and a BEAUTIFUL WOMAN. No kidding.

I'd be oh-so happy if it was about a clam and a beautiful feline, but sadly this is your history, not mine.

Read on.

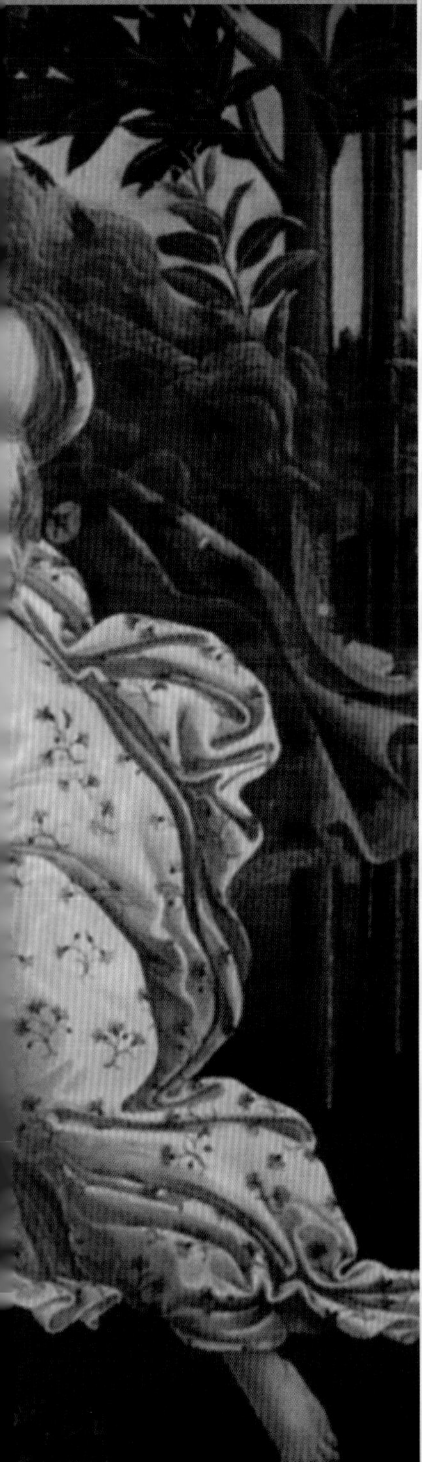

The Birth of Venus, 1483-85

Botticelli

1445-1510

We've landed back in Florence, Italy, to meet Botticelli (*Bo-ti-CHEL-lee*). I don't understand this guy. He painted a famous picture of a girl on a giant clamshell. Then he had everyone in the picture staring at *her* (see for yourself), but not the clam! C'mon, a giant clam is something you don't see every day. That clam could be the meal of a lifetime.

Botticelli represented the new artist of the Renaissance. Everything he painted was beautiful, an attempt to bring Humanism into art. Remember how Humanism focused on mankind's beauty and value? Botticelli and other artists of the early Renaissance began to paint subjects like characters from myth and legend as well as the religious figures that had been the subject of medieval art. In addition, Renaissance artists strove for a new, natural look.

Let's unbuckle and disembark in Florence. Here comes Botticelli, one of the famous artists you'll meet in the Renaissance. Feel the tip of your tongue tap as you say his name—Botticelli, Botticelli. You say that and I'll say: tuna, tuna, tuna. Tongue tapping, I'm heading for the tuna.

1

Allessandro di Filipepi (*Fee-lee-PE-pee*) was a small and sickly boy, born in Florence. Sandro, as little Allessandro was called, did not do well in school, so his father sent him to work for a goldsmith. Sandro preferred drawing to working with gold, but the precision design work helped him learn how to draw cleaner lines. Sandro was given the nickname "Botticelli," which meant little barrel or keg. After working with the goldsmith, he was sent to study with a famous artist, Fra Filippo Lippi. This was a life-changing moment for young Sandro, and he immersed himself in the new style of painting that was developing in Florence, one which tried to bring out the natural beauty of humanity.

1. Why was Sandro sent to work for a goldsmith?

2. Why might Sandro have not become a goldsmith?

3. How might learning to draw clean lines when working have helped him become an artist?

4. What do you think Sandro might have looked like if he was given the nickname "Botticelli?"

5. How might working with a famous artist have helped Botticelli?

2

By the time Botticelli was 25, he was popular with the rich nobles of Florence. His delicate paintings came to the attention of the Medici family. The members of this rich family ran Florence and were known for supporting the arts. They hired the young artist to paint a series of portraits and soon he was in demand among the rich. He set up a studio of his own, and set about trying to find a balance between the naturalist art of the classical Romans and Greeks and the heavily Church-influenced art of Italy. As part of the Medici court, he spent his days among the most talented people in the city. His fame grew, and he was known for his lovely style as well as the practical jokes he loved to play on his students.

1. How old was Botticelli when he came to the attention of the Medici family?

2. How might being hired by the powerful Medici family have helped Botticelli?

3. How might setting up his own studio have been important to Botticelli?

4. Why might Botticelli have wanted a balance between naturalist art and Church-influenced art?

5. Why might spending time with talented people have helped Botticelli with his art and fame?

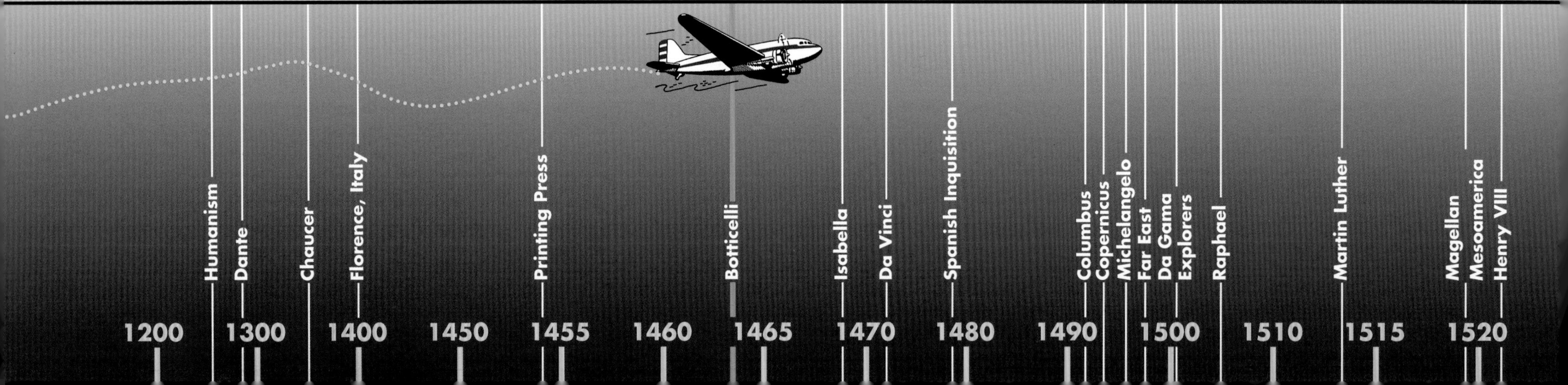
Humanism
Dante
Chaucer
Florence, Italy
Printing Press
Botticelli
Isabella
Da Vinci
Spanish Inquisition
Columbus
Copernicus
Michelangelo
Far East
Da Gama
Explorers
Raphael
Martin Luther
Magellan
Mesoamerica
Henry VIII
1200
1300
1400
1450
1455
1460
1465
1470
1480
1490
1500
1510
1515
1520

3

Botticelli had plenty of work and made loads of money, but he didn't handle his money well. He was often struggling, both with funds and with his poor health. In 1481, when he was 36 years old, Botticelli left Florence for the first and only time in his life. He had been invited to paint wall murals, known as *frescoes* (murals painted on fresh wet plaster), inside the Sistine Chapel in Rome. Only the greatest artists in Italy received such an honor. He chose to paint the trials of Moses and the temptation of Christ. Botticelli quickly painted three frescoes in the chapel. Though he was happy to be so honored, he returned to his beloved home in Florence as soon as he finished, refusing all offers to stay in Rome. This may have been due to his growing health problems.

1. **Where is the Sistine Chapel?**
2. **Do you think the Sistine Chapel was special? Explain.**
3. **Why might Botticelli have wanted to go to Rome?**
4. **Why might Botticelli have had to work quickly?**
5. **Why might having health problems have influenced Botticelli's decision not to stay in Rome?**

4

Botticelli spent several years during the peak of his career earning fine money. He painted religious subjects and portraits. He imagined scenes from mythology, giving them the ethereal (light and airy) look for which he became famous. His most famous painting, *The Birth of Venus*, is an example of his delicate and unique style at its best. The figure of the goddess Venus appears to be almost floating in the air as she steps out of a giant clamshell. Around her, everyone is in awe of her beauty. Botticelli used bold outlines and soft colors to give the main figure an almost transparent, ghostly look. This helped to illustrate that Venus, the goddess of love, was divinely lovely, beyond any human woman.

1. **What is the name of Botticelli's most famous painting?**
2. **Why might Botticelli have imagined scenes from mythology to paint?**
3. **Why might Botticelli have painted Venus to look like she was almost floating in the air?**
4. **How did the use of soft colors and bold outlines affect his painting of Venus?**
5. **Why do you think Botticelli might have wanted Venus to look divinely lovely?**

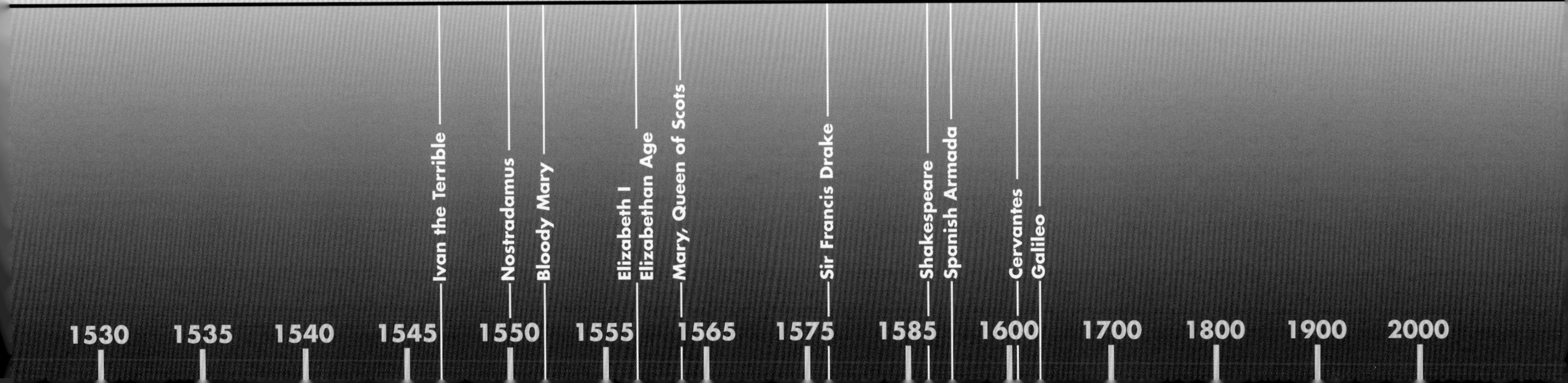
Ivan the Terrible
Nostradamus
Bloody Mary
Elizabeth I
Elizabethan Age
Mary, Queen of Scots
Sir Francis Drake
Shakespeare
Spanish Armada
Cervantes
Galileo
1530
1535
1540
1545
1550
1555
1565
1575
1585
1600
1700
1800
1900
2000

5 In the 1490's, when Botticelli was in his 50's, the Medici family fell from power, leaving the artist with little money or work. A mad priest named Savonarola who wore dark robes and had a hook nose and beady black eyes, had taken over the city. He enforced a strict moral code that all artists were allowed only to paint scenes from the Bible: no myths, legends, or portraits. Botticelli, already very religious, followed the priest with zeal. Legend has it that the artist burned some of his mythical, earlier works to please Savonarola. Penniless and living off the kindness of friends, Botticelli continued to paint until his death at age 65.

1. **What was the name of the scary priest?**
2. **Why do you think Botticelli wanted to please Savonarola?**
3. **Why might Botticelli have burned some of his earlier paintings?**
4. **Why do you think Botticelli's later paintings became less fanciful?**
5. **Why do you think Botticelli died penniless?**

Detail from *Allegory of Spring*, 1481-82 *(left)*; detail from *Adoration of the Magi* includes a self-portrait peering out at the viewer, ca. 1475 *(top, right)*; *The Madonna of the Magnificent*, 1483-85 *(right)*

Ivan says—

The word is that when Florence was ruled by the fanatical priest Savonarola, Botticelli actually burned some of his paintings. Luckily, he didn't burn that clamshell painting of the birth of Venus. Whew. Close call. Who knows, maybe on burning day, someone moved it out of the way. By the way, somebody burned Savonarola—at the stake.

Ah, but I digress in my imagery, here's more news. Botticelli was never good with money and he was too modest to even sign his own paintings. However, his work is sometimes thought of as the perfect example of Renaissance beauty. The soft colors and lines make every single thing in his paintings look ethereal, mythical, and beautiful.

Well, enough of Venus and clamshells. I've got to run to catch that flight attendant on IMAGINE AIR and get a little snack before we take off for Spain. Wait until you read about their queen! Now, as a king, I've considered finding a queen to keep me company. But then I came to my senses. A queen would mean sharing my DISH. Nope. *O solo mio*!

IVAN

36

Flight 7

The Reception of Columbus imagines the explorer presenting goods and people from the New World to Queen Isabella.

Isabella of Spain

1451-1504

Your next Flight is about a very important queen named Isabella. Isabella ruled Spain in the late 1400's and she was a little headstrong. Women in those days were usually not as strong-willed as Isabella, but when she set her mind on doing something, she did it. She did some good things and some very bad things. I mean, what do you think of this for bad? She made all her people become Catholic like her or hit the road, Jack. Not good. I like to be able to believe whatever I want. It is one of those freedoms I cherish.

Isabella did some good things too, as you'll soon visualize, and here's the one she's probably most remembered for: She sent Christopher Columbus on his trip to find the New World! Yup. Read and see why she's important in your human history.

As for trips, while you get to know Isabella, I'll be on a trip of my own. Let's see, shall I make a trip to the refrigerator, or maybe the fish tank, or maybe the birdcage, or maybe just a trip to check my Dish for some leftover morsels.

Gotta go. *Hasta la vista,* baby.

1

One of the strongest rulers of the Renaissance was Isabella I of Castile, a large kingdom in Spain. Isabella paved the way for future Queens. When she was just three years old, her older half-brother Henry IV became King. The young princess lived away from the court with her mother until she was 13, when Henry had her and her other brother, Alfonso, brought to live in the castle. Henry claimed to want to educate the children, but more likely he wanted to keep them under his watchful eye. Even at the royal court, Isabella and Alfonso were the focus of ambitious men who fought over who would sit on the throne next and who would control that ruler. After Alfonso died (possibly poisoned), some nobles offered to get rid of Henry and make young Isabella Queen, but she refused to stand against him. Henry rewarded her loyalty by making her his sole heir.

1. **What kingdom did Isabella rule?**
2. **Why might it be dangerous to be a princess of Spain?**
3. **Why might Alfonso have been murdered and by whom?**
4. **Why might the nobles have wanted young Isabella, not Henry, to be the ruler?**
5. **Why do you think the nobles wanted to control the ruler?**

2

Many members of royalty wanted to marry the future Queen of Castile. But Isabella wished to marry her cousin Ferdinand, the Prince of Aragón, a smaller kingdom in Spain. Even as a teen, she had a vision for uniting the countries of Spain into one nation. It was unusual for a woman to choose her own husband because marriage was often used as a way to link countries or gain territory. Henry did everything he could to force her to marry the King of Portugal, Alfonso V, threatening to imprison her if she did not. But Isabella, only 18, arranged a secret meeting with Ferdinand. Henry heard about the meeting and sent his guards to arrest the young Prince Ferdinand. Ferdinand, dressed as a servant, crossed the country at great peril to get to Isabella. Four days later, they were married. Their marriage in 1469 was the first step to unite Spain into one country.

1. **Who did Isabella want to marry and where was he from?**
2. **Why do you think many members of royalty wanted to marry Isabella?**
3. **Why do you think Henry wanted to decide who Isabella married?**
4. **Why do you think Ferdinand dressed as a servant to go meet Isabella?**
5. **Why was it smart of Isabella to marry Ferdinand?**

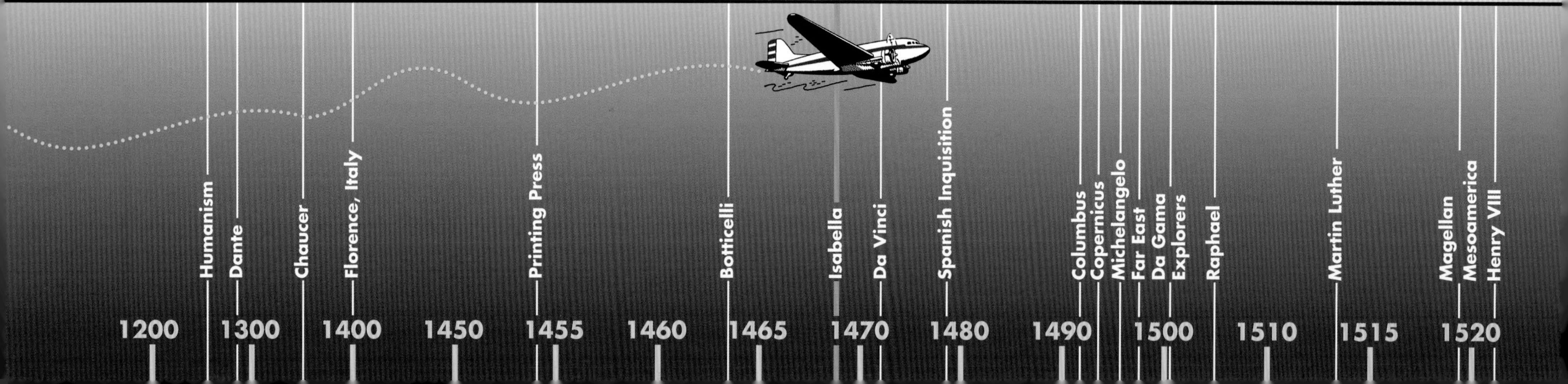

Humanism
Dante
Chaucer
Florence, Italy
Printing Press
Botticelli
Isabella
Da Vinci
Spanish Inquisition
Columbus
Copernicus
Michelangelo
Far East
Da Gama
Explorers
Raphael
Martin Luther
Magellan
Mesoamerica
Henry VIII
1200
1300
1400
1450
1455
1460
1465
1470
1480
1490
1500
1510
1515
1520

3

After King Henry IV died in 1474, Queen Isabella and King Ferdinand went to work securing all parts of Spain under their rule. They sent their armies to invade the south, which had been ruled by the *Moors* for 800 years, taking town after town. Although she was pregnant, Isabella supervised the invasion personally, even visiting the army camps in specially made armor. She was in constant danger, and at one point barely escaped being killed by an assassin. Finally Granada, the last stronghold of the Moors in Spain, fell to her armies. The young Queen was a devoted *Catholic*, and she believed she should rid Spain of the Moors and other people who followed the religion of *Islam*. She also ordered all *Jewish* people of Granada (about 180,000) to convert to her religion or get out of her country.

1. **What religion was Isabella?**
2. **Why do you think Isabella and Ferdinand wanted to secure all parts of Spain?**
3. **Why might Isabella have supervised the invasion personally?**
4. **Why do you think Isabella wanted to rid Spain of followers of Islam and the Jewish people?**
5. **How do you think the Jewish people felt about leaving or converting?**

4

At this same time, Christopher Columbus presented his case to Isabella and Ferdinand for a new sea route to the Far East. This was important because Spain lagged behind Portugal in the search for trade with the Far East and India. With Spain now united and strong, Isabella turned her attention to discovering new worlds to rule. Isabella agreed to finance the voyage that she saw as a genius idea by Columbus. Columbus never made it to the Far East, but he found the Americas instead. This New World provided a huge amount of resources and wealth for Spain, as well as land for colonies. Spain grew rich and powerful, and Isabella used some of this money to work on improving her country.

1. **Who did Isabella finance a voyage for and where did he really want to go?**
2. **Why do you think Isabella became interested in exploration?**
3. **Why might Columbus have needed the Queen's funding to go on a voyage?**
4. **Why do you think Isabella agreed to finance the trip?**
5. **Why might having land for colonies have benefited Spain?**

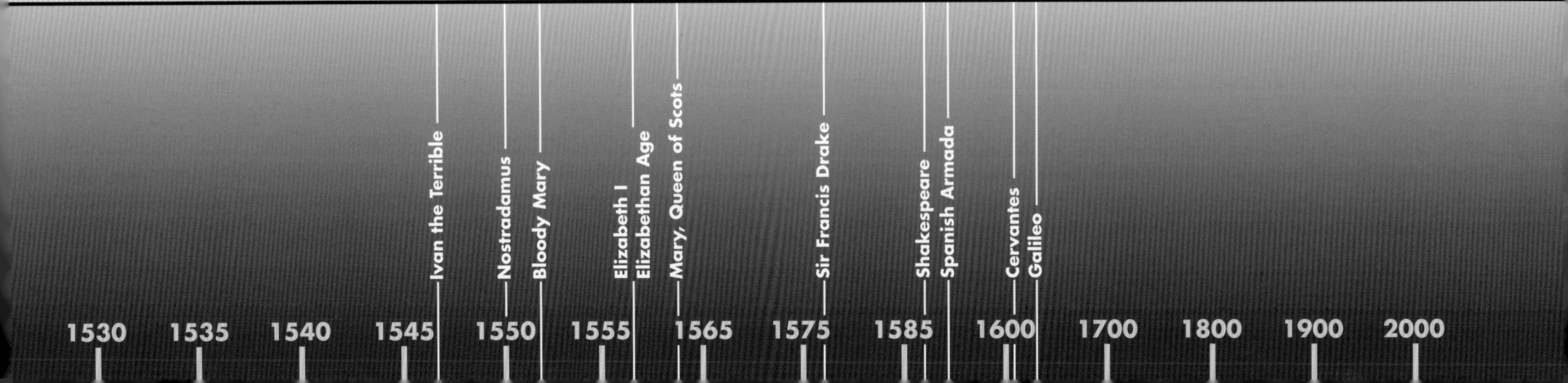
Ivan the Terrible
Nostradamus
Bloody Mary
Elizabeth I
Elizabethan Age
Mary, Queen of Scots
Sir Francis Drake
Shakespeare
Spanish Armada
Cervantes
Galileo
1530
1535
1540
1545
1550
1555
1565
1575
1585
1600
1700
1800
1900
2000

Wedding portraits of Isabella and Ferdinand *(left)*; a tapestry from Lérida Cathedral depicts the rulers on the throne, ca. 1400's *(right)*

5

Isabella was well educated, and had her five children, as well as their friends, taught in a palace school. She read and studied law, which led to a unified code of laws for Spain. She had new roads built and public buildings repaired. She was smart at managing the finances of the kingdom and she was even known to mend her husband's clothes as they wore out. However, her fanatical zeal for the Catholic religion led to the death and suffering of millions in the Spanish Inquisition. In 1504, at age 53, Isabella lay dying and proclaimed suddenly that the natives of the New World were not to be mistreated. It was too little too late, and her words were ignored by greedy explorers.

1. **What was Isabella a fanatic about?**
2. **Why was it good that Isabella was well educated?**
3. **Why would it be unusual for Isabella to mend her husband's clothes?**
4. **Why do you think Isabella's order not to mistreat the natives of the New World was ignored?**
5. **Why do you think Isabella made the proclamation on her deathbed and not earlier?**

Columbus' first meeting with Isabella and Ferdinand, as imagined by Henry Nelson O'Neill *(left)*

Ivan says—

Isabella was both sweet and sour—some good and some bad.

Isabella made some great decisions—like setting up the law code and uniting her country. But let's talk about Isabella's worst decision…to make all of Spain one religion. This is scary stuff. All over Europe, the Roman Catholic Church was trying to recruit new members and stamp out other religions. Isabella decided to set up her own investigation, the Spanish Inquisition. She set up courts and inquisitors (judges) to talk to the people and determine whether they were Catholic or otherwise.

Bite your tongue and get ready for the big, country-wide question-and-answer session that lasted hundreds of years. Any wrong answer could lead to death. So say nothing. Just read.

Me? I'm not saying nothing. My mouth is full, and it's not polite to talk with your mouth full.

A painting shows the Inquisition questioning the accused, ca. 15th c.

The Spanish Inquisition

1478-1834

Unbuckle and be careful. This Flight is full of horrible images, but it is an important part of history, so grit your teeth.

The Spanish Inquisition was part of a madness sweeping across Europe that drove everyone to look for witches and devils among their own neighbors. The Roman Catholic Church had set up the Inquisition to find, try, and punish witches. In Spain, King Ferdinand and Queen Isabella wanted everyone to follow their religion, and set up their own Spanish Inquisition. Not all the people of Spain wanted to change their religion, so what followed was hundreds of years of people being sent out of the country, put on trial, or killed.

This is something I don't understand about humans. Sometimes rulers and people in power do terrible things in the name of their country or religion. Sad, sad.

Teeth clenched? Okay, let's read and visualize the Spanish Inquisition. Grit and go. Hmmm. Grits.

1

The Spanish Inquisition was a court set up by Isabella of Spain to find, put on trial, and punish non-Catholics in her country. Spain had long been home to both Muslims and Jews, as well as Catholics. But thc unification of the country under Queen Isabella meant that they were not welcome unless they converted to Catholicism. Many people fled in fear for their lives while others practiced their religion in secret. They met at night or in secret bunkers, while in public they attended Catholic mass. They pretended to be Catholic, even though getting caught might mean death. They felt it was worth the risk to keep their homes and businesses. Some of these families had lived in Spain for generations and did not want to give up their homeland.

1. **What was the Spanish Inquisition?**
2. **Why might Isabella have wanted Jews and Muslims to convert?**
3. **Why do you think many fled rather than become Catholic?**
4. **Why might some people have chosen to stay and practice their religion in secret?**
5. **Why was it important some attended Catholic mass in public?**

2

The Queen and her advisors in the Catholic Church did not believe that the new converts were true Catholics. They thought that many were *heretics* (those who went against the rules of the Catholic Church). They were right in guessing that some of the "converted" people had really stayed true to their own religion in secret. She also believed that anyone who would try so hard to go against the Queen's wishes could be a danger to the Crown. Isabella and Ferdinand asked the highest authority in the Church, the Pope, for permission to rid their country of non-Catholics. With his blessing, the well-meaning rulers then chose pious (very religious) churchmen to serve as judges, called inquisitors, in the Spanish Inquisition. Systems to arrest, question, and punish non-Catholics were set up in the cities of Spain.

1. **What is a heretic?**
2. **Why might the Catholic Church think that the converts were not true Catholics?**
3. **Why might the Queen feel she had to set up the courts?**
4. **How might non-Catholics pose a danger to the Crown?**
5. **Why do you think only pious churchmen were chosen to serve as judges?**

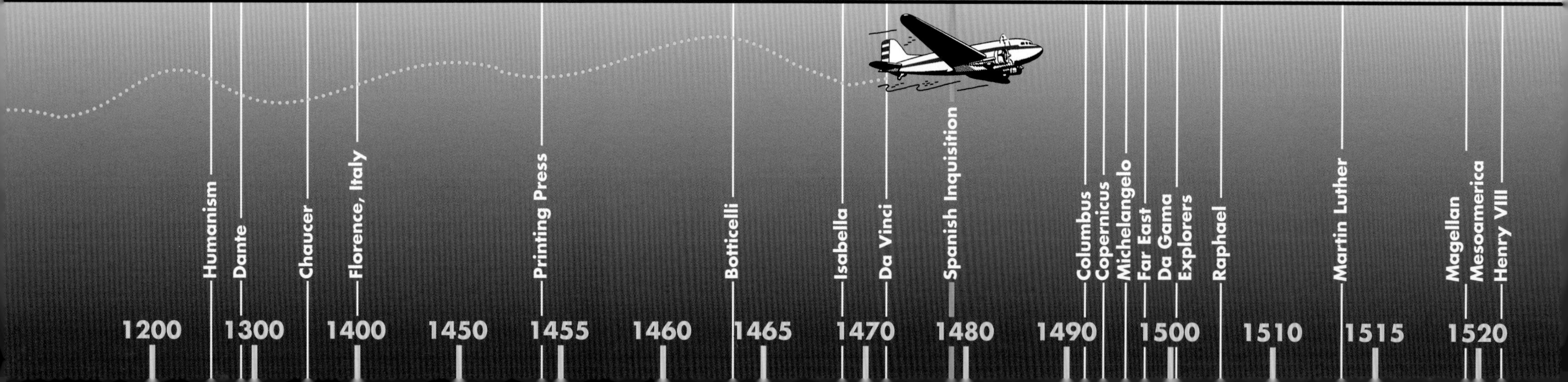

Humanism
Dante
Chaucer
Florence, Italy
Printing Press
Botticelli
Isabella
Da Vinci
Spanish Inquisition
Columbus
Copernicus
Michelangelo
Far East
Da Gama
Explorers
Raphael
Martin Luther
Magellan
Mesoamerica
Henry VIII
1200
1300
1400
1450
1455
1460
1465
1470
1480
1490
1500
1510
1515
1520

3

Isabella's priest, Father Torquemada (*Tor-kay-MAH-dah*), took on the job of becoming the Grand, or head, Inquisitor for the Spanish Inquisition. He had been raised to a high position in the court by Isabella, but he refused any titles or glory, preferring to remain a humble friar. He organized a system that gave offenders 30 to 40 days grace period to surrender. Catholic citizens were asked to report anyone who acted differently, including those who washed their hands before meals or did not eat pork (rules in some other religions). Muslims and Jews had rules like these that they followed. If someone wore clean clothes and did not work on Saturdays, they were suspect.

1. **Who became the Grand Inquisitor?**
2. **Why might Torquemada refuse titles and glory?**
3. **Why might citizens have reported on other citizens?**
4. **Why do you think a person who washed their hands before meals would be considered suspect?**
5. **Why might Torquemada have agreed to run the Inquisition?**

4

Torquemada has been described as being cruel during his 14 years of running the trials. The Inquisition had people arrested, and taken to the courts to be examined for *heresy* (speaking against the Church) in the presence of two priests. If the frightened person confessed to being non-Catholic, the kingdom claimed all their land and goods. Some confessors were allowed to repent and live while others were killed. If they did not confess, they were tortured until they did, or until they died. Many people suffered under the Spanish Inquisition. Muslims and Jews were forced to leave the country where their families had lived for generations, or to die horrible deaths at the hands of torturers or executioners. Men, women, and children were all under threat of pain or death, so many people chose to leave Spain.

1. **How long did Torquemada run the Spanish Inquisition?**
2. **Why do you think someone would confess if they weren't guilty?**
3. **Why do you think some people were executed?**
4. **Why might someone have been allowed to live after their trial?**
5. **How do you think the Muslims and Jews felt about leaving Spain?**

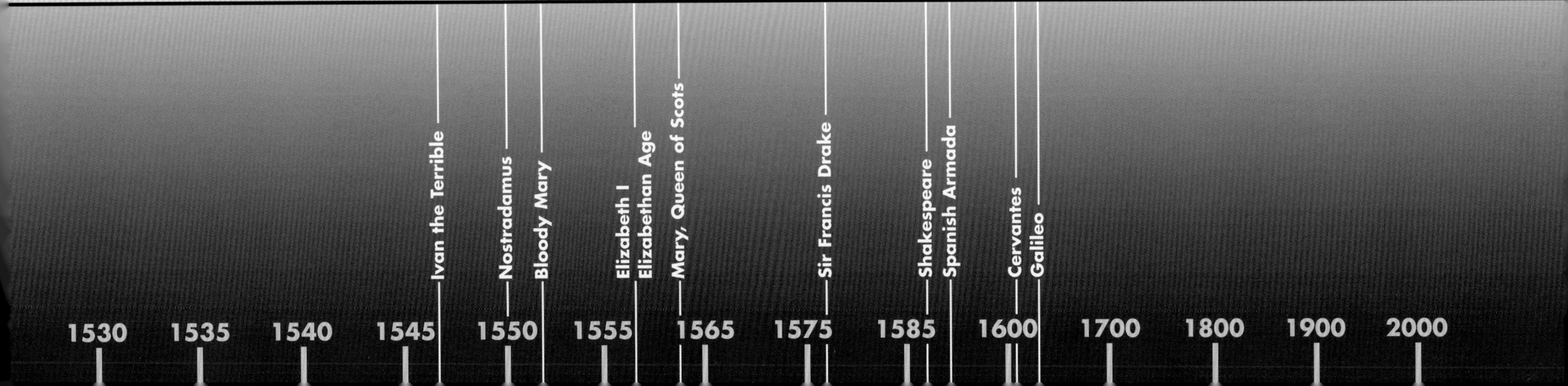
Ivan the Terrible
Nostradamus
Bloody Mary
Elizabeth I
Elizabethan Age
Mary, Queen of Scots
Sir Francis Drake
Shakespeare
Spanish Armada
Cervantes
Galileo
1530
1535
1540
1545
1550
1555
1565
1575
1585
1600
1700
1800
1900
2000

Goya's painting of the Inquisition *(left)*; a woodcut allegory for the burning of Jews by the Inquisition *(right)*

EXURGE DOMINE ET JUDICA CAUSAM TUAM PSALM. 73.

5 The horrible trials of the Spanish Inquisition finally ended in 1834, after more than 350 years. Nearly 200,000 people had been found guilty of heresy. Of these, over 14,000 had been killed. Over five million people had been forced to leave Spain. They had to leave most of their friends, businesses, and belongings behind. They were not allowed take any gold or silver with them. Most had trouble finding any place that would welcome them, now that they had been branded as outsiders. Many people died of hunger or homelessness.

1. **How many people were forced to leave Spain during the Spanish Inquisition?**
2. **Why do you think they had to leave most of their belongings behind?**
3. **Why might not being allowed to take gold and silver with them be a problem?**
4. **Why might it be difficult for someone who was forced to leave to find a new home?**
5. **Why do you think the Spanish Inquisition lasted so many years?**

Don fernando y doña ysabel
Reyes de castilla y de aragon.

The banner of the Spanish Inquisition *(center left)*; wedding portrait of Isabella and Ferdinand *(left)*; a woodcut shows the Inquisition at work *(right)*

Ivan says—

A pretty dreadful piece of history, isn't it? It makes my whiskers curl just thinking about what those poor people went through. Catholic, Muslim, Jewish…it's all the same to me.

In addition to non-Catholics, the Spanish Inquisition went after scientists as well. Galileo, an astronomer who discovered that the planets revolve around the sun, had to face the Inquisition and lived under house arrest until his death. You'll meet him at the end of our long journey.

We've looked over Isabella's worst decision, the Spanish Inquisition. Now let's talk about Isabella's greatest decision…to finance the voyage of a guy who was completely wrong in his travel plans and calculations. This big mistake led to the discovery of the New World—that's America to you and me.

CAT NIP
Fresh
Meow Munch
Kitty Krisps
NEW

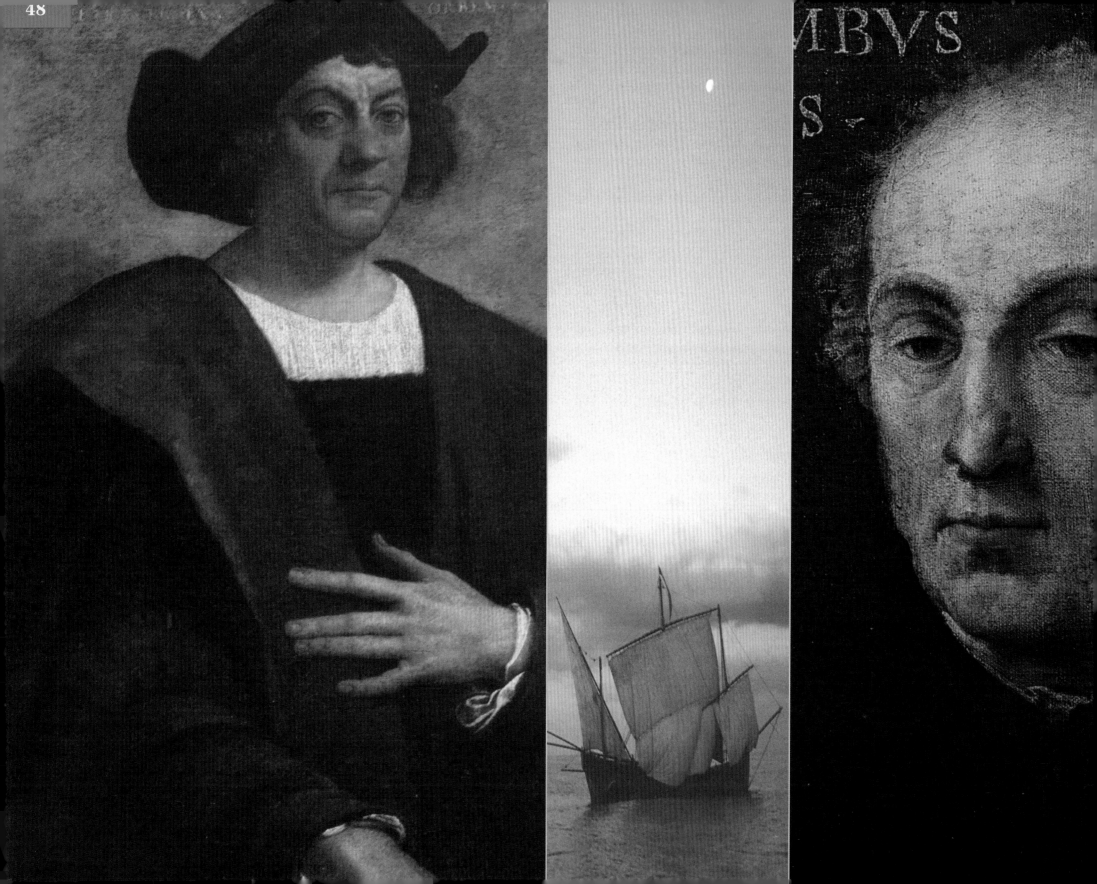

MBVS
S

Flight 9

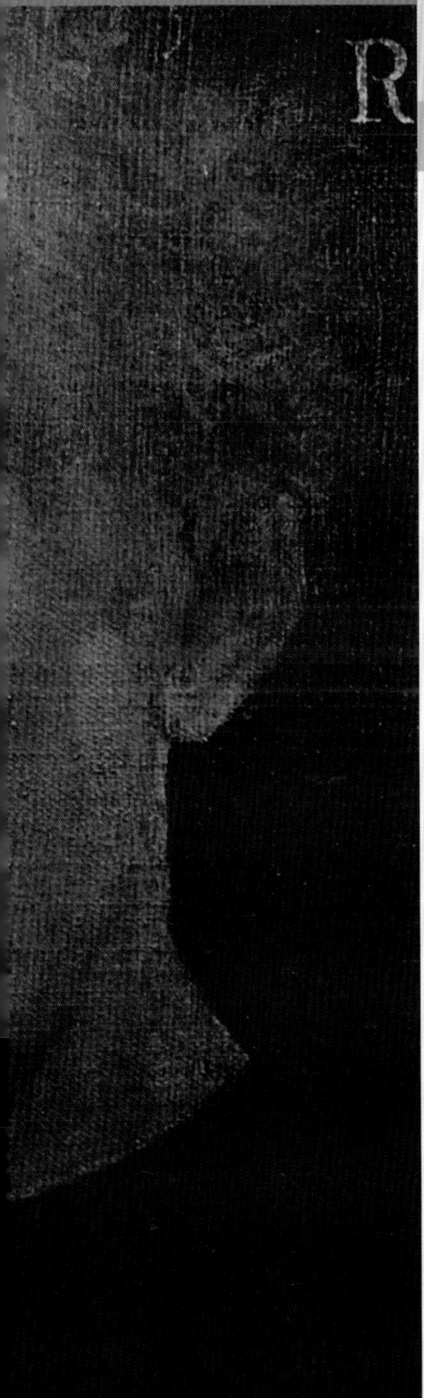

Columbus in his youth *(left)*; a replica of the *Santa Maria (center)*; Columbus in his old age *(right)*

Columbus

1451-1506

Holy mistake! This Flight is about a famous flub. Christopher Columbus became famous for making one very big mistake. He was busy trying to get to China and India when he discovered the New World—America—instead.

Chris's problem was that he thought the world was a lot smaller than it really was. Picture a tennis ball to represent the world. Now picture Columbus holding a golf ball. That's the size he thought the world was! Of course, that's not as bad as the humans who thought the world was flat like a pancake. They thought if you sailed too far in one direction, you would fall right off the edge of the world.

Here's news. Chris wasn't the first explorer from the Old World to set foot in the New World. Nope. The truth is that the Viking, Leif Eriksson, beat him by around 500 years. But the Vikings didn't stay—so let's give it to Chris. He changed the world by starting the first trading camps and permanent colonies there. He paved the way for all the explorers and pioneers and colonists—and their cats who followed.

Get your life vest. You read and visualize. I'm heading to the aquarium for a little sailing myself.

CHINA
AMERICA

1

Christopher Columbus was raised on the coast of Italy. His father was an Italian wool merchant and a weaver, but the little boy didn't want to join the family business. Like other young men in port cities, he dreamed of sailing to faraway lands on the big wooden ships he saw at the docks. At 14, he got his wish, as he began sailing on ships in the Mediterranean Sea and Atlantic Ocean. During this time, he learned all he could about winds and currents. After hearing tales of riches in the East, Columbus decided to search for a new sea route. All he needed was someone with money to fund his ships, supplies, and men.

1. Where was Columbus from?

2. Why do you think a young man in a port city might want to sail?

3. How might Columbus' experience on ships have prepared him for his later journeys?

4. Why might learning about winds and currents have been important for Columbus?

5. How do you think hearing tales of riches in far off lands influenced young Columbus?

2

Columbus had been all over the eastern seas, and was a longtime veteran of sailing by the time he was 23. Like most people, he knew the world was round. Columbus also thought the world was a bit smaller than it actually is, so he thought he could get to the East quicker by sailing west, not east. He was certain he would be sailing over open sea, and that this would take only a short time. He took his radical idea to King Alfonso V of Portugal and asked him to finance the voyage. The king denied his request, mainly because he thought Columbus was wrong about how long the trip might take. Frustrated, the sailor left Portugal in 1485, in search of someone else to support his voyage.

1. Where did Columbus want to go?

2. Which way did Columbus think he should sail and why?

3. Why do you think Columbus went to a king about his trip?

4. Why might Columbus' idea have been considered radical?

5. What might happen to the crew and ships if the trip lasted much longer than Columbus thought it would?

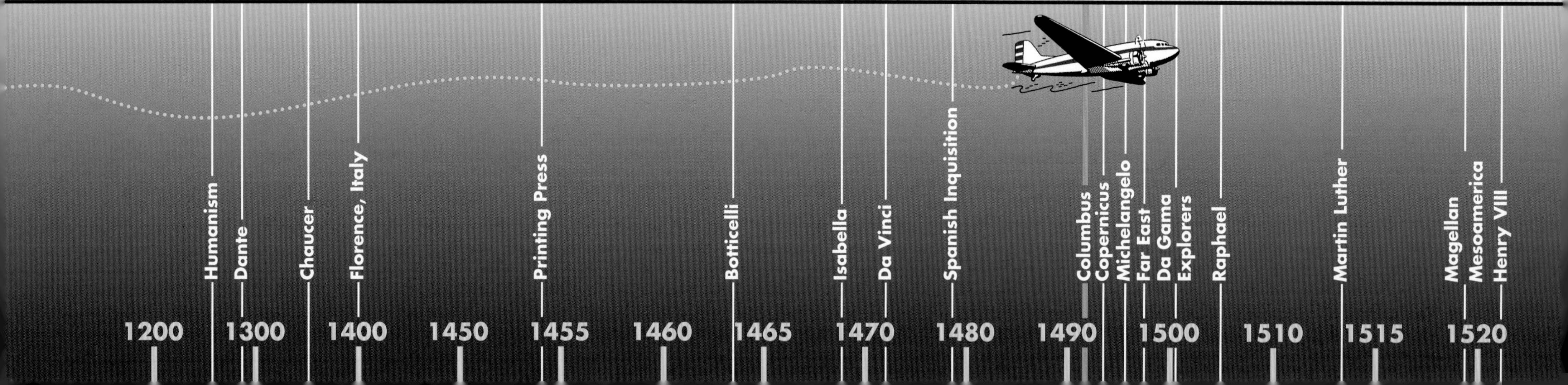
Humanism
Dante
Chaucer
Florence, Italy
Printing Press
Botticelli
Isabella
Da Vinci
Spanish Inquisition
Columbus
Copernicus
Michelangelo
Far East
Da Gama
Explorers
Raphael
Martin Luther
Magellan
Mesoamerica
Henry VIII
1200
1300
1400
1450
1455
1460
1465
1470
1480
1490
1500
1510
1515
1520

3 Columbus went to Spain to ask Queen Isabella and King Ferdinand for money for his voyage. Several times, he was turned down, as the royals were busy managing armies to unite Spain under their rule. Columbus, nearly penniless after several failed bids, caught the notice of a priest named Friar Perez. Perez fed and sheltered the sailor, and then personally went to Isabella to plead Columbus' case. Finally, Isabella agreed to pay for the voyage, believing Columbus' maps to be right. Soon Columbus hired a crew of 85 sailors for his three ships and was on his way, sailing due west, to the Far East.

1. **Where did Columbus go to seek money for his voyage?**
2. **Why do you think Columbus was nearly penniless from several failed bids?**
3. **Why might Friar Perez's involvement have been important?**
4. **Why do you think Columbus needed three ships?**
5. **Do you think the sailors Columbus hired believed in his route?**

4 On August 6th, 1492, Columbus and his men sailed west on his ships the *Niña*, *Pinta*, and *Santa Maria*. The ships carried enough food and water to last one year. The sailors spent months at sea without any sign of land. Columbus kept two journals, one that recorded the actual months that passed and one that was a fictional accounting that described the voyage as taking fewer months. Finally, the crew spotted birds flying above them and they knew they were near land. They came to a lush green island. Columbus, using his mistaken calculations, thought he had reached the Far East, but he was actually now in a part of the world that no modern European had ever seen. He visited several more islands, and carefully packed all kinds of new food, plants, and animals into his ships' holds.

1. **What were the names of Columbus' ships?**
2. **Why might the amount of food the ships carried be important?**
3. **Why might birds have indicated the nearness of land?**
4. **Why might Columbus have kept a journal that showed that he took fewer months?**
5. **Why do you think they had animals on the ships?**

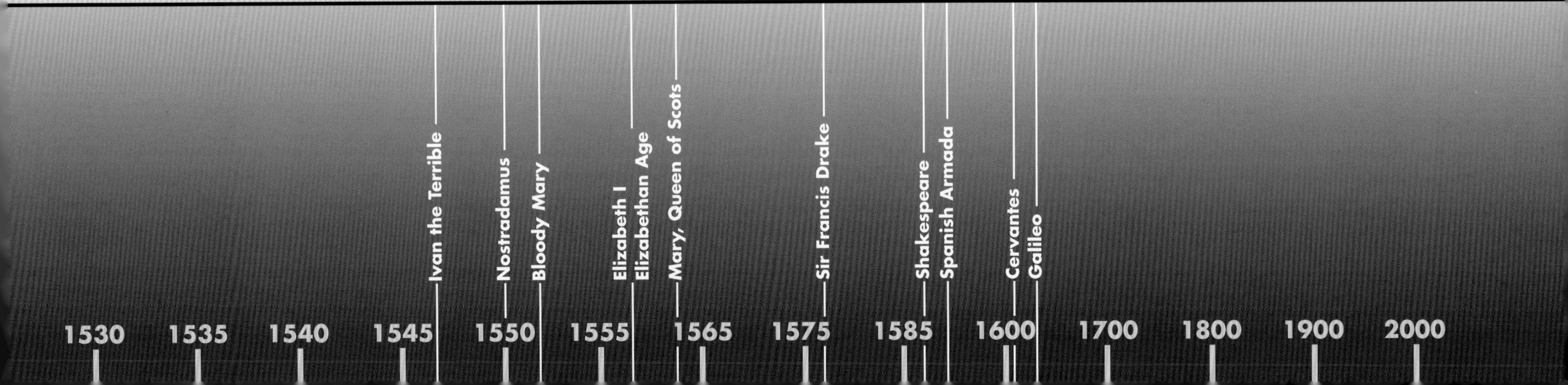
Ivan the Terrible
Nostradamus
Bloody Mary
Elizabeth I
Elizabethan Age
Mary, Queen of Scots
Sir Francis Drake
Shakespeare
Spanish Armada
Cervantes
Galileo
1530
1535
1540
1545
1550
1555
1565
1575
1585
1600
1700
1800
1900
2000

Caiquos
Ile de la Tortue
Ste Isabelle
Cap Francois
Cap Cabron
ISLE St DOMINGUE OU ESPAGNOLE
Conception de la Vega
St. Domingo ou St. Dominique
Isle a Vache deserte ou Ybaca
Ouest
Est
GOLFE DE MEXIQUE

A map of the area Columbus is thought to have landed at *(above)*

5 On the island of San Salvador, a group of native people came to meet the strangely dressed visitors. Using a sort of sign language, Columbus tried to confirm that they were in China, and when he couldn't, he said they were anyway. They explored several islands before returning in 1493 to Spain with corn, tomatoes, *cacao* (*ca-CAY-o*, what chocolate is made from) gold, and even some natives. He sailed back in 1498 and again in 1502 to the New World with pigs, wheat, chickens, horses, and bananas. He kept trying to prove that his route was correct, but it was not. At the time of his death, in 1506, Columbus still kept insisting that he had reached China, though many now knew otherwise. He had discovered the New World—America.

1. Where did Columbus believe he had landed?

2. Why might the native people have come to meet Columbus and his crew?

3. Why do you think Columbus needed sign language to communicate with the natives?

4. Why do you think Columbus brought cacao, tomatoes, corn, and natives back to Spain?

5. Why do you think Columbus insisted to his dying day that he had reached China?

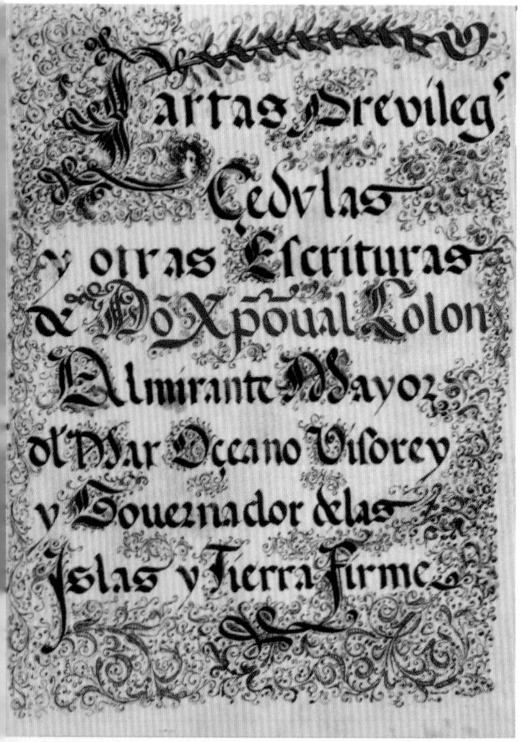
Cartas Previleg'
Cedvlas
y otras Escrituras
de Dō Xpoual Colon
Almirante Mayor
dl Mar Oceano Visorey
y Gouernador delas
Islas y Tierra firme.

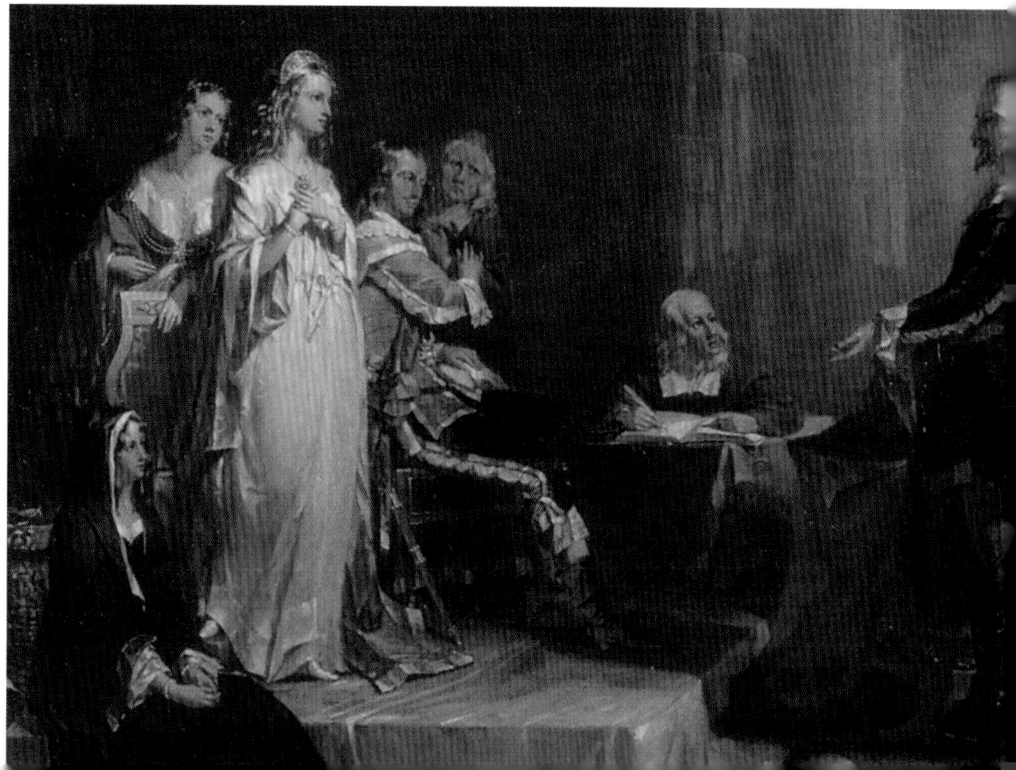

A page from the agreement, called *The Capitulations*, between Columbus and the Queen of Spain *(left)*; *Columbus Before the Queen*, 1841 *(right)*

Ivan says—

Columbus tried to use Marco Polo's book *Travels* to help him locate China. But Marco Polo had gone east, and over land, not west over water. So Chris missed his mark but landed somewhere even more important.

Maybe one of the great gifts of Columbus was that he brought cacao, the stuff from which chocolate is made, back to Spain. It took years before anyone but the royals were allowed to have any, and even then it was a bitter drink, not the candy I know and love. Chocolate candy came a long time later, when a Swiss fellow added milk and sugar to the bitter powder.

Off sweets and on to an animal lover and procrastinator, two of my other favorite things. Let's meet one of the most famous artists of the Renaissance, or even all time—Leonardo da Vinci.

Chocolate

Smiling mysteriously, Ivan heads to the candy box.

(clockwise from left) portrait of Isabella d'Este, ca. 1490; self-portrait, ca. 1514; *Un Condottiero*, ca. 1472; Leonardo's design for a machine, ca. 1488; *Head of a Tousled Young Woman*, ca. 1490

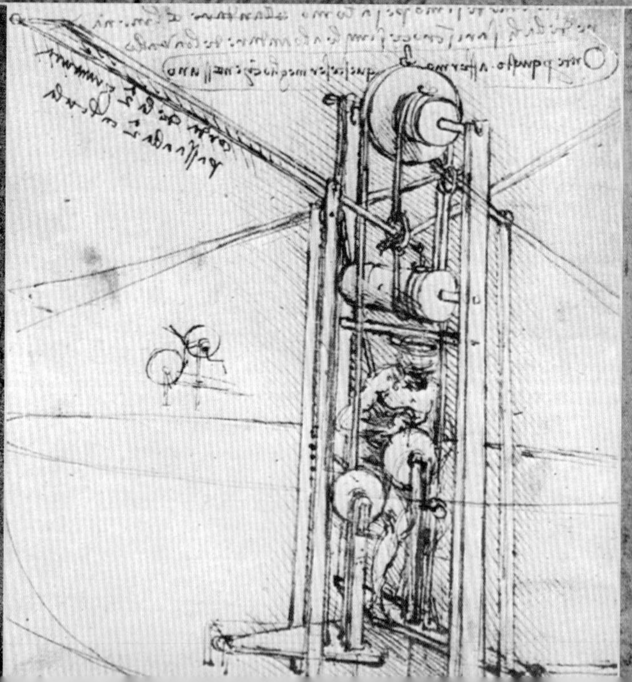

Flight 10

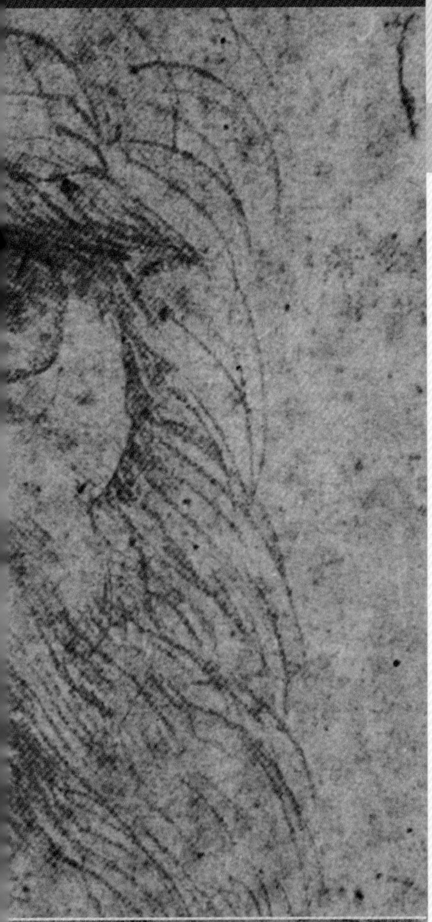

Leonardo da Vinci

1452-1519

Your next two Flights are all about one Italian man. Two Flights! Leonardo da Vinci (*da VIN-chee*) was a great artist, an inventor, and most importantly of all, he loved animals. I'm sure cats were his favorite. He was interested in everything and did it all, which is what we mean when we call someone a Renaissance Man.

Da Vinci created the most famous painting in the world. This great work of art is called the *Mona Lisa* (pg. 58). Experts are still trying to figure out who the girl in the painting is (some say it is da Vinci in a dress, while others think it is an noblewoman), and why she's smiling so mysteriously.

The *Mona Lisa* was stolen once from its place in the Louvre museum in Paris, France, and was lost for two years. The Louvre got it back, and now it is protected by glass, guards, and alarms.

Speaking of alarms, I set off the alarm on the refrigerator last night and had to sleep outside in the garage. Not good, not good at all. You read about da Vinci. I'm heading for da Dish.

1

Leonardo da Vinci was born near Florence, in 1452. His father took extra care in raising his gifted genius son who had many talents and a keen memory. At 14, Leonardo was sent to work for a famous painter, Verrocchio (*Ver-ROH-kee-oh*), where he studied the history of art and architecture. Together, the student and his teacher collected antiques, and kept them in the garden of the famed Medici family. But Leonardo was not influenced at all by classical art, unlike other artists of his time. He preferred instead to study living beings. By the time he was 25, Leonardo had his own art studio. Legend has it that Verrocchio stopped painting when he saw how much better Leonardo was than him.

1. **Where was Leonardo da Vinci born?**
2. **Why do you think Leonardo's father took extra care in raising him?**
3. **Why do you think Leonardo was sent to work for Verrocchio?**
4. **Why might it have been important that Leonardo studied the history of art and architecture?**
5. **How do you think Leonardo's study of living beings might have affected his artwork?**

2

Da Vinci's many interests helped shape his unusual lifestyle. His love of nature and animals led him to become a *vegetarian* who refused to eat meat. He often bought caged animals at the marketplace, with his only purpose being to set them free. Cats, birds, and dogs wandered his studio freely. He took home dead animals and reptiles when he found them on the roads, and dissected them to study their anatomy (body). This study of nature helped him learn to draw very realistically. So busy and intent was he working through the night and day, he often did not even notice when the dead creatures began to smell quite bad or the pets chewed up the furniture. He was happy in his chaotic home as long as he was learning.

1. **What animals wandered Leonardo's studio?**
2. **Why do you think it might have been unusual to be a vegetarian back then?**
3. **Why do you think Leonardo took home dead animals?**
4. **How might dissecting an animal have helped Leonardo make his drawing more realistic?**
5. **Why do you think Leonardo wouldn't eat meat but would dissect animals?**

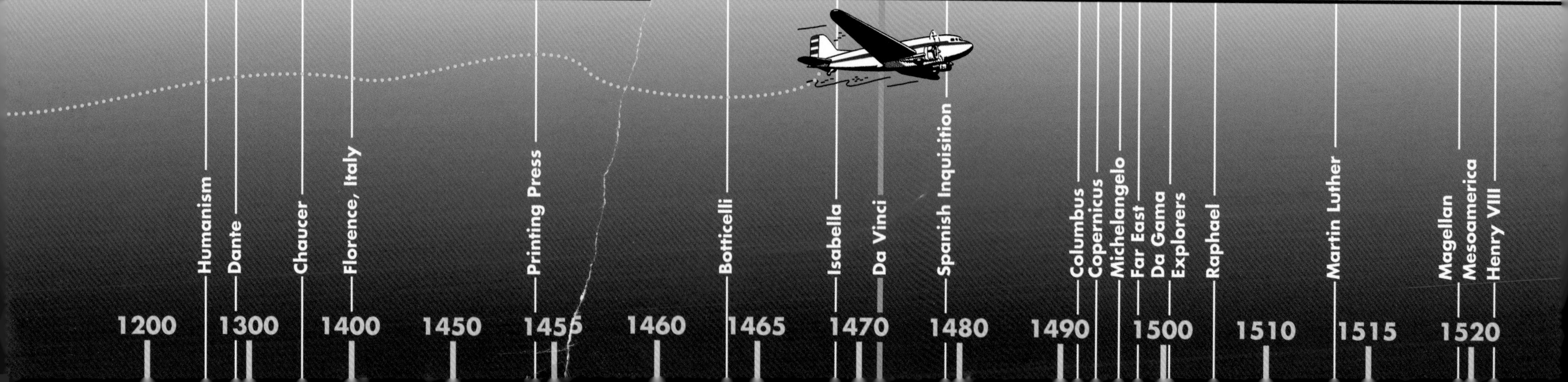
Humanism
Dante
Chaucer
Florence, Italy
Printing Press
Botticelli
Isabella
Da Vinci
Spanish Inquisition
Columbus
Copernicus
Michelangelo
Far East
Da Gama
Explorers
Raphael
Martin Luther
Magellan
Mesoamerica
Henry VIII
1200
1300
1400
1450
1455
1460
1465
1470
1480
1490
1500
1510
1515
1520

3

Da Vinci was known for the passionate way he lived his life. The handsome artist enjoyed his work more than anything. Once he even refused payment for a small painting, telling the patron that he did not paint for money, but for pure joy instead. Although he never married, Leonardo did adopt two orphaned boys. He taught them all about the art and science he loved, as he had been taught in his youth. Leonardo found inspiration in everything around him. He found it in the people he met, the animals he cared for, and the machines he used. To understand and improve the world became his lifelong desire.

1. **What was Leonardo's lifelong desire?**
2. **Why might people have said that Leonardo lived his life passionately?**
3. **Do you think it was common for an unmarried man to adopt two orphaned boys? Why or why not?**
4. **Why do you think Leonardo taught the boys about art and science?**
5. **How might Leonardo have worked on understanding and improving the world around him?**

4

When da Vinci was 43, he was asked to paint the wall of a dining hall in a monastery near Milan. After sizing up the huge wall, Leonardo began work on *The Last Supper* (pg. 203), one of the most famous paintings in the world. Always looking for ways to experiment, Leonardo came up with a new way to paint that would let him work slow. For the next two years, he worked to recreate the scene from the Bible in a way that had not been done before. He made the scene on the wall seem more life-like by arranging the disciples (Jesus' close followers) in groups, rather than in a line, with real expressions on their faces. Those who viewed the finished work were stunned at how Leonardo had found a way to make their eyes look at Jesus, making him the focus of the picture. It did not take long for people to applaud da Vinci for his masterpiece.

1. **What is the name of Leonardo's famous painting?**
2. **Why do you think Leonardo chose to paint a scene from the Bible?**
3. **Why do you think Leonardo painted the disciples differently than they had been painted before?**
4. **Why might Leonardo have wanted to draw people's attention to Jesus in the painting?**
5. **Why might Leonardo have wanted the disciples to have real expressions**

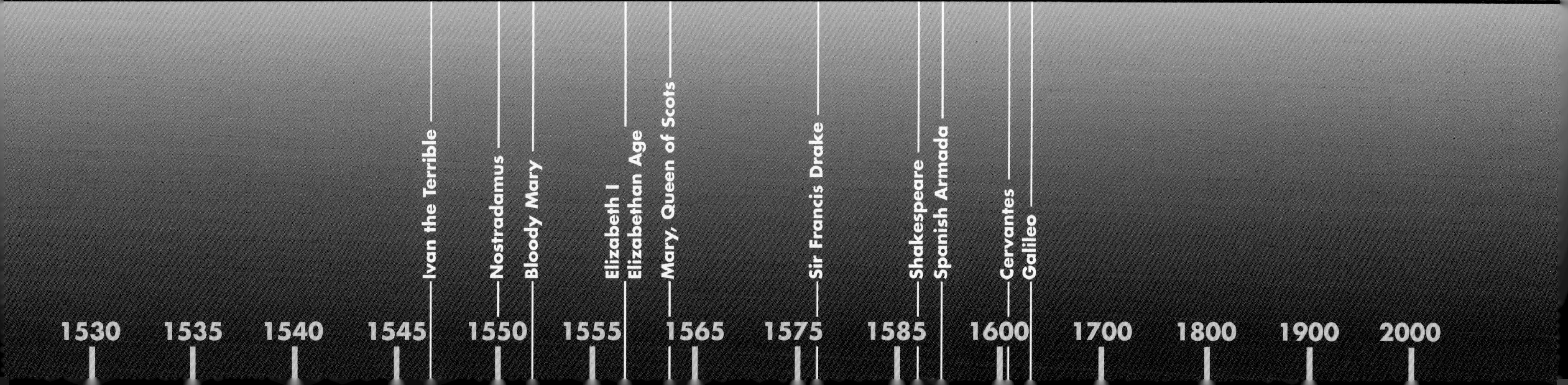
Ivan the Terrible
Nostradamus
Bloody Mary
Elizabeth I
Elizabethan Age
Mary, Queen of Scots
Sir Francis Drake
Shakespeare
Spanish Armada
Cervantes
Galileo
1530
1535
1540
1545
1550
1555
1565
1575
1585
1600
1700
1800
1900
2000

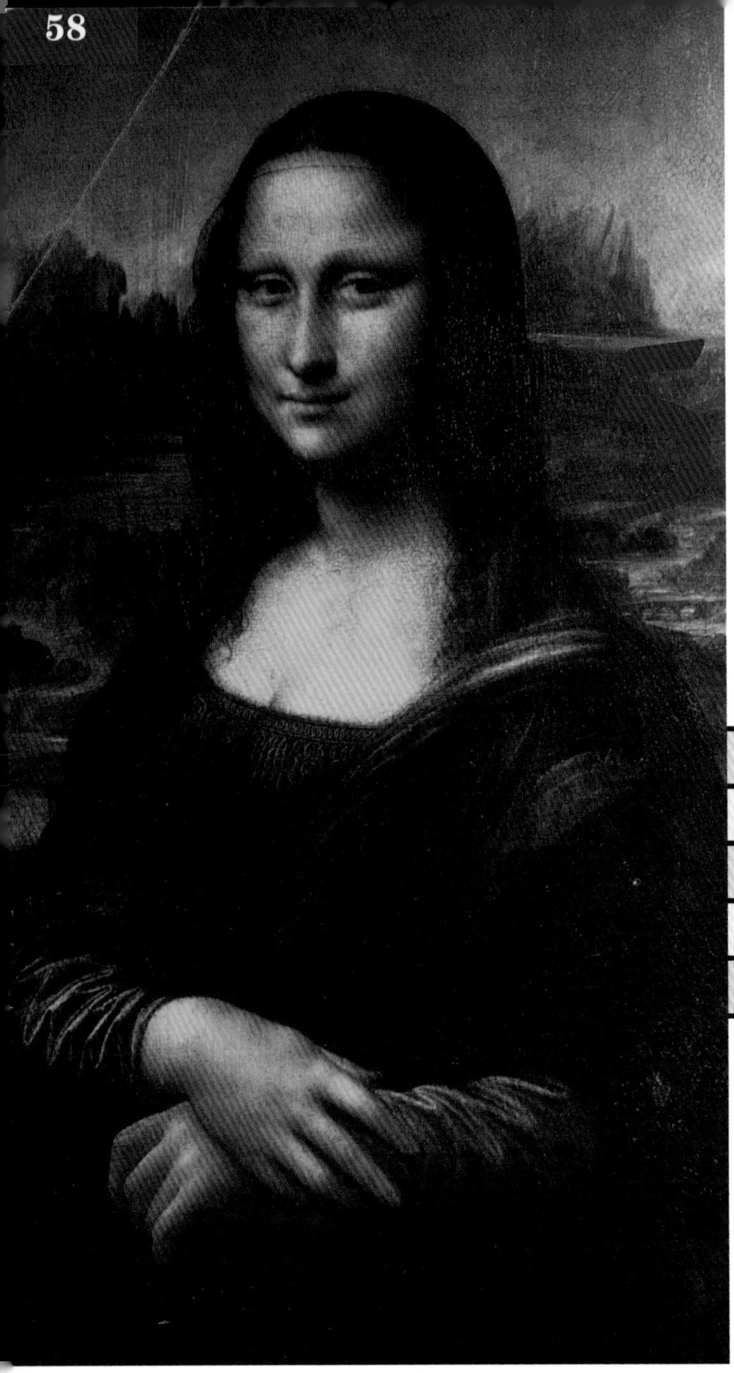

Mona Lisa, 1513-15 *(left)*; a study for the Equestrian Monument to Francesco Sforza, 1483-84 *(right, top)*; detail from *The Annunciation*, 1472-75 *(bottom)*

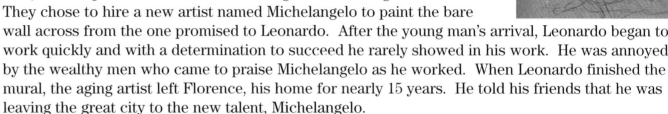

Da Vinci liked being known as the best artist of his time. In 1503, at the age of 51, he was asked to paint a large mural on a palace wall in Florence. One year later, he had not yet touched his brush to the blank wall, and his patrons were tired of waiting for him to begin his work. They chose to hire a new artist named Michelangelo to paint the bare wall across from the one promised to Leonardo. After the young man's arrival, Leonardo began to work quickly and with a determination to succeed he rarely showed in his work. He was annoyed by the wealthy men who came to praise Michelangelo as he worked. When Leonardo finished the mural, the aging artist left Florence, his home for nearly 15 years. He told his friends that he was leaving the great city to the new talent, Michelangelo.

1. How long did it take Leonardo to begin his work on the mural?

2. Why might people have wanted Leonardo to paint a mural in a palace?

3. Why do you think Leonardo became determined to succeed on this mural?

4. Why do you think Leonardo did not like to hear the wealthy men praise Michelangelo?

5. Why do you think Leonardo decided to leave Florence to Michelangelo?

Ivan says—

Awwww, what a talented guy. Da Vinci could write equally well left or right-handed, too. His notes have to be held up to a mirror to be read by anyone but him. No one knows if this was so that he could keep everything secret, or if writing this way helped him keep from smearing the ink with his own arm. Maybe he just liked to write backwards. To this, I can only say WOW, which my buddy da Vinci would have written backwards, as WOW.

Da Vinci, at one time, got a commission to build a monument to the Duke of Milan, a great man named Sforza. He designed a 40-foot-high horse statue, but he never got around to finishing it. He was too busy inventing, draining swamps, and figuring out the world. Sforza died before Leonardo had done much work.

Leonardo can't really be understood by just reading his life story. His true genius was in his ability to see how things work, to visualize, and to create new devices based on his pictures. For that, you fly on ahead!

I'm busy sketching mice for dinner...or as I like to call them, fast food.

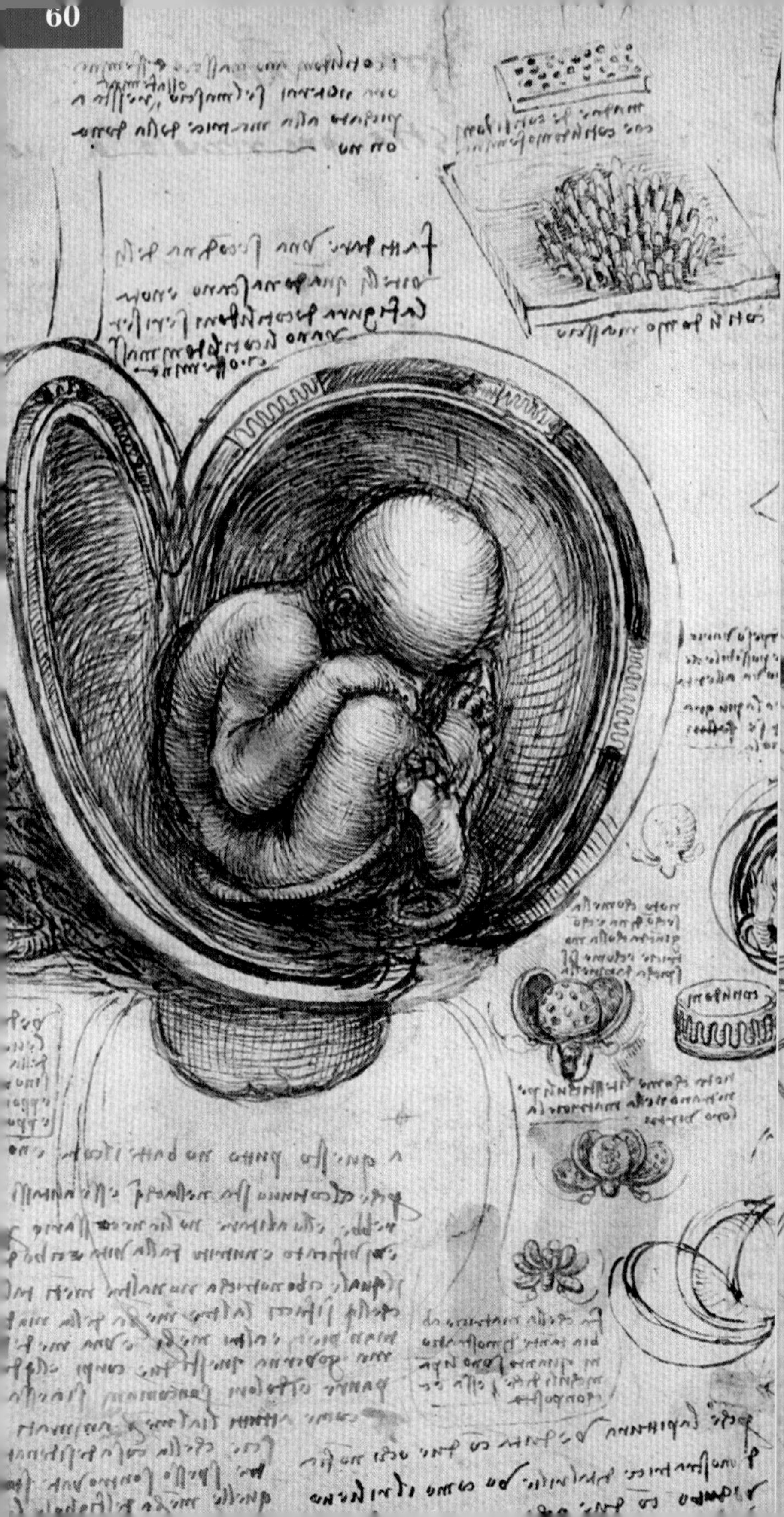

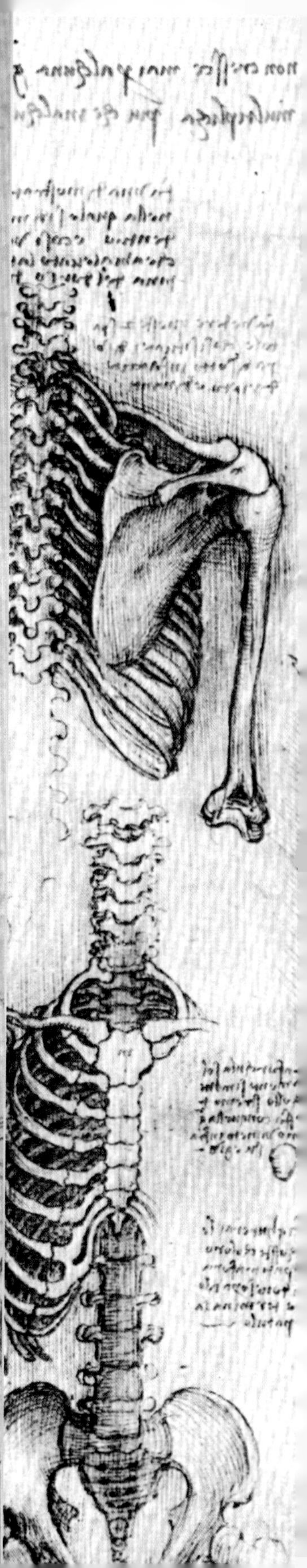

(from left) a study of a baby in a womb; designs for a life preserver, helicopter, and wing; studies of skeletons

Leonardo the Inventor

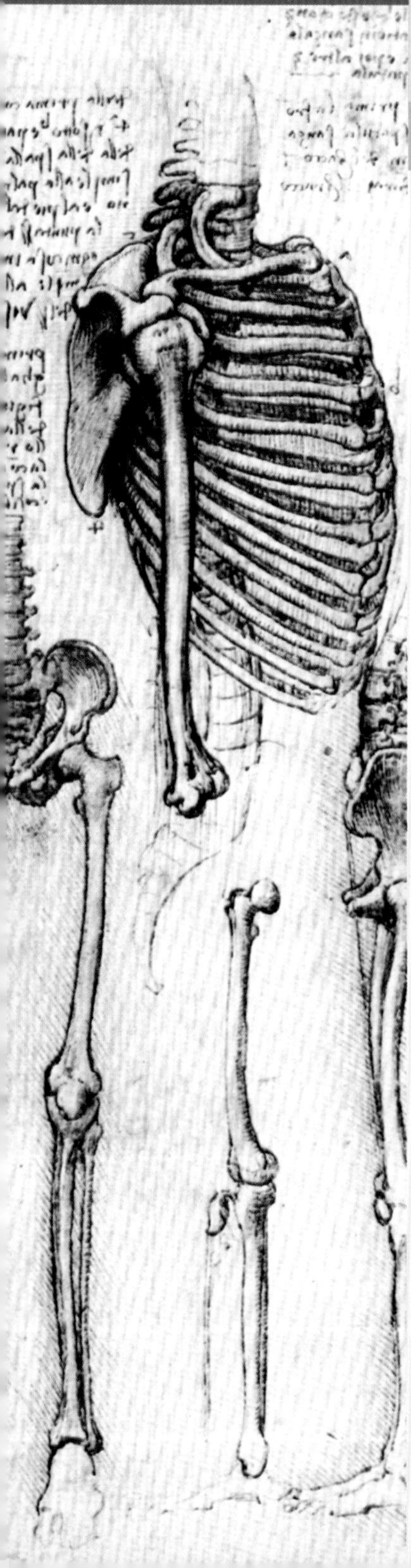

How do you describe the perfect Renaissance man? Leonardo da Vinci.

Da Vinci was many things: painter, humanitarian, engineer, inventor—it's a long list. It seemed like da Vinci could figure out anything, but he didn't always get it right. Only no one knew during the Renaissance, because most of the amazing contraptions he came up with were never built. In modern times, they have served as inspiration for the working models of things like submarines and helicopters. Back then? They might have looked like the ramblings of a madman.

Some of da Vinci's designs have now been built as he designed them, and some worked very well. Others had flaws that he would have easily seen and corrected had he made working models while he was alive.

Da Vinci was so ahead of his time that there are whole books written to suggest that he got his knowledge from either a heavenly place or another planet. Some say he had tons of secrets and put clues in all his works. Who knows?

1

Leonardo da Vinci's talents were not limited to art. He was also a clever *inventor* who was inspired by nature. In fact, in the middle of his life, he became uninterested in his art, and spent his days studying how things worked. He loved to watch birds in flight, and would spend hours drawing their wings. It was even said that Leonardo's eyes were like cameras. They could capture any image, at any time. After he began to understand more about the world around him, Leonardo worked to improve it, one invention at a time.

1. **What, besides art, was Leonardo known for?**
2. **What do you think the story meant about his memory when it said "his eyes were like cameras?"**
3. **Do you think having eyes like cameras might have helped him as an artist?**
4. **How do you think nature inspired him to invent?**
5. **Do you think it is important that an inventor be interested in how things work? Why or why not?**

2

Flight had always interested da Vinci. The time he spent studying birds gave him the idea that humans could also fly. After months of sketching different ideas, he came up with a group of machines that would allow humans to soar. He called his first invention the "flying ship." This shell-shaped ship had room for two people to sit inside and turn cranks that pumped the ship's bat-like wings, made out of wood and cloth. Leonardo also sketched the first model of a flying machine that became the helicopter. The thin wooden blades that spun at the top of this machine were designed to lift the flat platform and one person below, high into the sky. Even though these machines were never built in Leonardo's lifetime, he loved to think that one day humans would take flight.

1. **What was the name of Leonardo's first flying invention?**
2. **How might studying birds have helped Leonardo invent his flying machines?**
3. **Why do you think Leonardo made bat-like wings instead of using feathers?**
4. **Why do you think Leonardo's flying machines were never built during his lifetime?**
5. **How do you think Leonardo would feel about the many flying machines of today? Explain.**

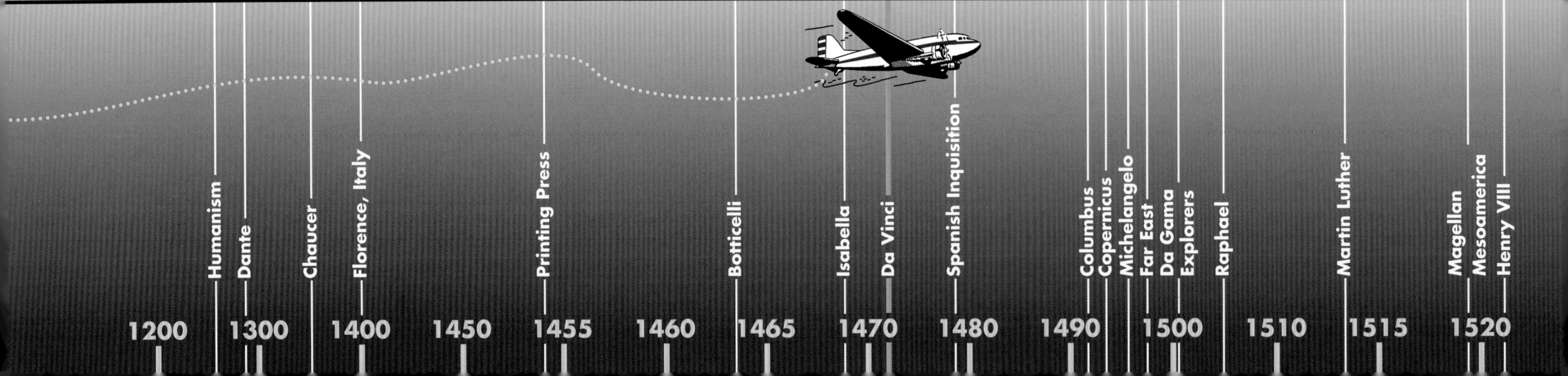

Humanism
Dante
Chaucer
Florence, Italy
Printing Press
Botticelli
Isabella
Da Vinci
Spanish Inquisition
Columbus
Copernicus
Michelangelo
Far East
Da Gama
Explorers
Raphael
Martin Luther
Magellan
Mesoamerica
Henry VIII
1200
1300
1400
1450
1455
1460
1465
1470
1480
1490
1500
1510
1515
1520

3

Da Vinci loved the human body. He wanted to know how it was put together and how it worked. To answer these questions, he spent his nights studying the insides of over 30 human cadavers (dead bodies). He was careful with his work, and made exact drawings of the internal organs and bones he saw. It was said that Leonardo avoided touching the blood from the cadavers, as he had seen that blood circulates through the body and had theorized that disease travels that way. He even built a glass model of a heart and pumped different colored waters through it to see how it worked. He did all of his research by candlelight and made only a few cuts to the body. He studied the bodies of a child, an adult, and an old man to track the changes caused by aging. His drawings were so accurate that they have been compared to x-rays taken 500 years later.

1. What did Leonardo avoid touching in the human cadavers he studied?

2. Why do you think Leonardo chose to study cadavers and not living people?

3. What internal organs might Leonardo have studied and drawn?

4. Why do you think Leonardo made a model out of glass?

5. Why might his drawings have been compared to x-rays taken 500 years later?

4

In 1482, da Vinci was hired as an engineer by the wealthy Duke of Milan, Sforza. He wanted Leonardo to build weapons that would give the Duke an advantage in future wars between Milan and other cities. Leonardo drew maps of Milan, developed good defense points, and sketched machines that could destroy any army. The maps were used years later when the French invaded the city. The Duke, though, did not value Leonardo's sketches. The weaponry, which included versions of tanks and machine guns, was too advanced, and was hard for him to understand. The war machines Leonardo invented for the Duke were ignored, and Leonardo fled Milan in 1499, at age 47, in order to escape the fighting he hated.

1. What did Sforza want Leonardo to build?

2. Why might the maps have been an important resource for the Duke once fighting began?

3. Why might Leonardo's sketches of weapons have confused the Duke?

4. Why do you think Leonardo hated fighting?

5. Why do you think Leonardo worked for the Duke if he hated fighting?

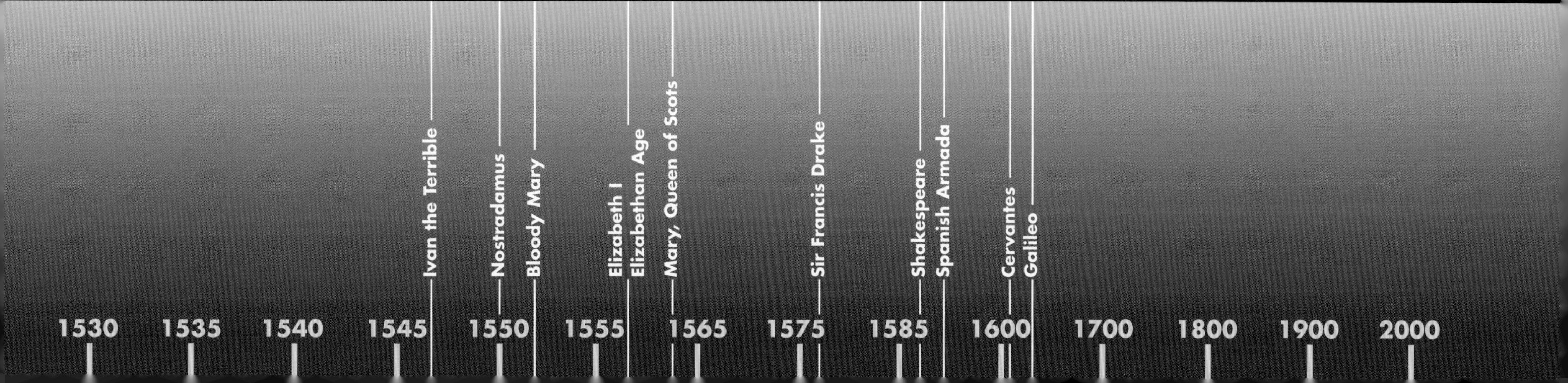
Ivan the Terrible
Nostradamus
Bloody Mary
Elizabeth I
Elizabethan Age
Mary, Queen of Scots
Sir Francis Drake
Shakespeare
Spanish Armada
Cervantes
Galileo
1530
1535
1540
1545
1550
1555
1565
1575
1585
1600
1700
1800
1900
2000

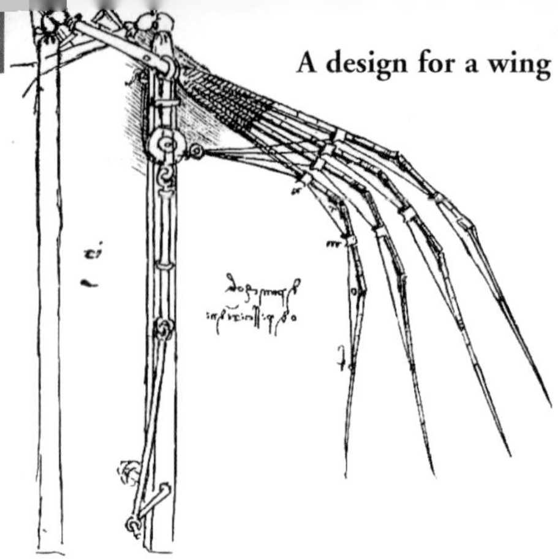

A design for a wing for flying *(left)*; study of a Star of Bethlehem and other flowers *(right)*

5 Da Vinci left his mark in the scientific world, although his wealth of notes weren't discovered until decades after his death in 1519, at age 67. He filled over 5,000 sketchbooks with inventions and detailed pictures of humans and animals. Also in the sketchbooks were massive amounts of notes that were all written backwards. They could be read only if they were held up to a mirror. Some say that Leonardo wrote backwards because he used his left hand (which was thought to be a sign of the devil's work) and did not want to smear his writing on the page. Others say that he liked secrets or had a wicked sense of humor. Whatever the case, the notes and sketches leave us with a clear idea of Leonardo's power of observation and his deep love for the world around him.

1. **How many sketchbooks did Leonardo fill?**
2. **Why do you think Leonardo filled so many sketchbooks with notes about his inventions?**
3. **What kinds of pictures do you think filled Leonardo's sketchbooks?**
4. **Why do you think Leonardo chose to write backwards in his sketchbooks?**
5. **How might Leonardo's sketches have shown us his power of observation?**

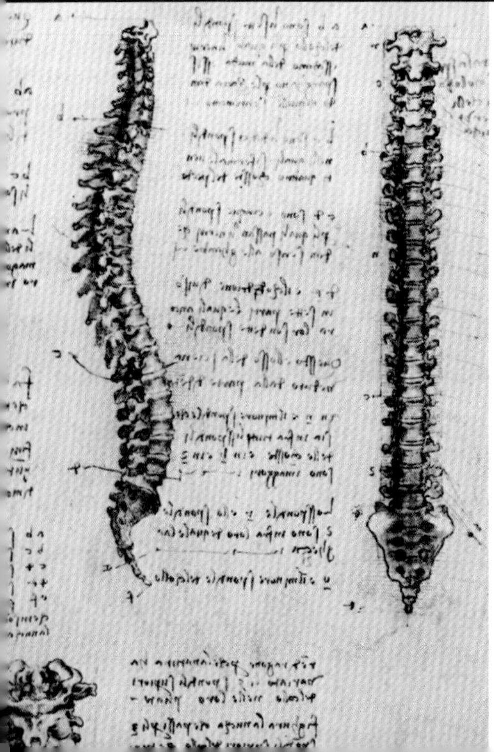

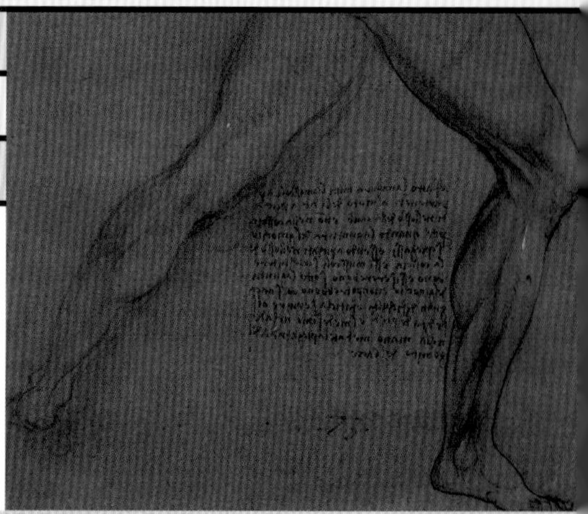

Sketches and notes on the spine: Leonardo was the first person to correctly draw and number the vertebrae *(left)*; study of a man's leg while lunging, chalk and ink on brown paper *(right)*; a design for a war machine *(bottom)*

Ivan says—

Leonardo filled his notebooks with all sorts of thoughts. For instance, one entry states that imagery is very important, like the pictures you and I make, and that a person should take notes or make drawings. Leonardo said, "A master falsely thinking his memory fit to remember all the shapes of nature's phenomena is but an ignorant wretch in my eyes. For nature abound in phenomena and our memory cannot embrace it all..." Also, he wrote on one page that "the sun does not move" in the sky, a theory that was proved by Galileo (you'll meet him in your last Flight).

It was said that if "Leonardo took a fancy for an interesting man with an unusual beard, he followed his man all day long and made so vivid a mental picture of him that, coming home, he drew him as if the man stood before his eyes."

Next, we visit that place that everyone was trying to sail to—the Far East. They had wonderful stuff that that was all the rage back in Europe. To the Far East you sail! I'm sailing to the refrigerator... then to dreamland.

HIGH RENAISSANCE

Emperor Akbar on a tiger hunt in India *(left)*; the insignia of a Ming official, the dragon on this robe is sewn with gold and silver threads and filaments of peacock feathers *(right)*

Flight 12

The Far East

1490's

We've learned about how trade rejuvenated Italy and then the whole of Europe, and that Columbus was looking for a safe sea passage to the Far East. Now let's meet the countries that were responsible for all the new goods coming into Europe.

The Far East has many countries and most, if not all, were involved with trade, but the key countries of the Renaissance period were China, India, and the Spice Islands. From the Spice Islands came—you got it—spices! China and India, both with a long and ancient history behind them, had developed better ways to make certain things, like pottery and cloth, so that the final results were much nicer.

Most of the trade with the East was done on the Silk Road. This overland journey included deserts and mountains, and was very difficult. Armed gangs patrolled the roads to steal from the long caravans. A trip to the East was expensive and often ended in an ambush by highwaymen. It was very important that a sea route be discovered. In the meantime, all the new prosperity in the Renaissance combined with the rediscovered love of the finer things in life had increased the demand for beautiful silks and porcelains from the East.

I, too, am a fan of the finer things in life. While you explore the Far East, I will go enjoy a fine fish from our fine aquarium.

1

Columbus, like many other sailors, was trying to set up a sea route to the Far East, where spices, fabrics, and other goods were produced that many people wanted in Europe. A land route, the Silk Road, had existed for centuries, but a direct sea route would be faster and safer. In the late 1300's, the Far East went through many changes of its own. The brutal *Mongols*, led by Genghis (*GENG-is*) Khan, had conquered China years before. Their fierce warriors easily overpowered simple farmers. A revolt of the starving peasants finally got rid of the Mongols. A new family took power. The *Ming Dynasty* ruled for almost 300 years. They eventually brought peace and prosperity to the Chinese people. They made a code of laws and supplied food for all to eat. China's people made fine silk, porcelain, and art, and sold them to traders from Europe where demand for fine things was high.

1. **Who once led the Mongols to conquer China?**
2. **Why might it have been important to find a sea route to the Far East?**
3. **Why do you think the peasants revolted against their leaders?**
4. **How might the Ming Dynasty's rule have improved China?**
5. **Why do you think Chinese goods were in high demand?**

2

In China, the Forbidden City was a huge collection of palaces built to house the Ming emperor and his family. Even though it was in the center of the busy capital city of Beijing, the Forbidden City was open to royals and their servants only. There was even a tall wall and deep moat to keep unwanted guests away. With over 10,000 rooms, the city took 14 years to build and was split into two parts. The Outer Court was where the emperor gave military orders and saw people. The Inner Court was where he lived with his family. All of the buildings in the city had yellow tiled roofs and thin red dragons painted on them. The colors and the fiery beasts stood for the emperor's power. From the City, the Ming oversaw China, with help from the money brought in by the traders.

1. **What were the names of the two parts of the Forbidden City?**
2. **Goods from China were in high demand in Europe. How might that have helped the Ming Dynasty and China?**
3. **Why do you think the royals wanted to keep people out of the Forbidden City?**
4. **Why might the Forbidden City have been built in the center of the capital city?**
5. **Why might the dragon be a good choice to represent the Ming's power?**

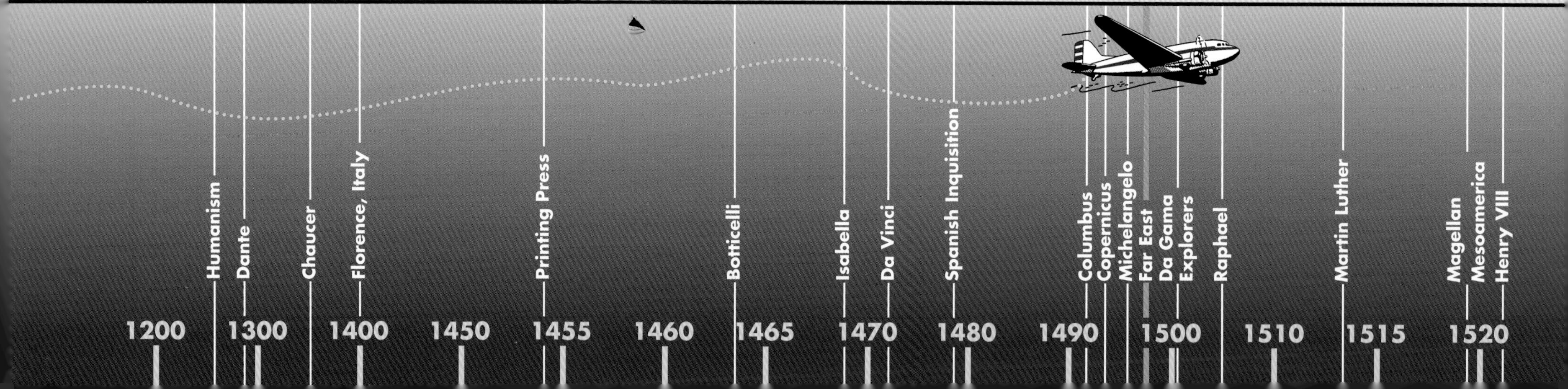
Humanism
Dante
Chaucer
Florence, Italy
Printing Press
Botticelli
Isabella
Da Vinci
Spanish Inquisition
Columbus
Copernicus
Michelangelo
Far East
Da Gama
Explorers
Raphael
Martin Luther
Magellan
Mesoamerica
Henry VIII
1200
1300
1400
1450
1455
1460
1465
1470
1480
1490
1500
1510
1515
1520

3

The people in many European countries demanded more and more Chinese products. The largest export was silk; a shiny, colorful, and soft cloth. Silk was prized among the rich to make fine clothes, drapes, and furniture. The new silks were very desirable and expensive. Chinese porcelain was valued for its beauty and strength. Clay was shaped, painted with pictures in blue and white, and baked into dishes and vases more delicate than most pottery. Porcelain was a luxury that only the wealthiest could afford. Chinese tea was made from the seeds of the sweet-smelling flowers of tea plants. Tea soon became a popular necessity for well-to-do European households.

1. **What was China's largest export?**
2. **Why might silk have been prized among the richest people in Europe?**
3. **How might China's porcelain be different from regular pottery?**
4. **Why might demand for Chinese goods have increased during the Renaissance?**
5. **Do you think tea plants grew in Europe? Why or why not?**

4

India, a country between Europe and China, was also opening its doors to trade with the West. Once only scattered local kingdoms, India was united by the *Mughal* (*MOO-guhl*) Emperor Akbar. The new empire was able to push India's borders to the Arabian Sea. Access to this busy waterway allowed for trade with the Europeans. Spices, used to flavor food and hide the bad taste of rotting meat, brought India great wealth. Small, hard, black peppercorns were ground to add flavor to foods. Pink ginger was used to season meats, and tiny brown cloves were used in desserts. Other exports were fragrant oils, like thick dark-yellow sandalwood oil, which royal and wealthy women applied to their skin after bathing.

1. **What was the name of the emperor who united India?**
2. **Why do you think it was important for India to gain access to the Arabian Sea?**
3. **Before trade with India, what might the food in Europe have tasted like?**
4. **Why might fragrant oils and perfumes be in demand in Europe?**
5. **Why might Europeans have also wanted products from India?**

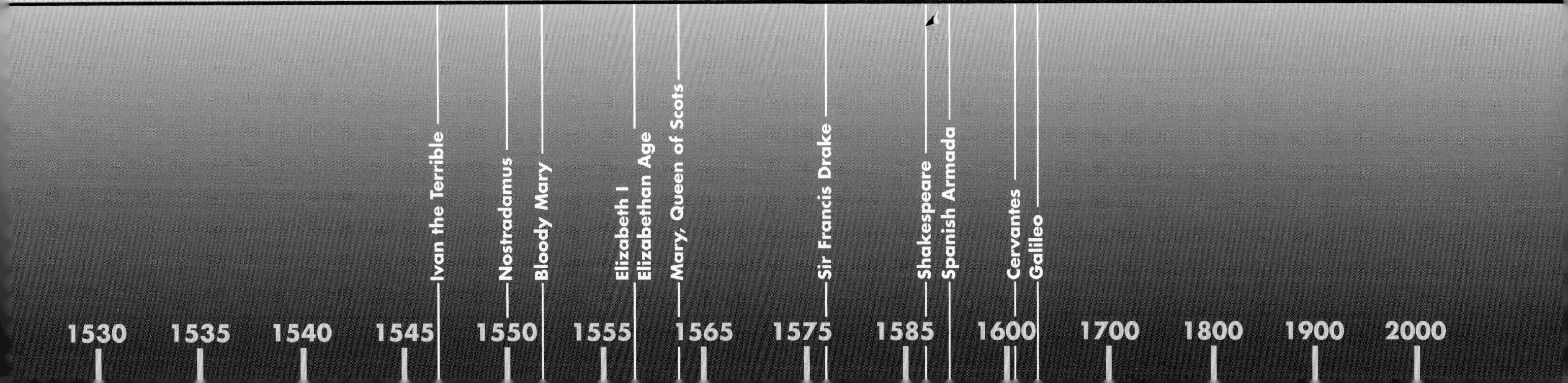
Ivan the Terrible
Nostradamus
Bloody Mary
Elizabeth I
Elizabethan Age
Mary, Queen of Scots
Sir Francis Drake
Shakespeare
Spanish Armada
Cervantes
Galileo
1530
1535
1540
1545
1550
1555
1565
1575
1585
1600
1700
1800
1900
2000

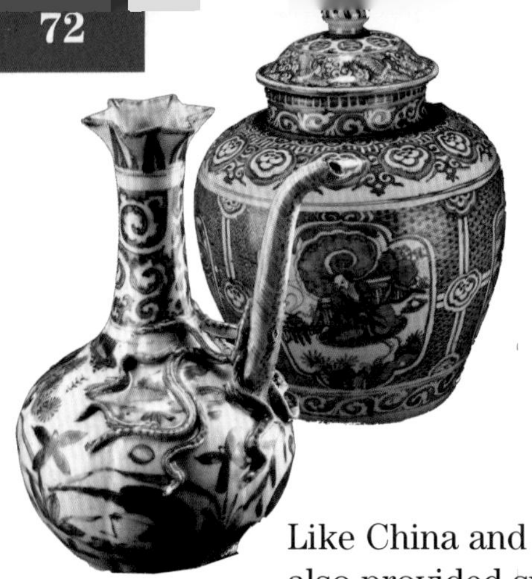

Ming porcelain, ca. 16th c. *(left);* trays of young silkworms are filled with mulberry leaves *(near right),* and once the fed worms have spun cocoons, they are loaded into barrels *(far right)*

5

Like China and India, the Spice Islands south of China also provided spices and foods. When trade with the countries in Europe was minimal due to the difficult overland route, the countries in the East were very isolated and arrogant. They thought that no other country was as fine as theirs, and disliked outsiders. However, when ships began arriving at their shores in the late 1400's, they soon changed their minds. They knew their silk, porcelain, spices, and perfumes could not be found anywhere else in the world, which meant that the Europeans would pay high prices for these goods. China and India were eager to grow, and saw that money could quickly bring them power. They and the Spice Islands remained in the center of trade and a source for bickering and war among the countries in Europe during the Renaissance and long afterwards.

1. Where were the Spice Islands located?

2. Why do you think the Far East countries had been isolated up to the Renaissance?

3. Why might the European ships arriving on their shores have changed Easterners' minds about outsiders?

4. Why do you think the Europeans paid such high prices for Eastern goods?

5. Why do you think European countries would fight over trade opportunities in the Far East?

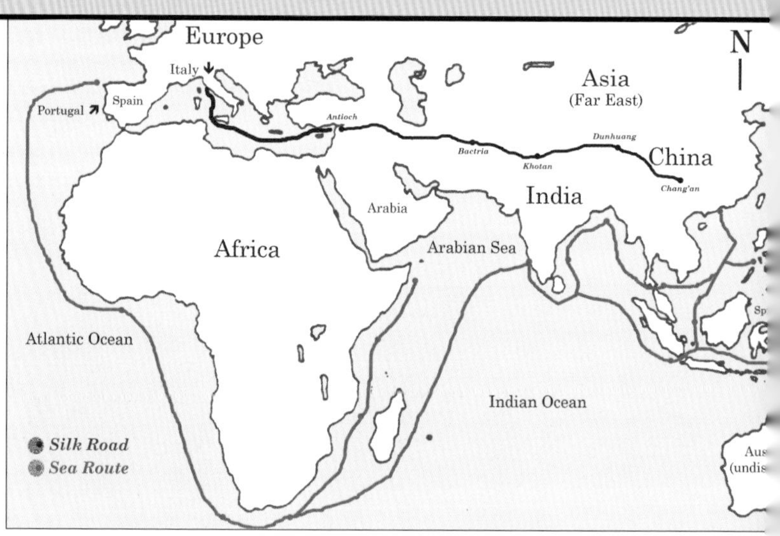

Europe
Italy
Portugal
Spain
Antioch
N
Asia
(Far East)
Dunhuang
Bactria
Khotan
China
Chang'an
India
Arabia
Africa
Arabian Sea
Atlantic Ocean
Indian Ocean
Silk Road
Sea Route

English trading ships in the Indian harbor of Tellicherry, known for its pepper and ginger spices *(left);* map of the Silk Road and the new sea trade routes (*right*)

Ivan says—

It wasn't just pretty things that were coming in through trade with the Far East. The Chinese had paper money, engineering ideas, printed books, and many other things. The Muslims, for years the rulers of India and the Near East, had highly advanced medical techniques. They were skilled astronomers, and loved to compile the things they learned in written form. Some of these made their way to Europe and thinkers there.

Here's a tidbit. In India, Emperor Akbar began a grand tomb for himself, with marble walls and tall minarets, but he died before it was completed. His son finished it for him. The rulers of China, the Ming dynasty, also built grand tombs. There is a road, the Sacred Way, that is lined with statues of animals like elephants, horses, and camels. At the last part of the road, also called the Avenue of Ghosts, there are carvings of soldiers, scholars, and officials. This impressive walk leads to 13 of the magnificent tombs. Each of the tombs holds an emperor, along with all of his wives, who were buried alive in order to serve him in the next world.

Arg. You read, I'll eat.

Greenland
European Explorers
Columbus 1492-1493
Cabot 1497
da Gama 1497-1498
Magellan
and de Cano 1519-1522
North America
NEWFOUNDLAND
Bristol
Europe
Nova Scotia
Lisbon
Cadiz
Asia
CUBA
HISPANIOLA
La Navidad
Atlantic
Ocean
Africa
Callcut
PHILIPPINES
Malindi
Indian Ocean
South
America
Mozambique
MADAGASCAR
Rio de Janeiro
Cape of
Good Hope
Australia
N
Treaty line of
Tordesillas
1494

Vasco da Gama

1469-1524

A sample of cotton cloth from Calicut, India; map of da Gama's voyage *(inset)*

Weee. We're flying to Portugal next. While Columbus really jump-started the whole exploration trend, it was Henry the Navigator, from Portugal, who did the hard work of finding new lands by sea. He did it for gold, glory, and Portugal. Prince Henry, a duke of Portugal in the 1400's, loved the idea of sailing, and spent his life making better maps and navigational systems. He never actually sailed anywhere himself, because who wouldn't prefer a nice comfy castle to a wet, crowded ship? Then again, castles are pretty drafty. Still, Henry was a homebody. He sent others sailing down the coast of Africa to try out his ideas while he stayed safely home in Portugal. Prince Henry and Columbus inspired many people to sail the seas in search of adventure. Some, like the star of your next Flight, did and found some remarkable things in the next years. Portugal's King Manuel wanted to continue the good work that Henry had started, and he teamed up with Vasco da Gama, our next explorer.

Da Gama traveled around Africa and up through India, and never made a friend. But he did manage to open up trade for Portugal with the Near and Far East and make his boss, King Manuel, very rich. I have a cousin named after Vasco. His name is Vasco da Gummer. He has no teeth. Get it? Awww...go sail a boat. I'm having a nice nap.

1

In the 1400's, Muslim traders controlled the cost and flow of silk, spices, and other goods from India to Europe. Portuguese King Manuel wanted to compete with these traders, so in 1497, he sent ships to set up trade. The crews were led by Vasco da Gama, a former naval officer, in an attempt to gain access to the rich markets in India. Da Gama sailed with 170 men in four ships far out into the Atlantic Ocean to catch the best winds. Then they raced south toward the tip of Africa to go around it and up to India.

1. **Who controlled the trade between Europe and Asia in the 1400's?**
2. **Why do you think King Manuel wanted to compete with the Muslim traders?**
3. **Why might King Manuel have chosen da Gama to lead this voyage?**
4. **Why do you think da Gama needed four ships instead of one?**
5. **Why do you think finding the best winds was important to da Gama?**

2

Vasco da Gama's four ships rounded the tip of Africa and sailed up its east coast. He stopped at a trading center and quickly discovered that he was not well prepared for this trip. The vendors were not interested in the cheap beads and bells that da Gama had brought to trade. He managed to buy some fresh fruit and vegetables for his crew before he was told to leave port or risk death. His men were under almost constant attack from Muslim trading ships. Further up the coast of Africa, they were able to find a guide to lead them to Calicut, India.

1. **Where did da Gama's ships sail first?**
2. **In what way do you think da Gama was not well prepared for this trip?**
3. **What about the vendors might have been unexpected by da Gama?**
4. **Why do you think da Gama was told to leave port?**
5. **Why might it have been important to the expedition to find a guide to lead them?**

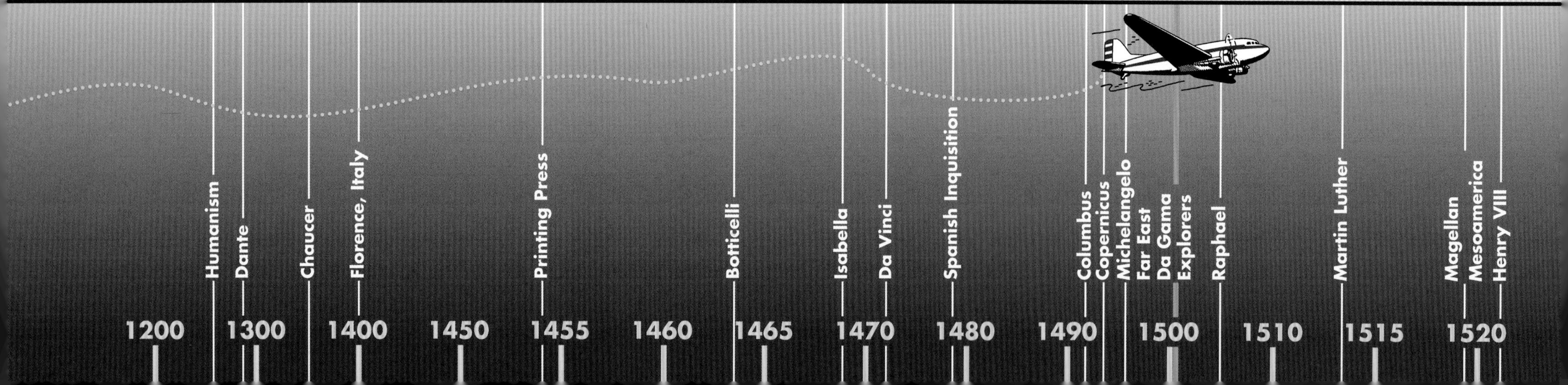
Humanism
Dante
Chaucer
Florence, Italy
Printing Press
Botticelli
Isabella
Da Vinci
Spanish Inquisition
Columbus
Copernicus
Michelangelo
Far East
Da Gama
Explorers
Raphael
Martin Luther
Magellan
Mesoamerica
Henry VIII
1200
1300
1400
1450
1455
1460
1465
1470
1480
1490
1500
1510
1515
1520

3

Calicut, India was not what da Gama expected. He found the culture rich and advanced. He asked to meet the ruler and was told to bring gifts, as was the custom. Da Gama gave the ruler hats, wash basins, cloth, oil, and honey. The ruler, who was wearing diamonds, rubies, emeralds, and pearls, felt insulted by the cheap gifts. None of the merchants were interested in the Portuguese goods either. Da Gama and his men left the port nearly empty handed.

1. **What was the ruler of Calicut, India wearing?**
2. **What do you think da Gama expected to find in Calicut, India?**
3. **Why do you think the ruler felt insulted by da Gama's gifts?**
4. **Why do you think the merchants weren't interested in the Portuguese goods?**
5. **Why do you think da Gama and his men left nearly empty handed?**

4

Da Gama had managed to get samples of spices, mostly pepper, before he left India in August, 1498. Sailing against the wind, the trip home to Portugal took over one year. Without fresh fruit for most of the journey, the sailors began to die of *scurvy* (a disease) and morale was low. When he was 30 years old, da Gama and 55 of his original crew of 170 sailors arrived back in Portugal. The trip had not been a total success, but King Manuel was pleased and named da Gama Admiral of the Sea of India.

1. **What main spice did da Gama take back to Portugal?**
2. **Why might sailing against the wind make the trip longer?**
3. **How do you think the long trip affected the sailors?**
4. **Why do you think the trip was not considered a total success?**
5. **Why might King Manuel have named da Gama Admiral of the Sea of India?**

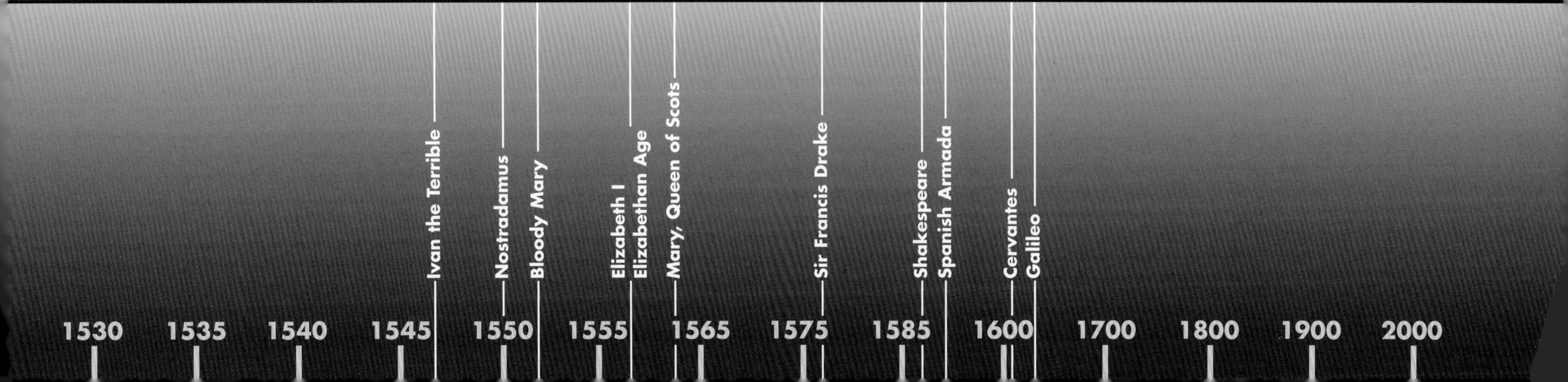
Ivan the Terrible
Nostradamus
Bloody Mary
Elizabeth I
Elizabethan Age
Mary, Queen of Scots
Sir Francis Drake
Shakespeare
Spanish Armada
Cervantes
Galileo
1530
1535
1540
1545
1550
1555
1565
1575
1585
1600
1700
1800
1900
2000

The new astrolabe, used to calculate latitude at sea, was a major reason for the increase in exploration.

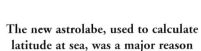

A portrait of da Gama as Admiral of the Sea of India

5 A larger trading voyage, led by Pedro Cabral, had greater success in India. He was able to bring two shiploads of spices back to Portugal. Some of his men stayed in India to set up trade, but soon after Cabral left, they were killed. King Manuel sent da Gama back to India with a fleet of 20 ships. Da Gama attacked Muslim ports and forced trade agreements to be signed. He set up armed forts at key sites in Africa and India so that the Portuguese were now firmly established in these countries.

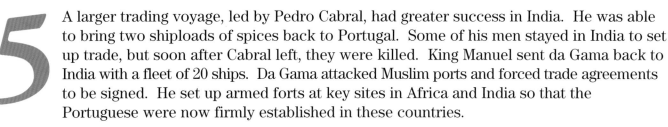

1. **Who led the larger trading voyage?**
2. **Why might King Manuel have sent da Gama back to India instead of Cabral?**
3. **Why do you think da Gama had 20 ships this time?**
4. **Why do you think da Gama set up forts?**
5. **How might da Gama's efforts have changed the future of Portugal?**

Ivan says—

Da Gama's father was supposed to make the initial trip to India, but he died shortly before they set sail, leaving Vasco in charge. Things might have turned out differently had Papa da Gama gone to India instead of da Gama junior. For one thing, Vasco was known to be cruel and stubborn. His bad attitude made him unwelcome in India.

Speaking of altitude—oops, added an L, see what one letter can do to your imagery—let's get in the air again and meet other great explorers. By this time, most all of Europe had changed, like Italy, and there were schools, museums, libraries, and art galleries all over the place. And Europe was suddenly not big enough for everyone, so many kings and queens gave a bunch of sailing captains money, and off they went into the great unknown to discover new lands, just like Columbus and da Gama.

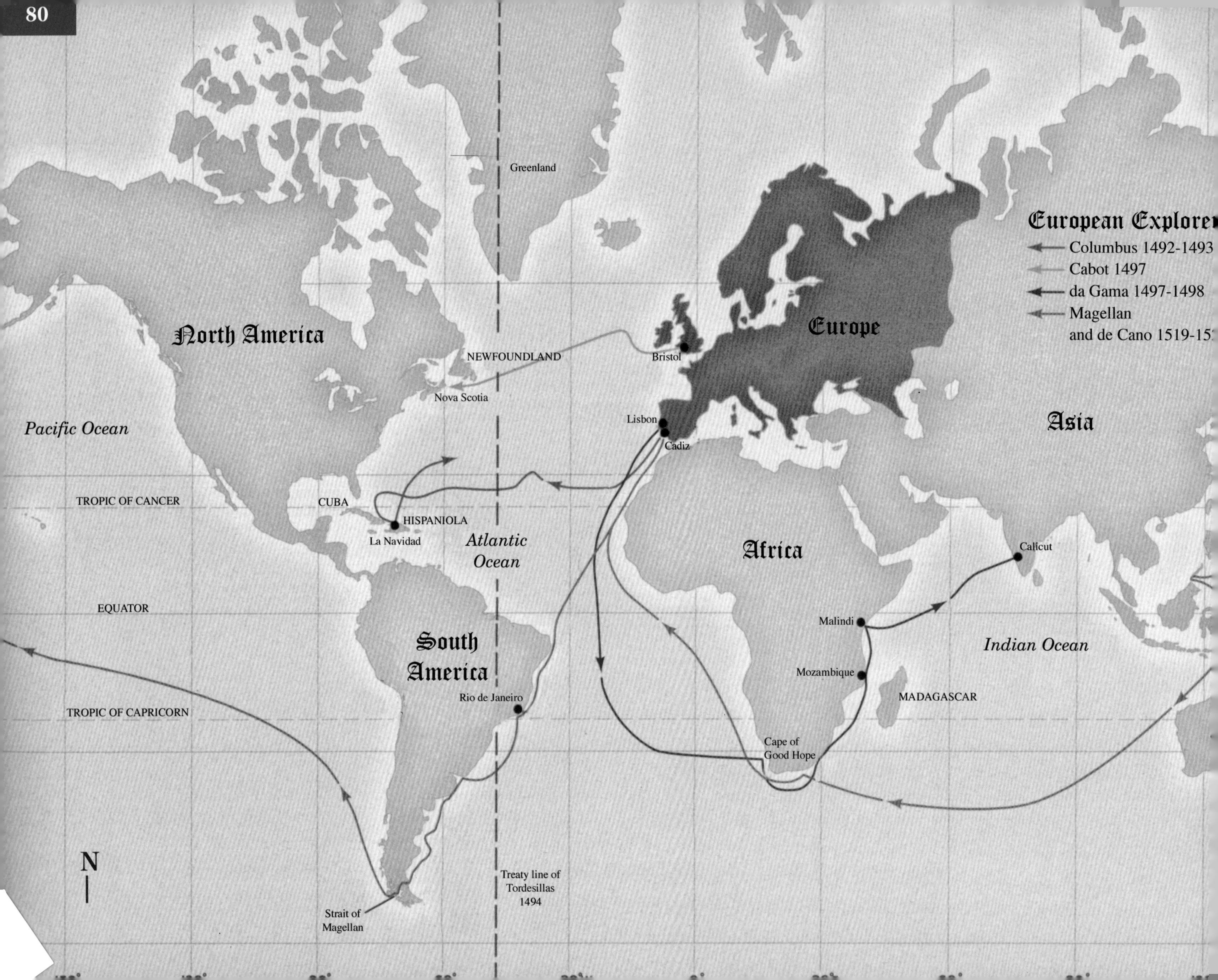
European Explorer
Columbus 1492-1493
Cabot 1497
da Gama 1497-1498
Magellan
and de Cano 1519-15
North America
Greenland
Europe
Asia
Africa
South America
Pacific Ocean
Atlantic Ocean
Indian Ocean
NEWFOUNDLAND
Bristol
Nova Scotia
Lisbon
Cadiz
TROPIC OF CANCER
CUBA
HISPANIOLA
La Navidad
Calicut
EQUATOR
Malindi
Mozambique
MADAGASCAR
Rio de Janeiro
TROPIC OF CAPRICORN
Cape of
Good Hope
N
Treaty line of
Tordesillas
1494
Strait of
Magellan

The Explorers

1400-1550

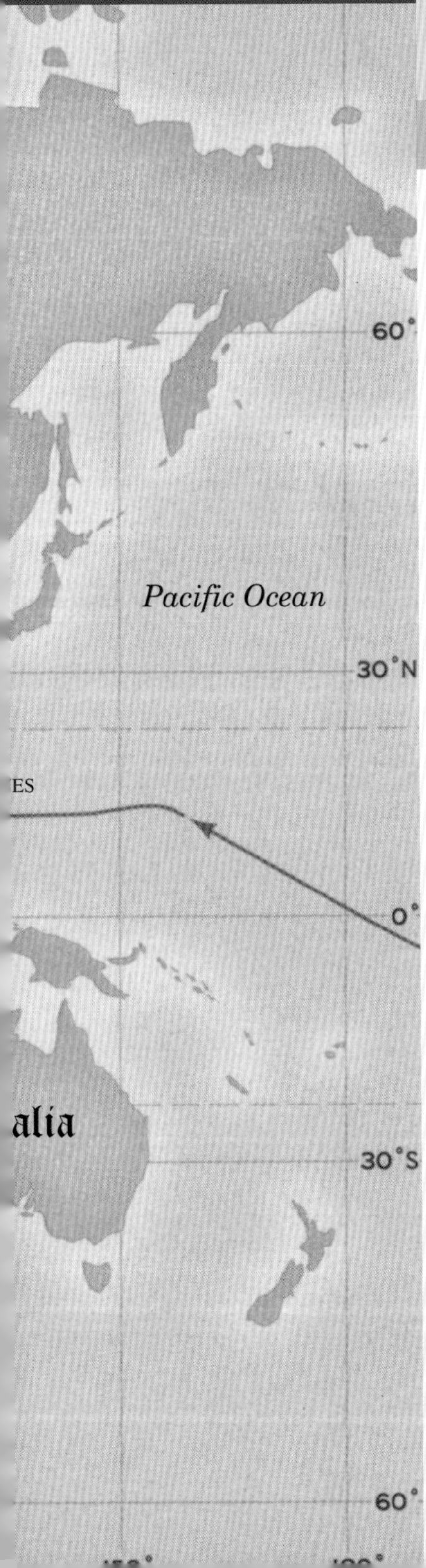
60°
Pacific Ocean
30°N
ES
0°
alia
30°S
60°

Your next Flight is about a bunch of guys you could call copycats. Their names are Vespucci, Cabot, Hudson, and Ponce de Leon, four important explorers from the 1400's.

After Christopher Columbus discovered the New World, other explorers started heading out to sea as soon as they could get their hands on a boat. Later voyagers included Magellan, and you've already visualized da Gama. Let's meet some more brave souls as the Age of Discovery begins.

Exploring was no walk in the park back then. People would be out to sea for months at a time with little food, and at the mercy of the winds and the weather. It's not like they had accurate maps—they were sailing into uncharted waters. If they found what they were looking for, they were happy, but the truth of the matter was that they were happy to find any land at all.

If you ask me, and I love it when you do, these humans were nuts. There was nothing but water all around them, as far as the eye could see. How crazy was that? Oh, well, let's discover the discoverers. Or, what say *you* discover them and *I'll* discover a can of sardines.

MADE IN INDIA
SHIP TO PORTUGAL

1

In 1493, Columbus returned to Spain from his voyage of discovery. Word spread quickly throughout Europe that he had reached Asia by sailing west. No one would know for several years that it was not Asia, and instead it was a New World of forests, fields, people, and animals. Soon many voyages of groups of large wooden ships stocked with food and water for a long trip were launched from ports in Spain, Portugal, and England. Explorers began sailing west in the hopes of reaching the Far East and all the riches that were there. Most of these trips were unsuccessful, and many men died. They had set out on endless oceans with no real idea of what they might find. A few others became famous and helped discover new lands throughout the world.

1. Where did people in Europe think Columbus had sailed to?

2. Why might Columbus' voyage have encouraged other explorers to sail west?

3. Why do you think it took several years before people knew that Columbus had not reached Asia?

4. Why do you think most of the new voyages were unsuccessful?

5. Why do you think the explorers are thought of as brave?

2

John Cabot (*CA-bot*) was an Italian mapmaker and trader living in England when he heard of Columbus' voyage. In 1497, with funds from English businessmen, Cabot sailed north in one small ship with 18 sailors. He had hoped to reach the Far East faster by sailing across the North Atlantic, but instead he landed somewhere on the coast of what is now Canada. He mapped all of the rugged coastline that he saw. Cabot returned to England and announced that he had reached Asia. Soon he was headed back with five ships given to him by the King, Henry VII. He was never heard from again.

1. Where did Cabot land?

2. Why might Cabot have started with one small ship?

3. Why might Cabot have thought he had reached Asia instead of the New World?

4. Why do you think Henry VII funded his next trip?

5. What do you think might have happened to Cabot?

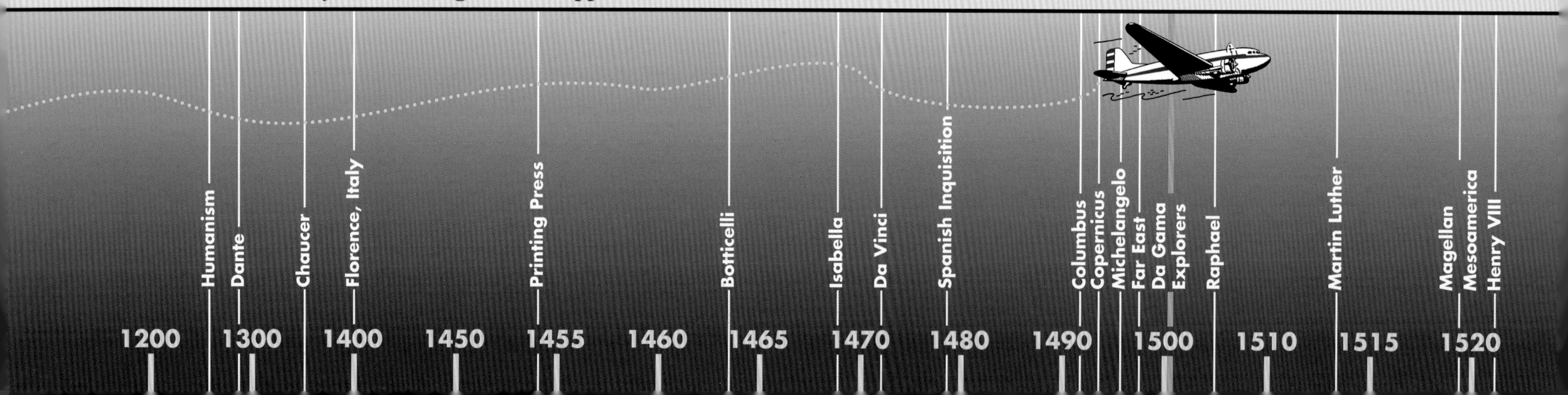
Humanism
Dante
Chaucer
Florence, Italy
Printing Press
Botticelli
Isabella
Da Vinci
Spanish Inquisition
Columbus
Copernicus
Michelangelo
Far East
Da Gama
Explorers
Raphael
Martin Luther
Magellan
Mesoamerica
Henry VIII
1200
1300
1400
1450
1455
1460
1465
1470
1480
1490
1500
1510
1515
1520

3

Another famous explorer was an Italian navigator named Amerigo Vespucci (*Ves-POO-chee*). He was inspired by Columbus, and got three ships from King Ferdinand of Spain. He made several trips to map the New World and explored the coast of what is now South America in the early 1500's. After one trip, he sent a letter to a friend in which he described in detail the people, land, and cultures he had seen there. This letter was published and became a popular read all over Europe. A German mapmaker who read it thought that Amerigo Vespucci was the first to discover the New World, and suggested it be named for the explorer. Soon the New World became known as America.

1. What was Vespucci's first name?

2. Why do you think Vespucci wanted to sail to the New World?

3. Why do you think Vespucci's friend published the letter?

4. Why might Vespucci's letter have become a popular read all over Europe?

5. Why might there have been confusion over who discovered the New World?

4

Juan Ponce de Leon (*le-OHN*), a rich Spanish noble, led a Spanish army when it conquered the native people of Hispaniola and Puerto Rico, islands to the southeast of North America. He served as a cruel governor of the colony for a time, responsible for terrible treatment of the natives. In 1513, Ponce de Leon led the search for an island that was rumored by natives to be full of riches. Legend says he was also looking for the Fountain of Youth, a natural water source that promised eternal life. Instead, he found and explored the coast of Florida, and brutalized the natives that lived there. Years later, Ponce de Leon returned with two hundred settlers, but the remaining natives attacked and wounded him.

1. What was Ponce de Leon looking for but didn't find?

2. Why do you think a rich noble might have wanted to travel to the New World?

3. Why do you think Ponce de Leon treated the native people with brutality?

4. Why might Ponce de Leon have been interested in finding the Fountain of Youth?

5. Why might the natives have attacked the settlers when Ponce de Leon returned?

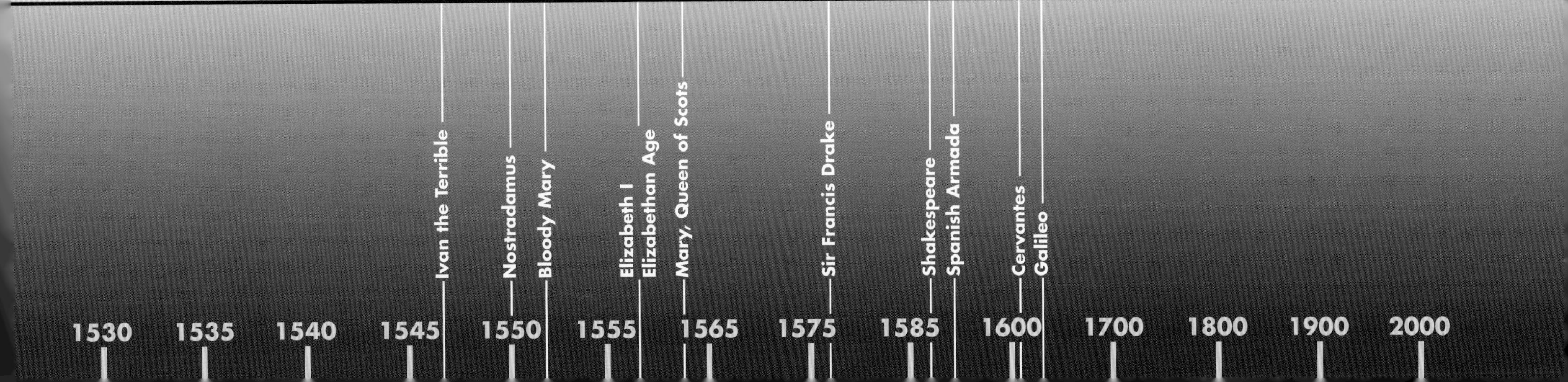
Ivan the Terrible
Nostradamus
Bloody Mary
Elizabeth I
Elizabethan Age
Mary, Queen of Scots
Sir Francis Drake
Shakespeare
Spanish Armada
Cervantes
Galileo
1530
1535
1540
1545
1550
1555
1565
1575
1585
1600
1700
1800
1900
2000

R.Holata
Outina

Henry Hudson's fate is imagined by painter Collier *(left)*; meetings between native cultures and explorers were often violent *(right)*

5

In 1607, Henry Hudson, an Englishman, tried to reach Asia by sailing north. Twice, Henry sailed past Norway before the cold and ice forced him to return. Then, on his third trip, he crossed the Atlantic to the coast of North America. He sailed from the Carolinas to New York and discovered the Hudson River before returning home. On his last voyage, he sailed north along Canada's rugged coast and into a large bay, now known as Hudson Bay. Tired of sickness and starvation, the crew mutinied and put Henry, his son, and a few loyal sailors in a small boat that was set adrift in the bay, in 1611. They were never seen nor heard from again.

1. **What did Henry Hudson discover along the New York coast?**
2. **Why do you think Hudson continued to sail after failing so many times?**
3. **Why do you think Hudson's crew mutinied?**
4. **Why might the crew have put Hudson's son in the boat with the others?**
5. **What do you think happened to Hudson?**

A gold mask of the type that drew explorers to the New World *(left)*; Cabot sets out on his voyage *(right)*

Ivan says—

There were lots of other guys just itching for a chance to sail in a rickety wooden boat across uncharted waters to lands unknown, at the risk of life and limb. Very brave, some say. Or very crazy, I say.

One guy who thought so was Bartolomeu Dias, who first found the route around the tip of Africa way back in 1487. In his 30's, he survived a terrible storm that blew his ship far off course. Imagine his surprise when he figured out that this had taken him around Africa, a route used by many others, like da Gama, in the future.

Another was the famed Coronado, who explored Mexico trying to find the legendary Seven Cities of Cibola (thought to be full of riches).

Back to our Cabot for an interesting tidbit. Cabot is believed to have discovered the Grand Banks, off the coast of Newfoundland, considered to be the best fishing area in the world. He wrote that you could just dip a bucket over the side of the boat and pull out as many fish as you wanted! Someone get me a map and a bucket.

NON PAREM PAVLO GRATIĀ · REQVIRO
VENIAM PETRI NEQ. POSCO, SED QVAM
IN CRVCIS LIGNO DEDERAS LATRONI
SEDVLVS ORO

Nikolaus
the room
work

Copernicus

1473-1543

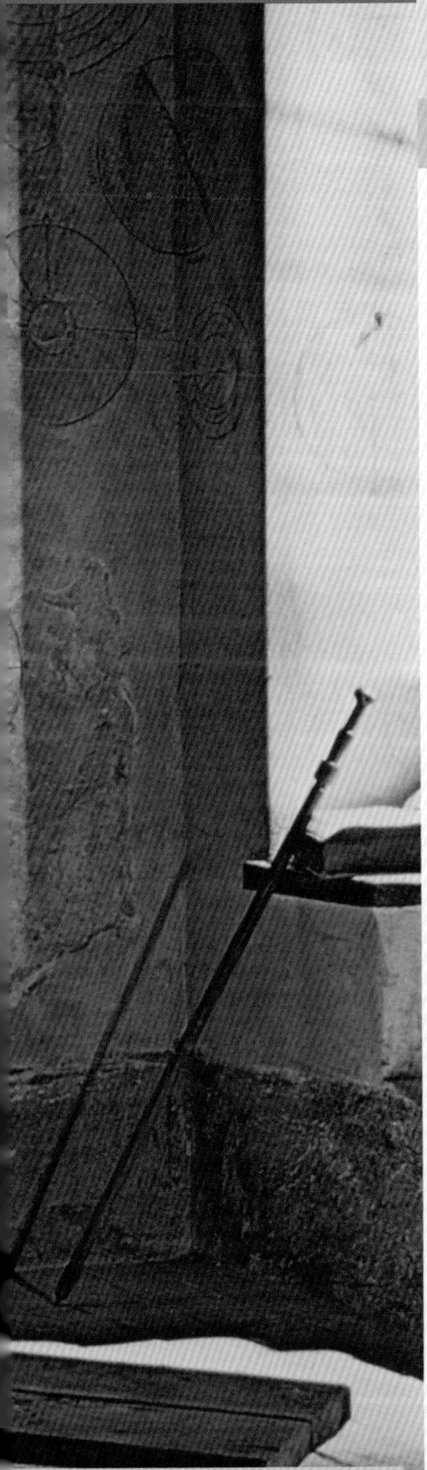

:us, from his epitaphic plaque *(left)*;
pernicus did much of his astronomical
his drawings on the walls *(right)*

While folks were running off to discover new lands, Copernicus (*Coh-PER-ni-cus*) was rocking the foundation of the Church in the old land. People had accepted certain things about the universe as facts for so long that no one ever questioned them. Then one man came along and proved some of those "facts" to be dead wrong.

It's funny the way people get so attached to their ideas. Like that whole black-cat-equals-bad-luck myth; the only bad luck I've ever had with a black cat was when one caught me in his food dish. In fact, long before black cats were thought to be bad luck, they were considered good luck.

Speaking of myths and mysteries of the universe, Copernicus' original manuscript about the universe was lost for years before it finally turned up in Prague in the 1800's, nearly four hundred years after it was lost. He had messy handwriting, and had revised his book over and over again—in Latin.

Too much for me, I'm getting tired just thinking about writing a book over and over. I'll have a nap while you figure out the universe with the shy genius, Copernicus.

1

Nikolaus Copernicus was born to a middle class family in Poland. When he was only ten his father died, so his uncle raised him and enrolled him in the best schools. The shy bright young man attended the University of Kraków, and then his uncle decided that Nikolaus should have a career in the Church. This would allow him to earn a good income and continue to study. Soon he was off to Rome, Italy, the center of the Catholic religion, to study Church law.

1. Where was Copernicus born?

2. Why do you think his uncle sent Copernicus to the best schools?

3. Why do you think Copernicus' uncle was deciding his career?

4. Why might going to Italy have been important to Copernicus?

5. What is the main idea of all this imagery?

2

In Italy, Copernicus rented a room in the house of a math professor. This man was an avid astronomer, and soon Copernicus was also observing the stars. He assisted the professor with his math classes. Three years later, Copernicus was teaching math and astronomy on his own in Rome. But his uncle disapproved of this line of work. So Copernicus changed his focus to medicine. He returned home to Poland to work as a doctor, pleasing his uncle. However, astronomy remained his favorite hobby and the quiet and studious man spent his free time gazing up at the stars. He read earlier works on the universe by Ptolemy and Aristotle, and wrote notes and calculations all over the walls of his room.

1. What subjects did Copernicus teach in Rome?

2. Why might Copernicus have started observing the stars?

3. Why do you think Copernicus felt he had to please his uncle?

4. What do the notes all over the walls in his room tell you about Copernicus?

5. How do you think his uncle felt about Copernicus' "hobby" and the notes in his room?

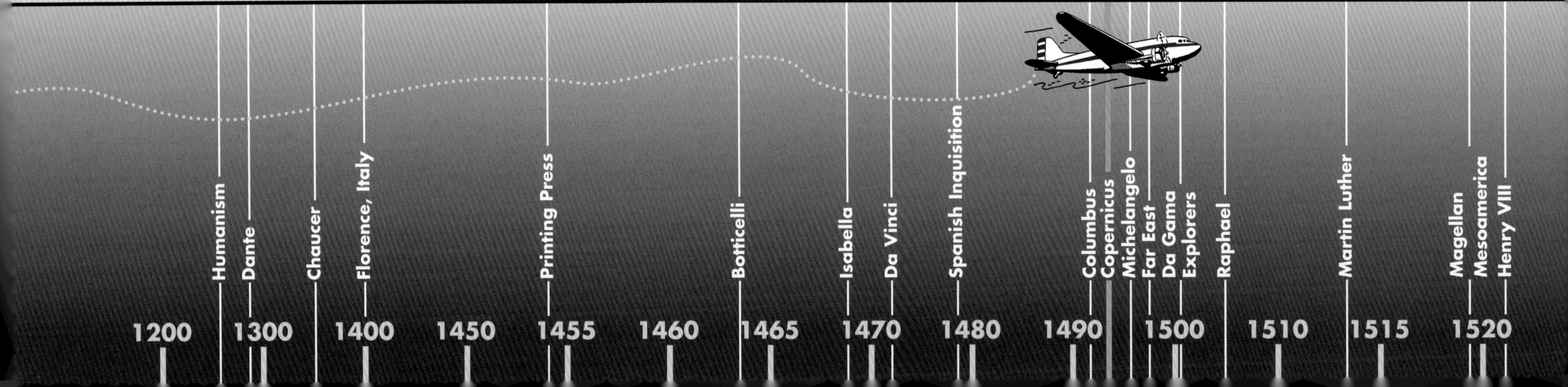
Humanism
Dante
Chaucer
Florence, Italy
Printing Press
Botticelli
Isabella
Da Vinci
Spanish Inquisition
Columbus
Copernicus
Michelangelo
Far East
Da Gama
Explorers
Raphael
Martin Luther
Magellan
Mesoamerica
Henry VIII
1200
1300
1400
1450
1455
1460
1465
1470
1480
1490
1500
1510
1515
1520

3

Copernicus studied the stars and planets, taking detailed notes that he kept in secret notebooks. Most people believed the sun and the planets revolved around the Earth at that time, a view the Church supported. Copernicus discovered that the planets, including the Earth, revolved around the sun. He was not the first person to believe this, but no one was allowed to contradict the Church or the Kings and Queens and expect to live. His ideas were revolutionary for that time. In addition, he managed the diocese (an area of land governed by a church) where his late uncle had been bishop, so he could have been imprisoned or even killed if anyone found out about his hobbies. But, many learned scholars and men of the Church leadership wanted him to publish.

1. What did most people believe the planets revolved around at the time of Copernicus?

2. Why do you think Copernicus kept his notes secret?

3. Why do you think his ideas were considered revolutionary?

4. Why didn't people want to contradict the Church?

5. What might have happened if his ideas were published?

4

For many years, Copernicus kept writing and rewriting his theory of the planets' orbits. He continually sought proof of his theory, but without the telescope, a tool not yet invented, he had to rely on his naked eye. Unable to prove his ideas, he only shared his thoughts with a few trusted friends. As a good Catholic, he was not trying to go against Church law, so he didn't want to publish until there was visual proof of his ideas. The lack of tools made finding proof to back up his mathematical theories impossible. He simply kept his thoughts to himself, but rumors of Copernicus' theory had begun to spread among academic people, attracting the attention of many.

1. What tool did Copernicus need to find proof for his theory?

2. Why do you think Copernicus kept writing and rewriting his theory of the planets' orbits?

3. Why do you think he only shared his ideas with a few friends?

4. Why do you think a telescope might prove his theories?

5. How might rumors of his ideas have begun to spread?

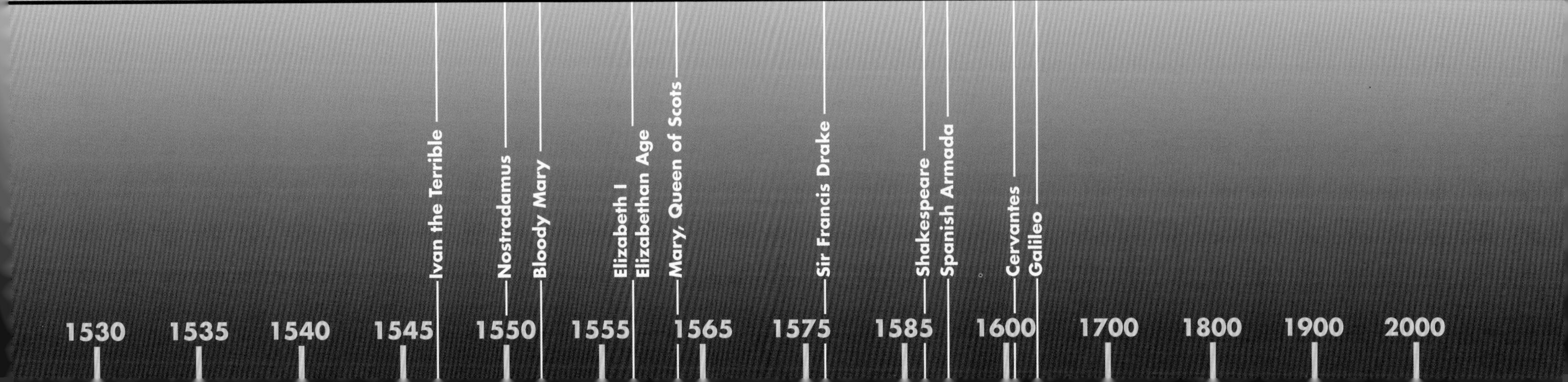
Ivan the Terrible
Nostradamus
Bloody Mary
Elizabeth I
Elizabethan Age
Mary, Queen of Scots
Sir Francis Drake
Shakespeare
Spanish Armada
Cervantes
Galileo
1530
1535
1540
1545
1550
1555
1565
1575
1585
1600
1700
1800
1900
2000

A page from *De Revolutionibus* details the heliocentric theory, Copernicus' idea that the planets orbited the sun *(right)*

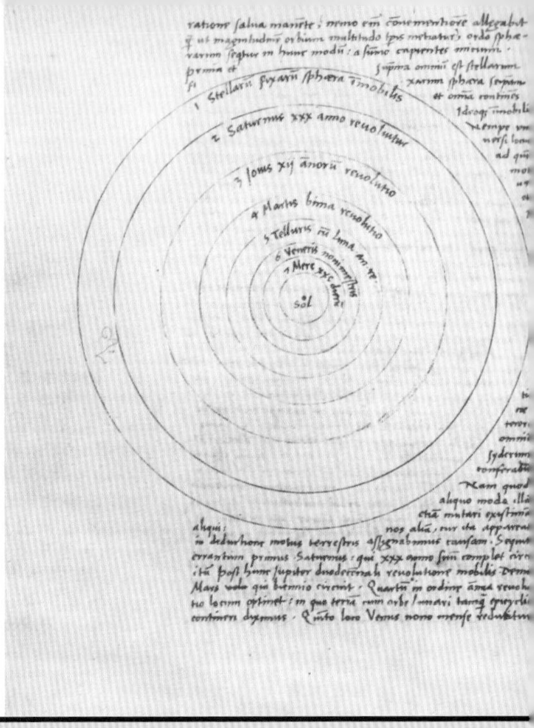

5 In 1539, when Copernicus was 66 years old, a math professor named Rheticus left his teaching job to study with Copernicus. The scholar stayed for two years, during which time he was able to convince Copernicus to write a book. That work, *De Revolutionibus*, was about his heliocentric (sun-centered) theory of the universe. The book was finally published in 1543. Against the wishes of the 70-year-old author, the publisher added a preface to help calm the Church. It stated that the ideas in the book were only theory, not facts. At this time, Copernicus suffered a stroke that left the right side of his body paralyzed and his mind weakened. Copernicus, a quiet man who never sought fame, received a copy of his book only a few hours before he died. The Church, meanwhile, insisted on changes that would make clear the heliocentric system was not fact before the book went out to the public.

1. What was the name of Copernicus' book?

2. Why do you think Rheticus wanted to study with Copernicus?

3. Why do you think Copernicus finally wrote a book about his theory?

4. How did the added preface help keep Copernicus out of trouble?

5. How might have Copernicus' one book changed the way people look at the universe?

PLANISPHÆRIVM
Sive
ORBIVM MVNDI
PTOLEMA
NO DI
PTOLEMAICVM
Machina
EX HYPOTHESI
ICA IN PLA
SPOSITA

The map of the universe as Ptolemy believed, with the Earth at its center, served as fact for hundreds of years *(left)*; Galileo Galilei, pictured here, was inspired to prove Copernicus' theory correct years later *(right)*

Ivan says—

Copernicus was such a quiet and studious fellow that not too much is known about his personal life. He did have a big impact on some thinkers in the future, notably the great Renaissance scientist Galileo. Galileo and Copernicus agreed about planets and gravity.

Copernicus was also a very kind man, who gave medical care to the poor at no charge. And he served the Church in any way he could. He even dedicated his book to the Pope. In 1616, 73 years after its publication, the work of Copernicus was banned for a time by the Catholic Church. Nine sentences which made the heliocentric theory seem fact, had to be taken out or changed before the book could be sold again.

Meanwhile, you go on to the next Flight, to meet a master. Let's fly back to Italy, get your imagery going. I'm getting my taste buds going.

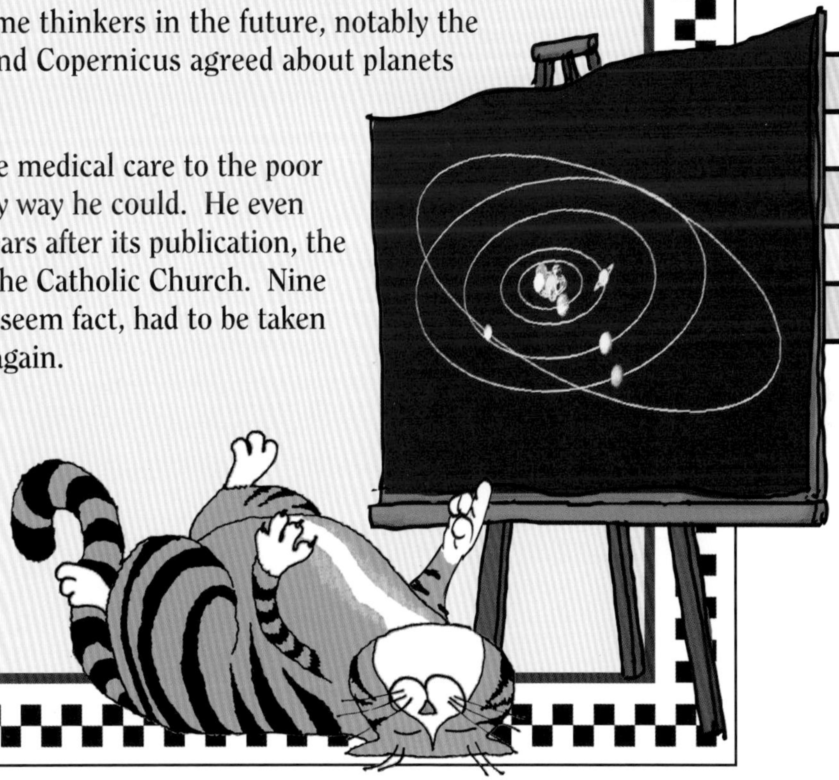

Flight 16

Michelangelo

1475-1564

The ceiling of the Sistine Chapel, painted by Michelangelo between 1508 and 1512

Buckle up. We're flying back to Italy for two flights. That's right. Two flights on the famous Michelangelo (*MEE-kul-an-gel-loh*). He is famous in history and deserves a lot of your imagery. Michelangelo did it all—draw, paint, sculpt, and design buildings.

Michelangelo is most famous for a statue and a ceiling. That's right, I said a ceiling. He painted and covered the ceiling of the Sistine Chapel in Rome with beautiful pictures illustrating scenes from the Bible.

Even though he lived nearly 500 years ago, Michelangelo's work still influences artists today. Oh, yes. He talked of seeing the figure trapped in the block of marble, and how he would carve the stone to free the figure within. He would run his hands over the cool marble until he was sure of the figure inside waiting to be released.

Wait until you visualize what he did. Oh, my aching neck. You read on. I'm heading for a massage with a little fish oil. Oh, yeah.

1

Michelangelo Buonarroti was one of the greatest artists of the Renaissance. Though he came from humble beginnings, he became one of the most famous men of his day. He was dedicated to hard work and would not stop until he was sure his art was as close to perfect as he could ever hope to get it. Michelangelo hated when people watched him or spoke to him while he worked. He would often let people know with loud shouts what he thought of their criticisms of his unfinished art. He passionately believed that an artist should be free to create with no direction or criticism. His first love was sculpting, and he liked to chip at the white stone blocks all night long. It was the only time he could be alone.

1. **What was Michelangelo's first love?**
2. **Why do you think it was important for Michelangelo to be dedicated to hard work?**
3. **Why do you think he hated when people watched him work?**
4. **Why do you think he did not want direction or criticism for his work?**
5. **Why do you think Michelangelo preferred to be alone while sculpting?**

2

Michelangelo was born in a small village near Florence, in 1475. His mother was ill for years, and died when he was only six years old. His father had brought in a woman from a family of stonecutters to help take care of him. Years later he would claim that his love of sculpting came from this second family. Then, at the age of 12, he left home against the wishes of his father to study art with a famous local painter. His father was angry that Michelangelo would give up a future in banking to pursue a living as uncertain as that of an artist. But the young man's stubborness and talent surprised everyone. Just a year later, at 13, Michelangelo enrolled in a sculpting school. Soon he was invited to live and work in the home of Lorenzo de'Medici, the most powerful man in Florence.

1. **What did the family that helped raise Michelangelo do for a living?**
2. **How do you think his second family influenced Michelangelo to become a sculptor?**
3. **Why do you think Michelangelo went to study with a famous painter?**
4. **Why might his father have wanted him to be a banker and not an artist?**
5. **Why do you think Lorenzo de'Medici invited the artist to live and work at his home?**

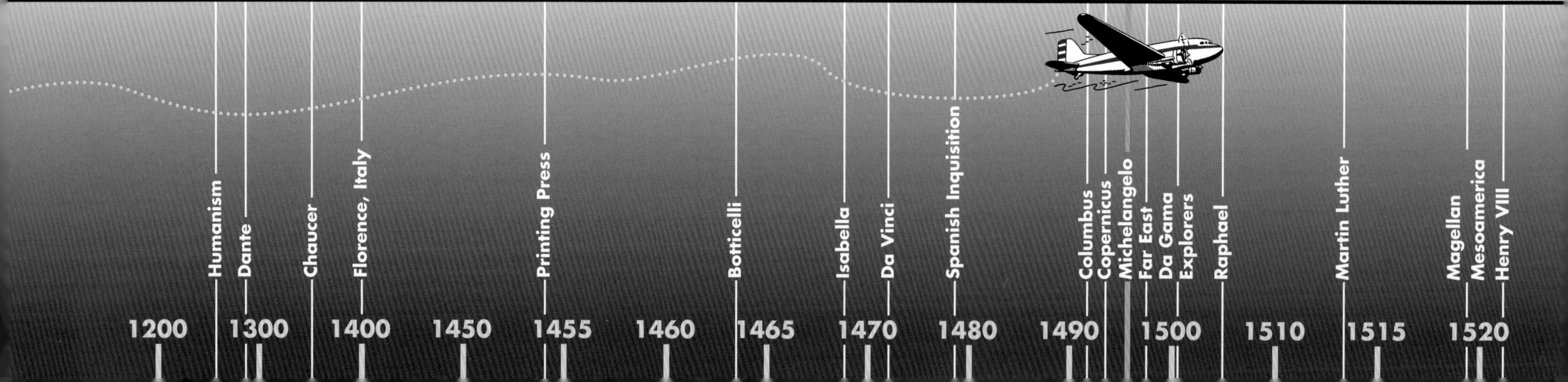
Humanism
Dante
Chaucer
Florence, Italy
Printing Press
Botticelli
Isabella
Da Vinci
Spanish Inquisition
Columbus
Copernicus
Michelangelo
Far East
Da Gama
Explorers
Raphael
Martin Luther
Magellan
Mesoamerica
Henry VIII
1200
1300
1400
1450
1455
1460
1465
1470
1480
1490
1500
1510
1515
1520

3

When he was young, Michelangelo was known more for his ego and short temper than his art. He offended many people and made fun of other artists. His distaste for Leonardo da Vinci was well known. It is said that on one occasion the two met on a bridge in Florence. Michelangelo wanted to embarrass the older man, so he asked da Vinci to quote a passage from Dante's *The Divine Comedy*. When da Vinci refused to answer, the young sculptor just laughed at him and walked away, satisfied. Most people couldn't stand this kind of attitude, so Michelangelo didn't make very many friends. But the few friends he did have were very loyal to him. One of those friends was the powerful Roman Catholic Church leader, Pope Julius II.

1. **What was the name of the Pope who was Michelangelo's friend?**
2. **Why do you think Michelangelo might have made fun of other artists?**
3. **Why do you think he may have wanted to embarrass da Vinci?**
4. **Why do you think he wouldn't have very many friends?**
5. **Why might it have been important to have a friend like Pope Julius II?**

4

Pope Julius II hired Michelangelo to paint the ceiling of the Sistine Chapel. The other artists who worked for the Pope at the time didn't like the brash newcomer with the big ego. They were jealous of the special friendship between Michelangelo and the Pope, who thought Michelangelo's talent was a gift from God. They knew that Michelangelo loved sculpting more than painting and that he was a better at it. So they convinced the Pope to ask him to paint the entire Sistine Chapel ceiling. Michelangelo tried to get out of the job, but couldn't. The other artists were elated when they saw him hesitate. They thought that he would do such a poor job that the Pope would have to call in Raphael, the best painter of that time, to fix it. They hoped that the Pope would be furious with Michelangelo. But their plan backfired, and Michelangelo devoted himself to creating a masterpiece on the ceiling.

1. **What did Pope Julius II hire Michelangelo to paint?**
2. **Why might the Pope have had a special friendship with Michelangelo?**
3. **Why might the other artists have wanted to make Michelangelo paint?**
4. **Why do you think Michelangelo tried to get out of the job?**
5. **Why do you think Michelangelo devoted himself to creating a masterpiece?**

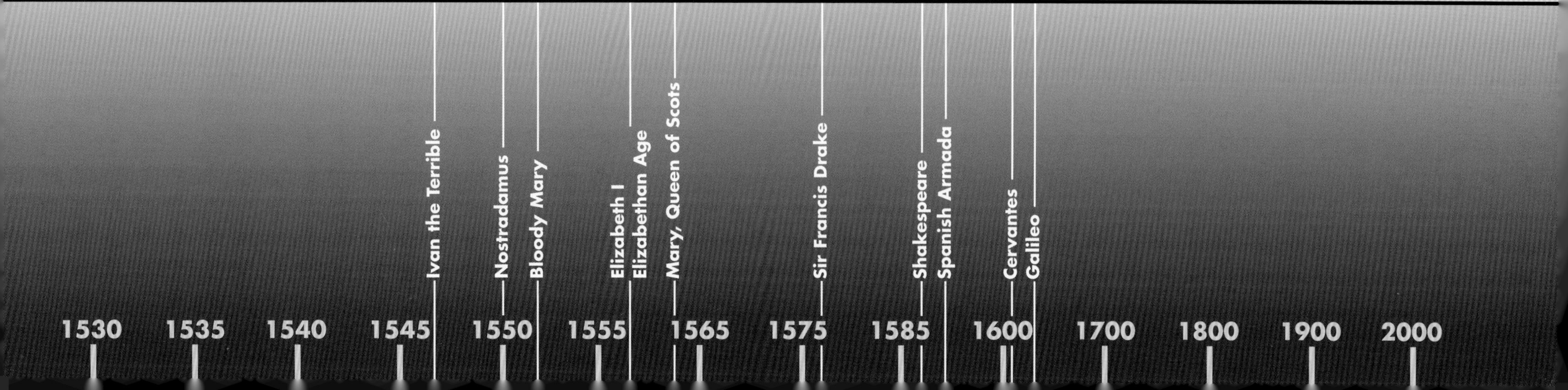

Ivan the Terrible
Nostradamus
Bloody Mary
Elizabeth I
Elizabethan Age
Mary, Queen of Scots
Sir Francis Drake
Shakespeare
Spanish Armada
Cervantes
Galileo
1530
1535
1540
1545
1550
1555
1565
1575
1585
1600
1700
1800
1900
2000

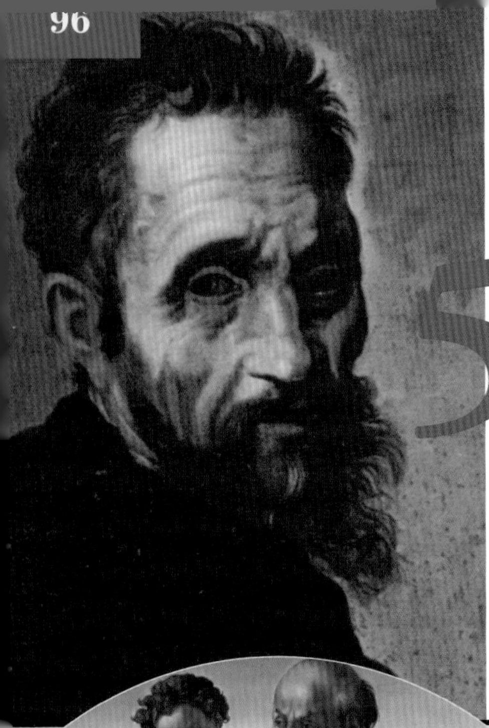

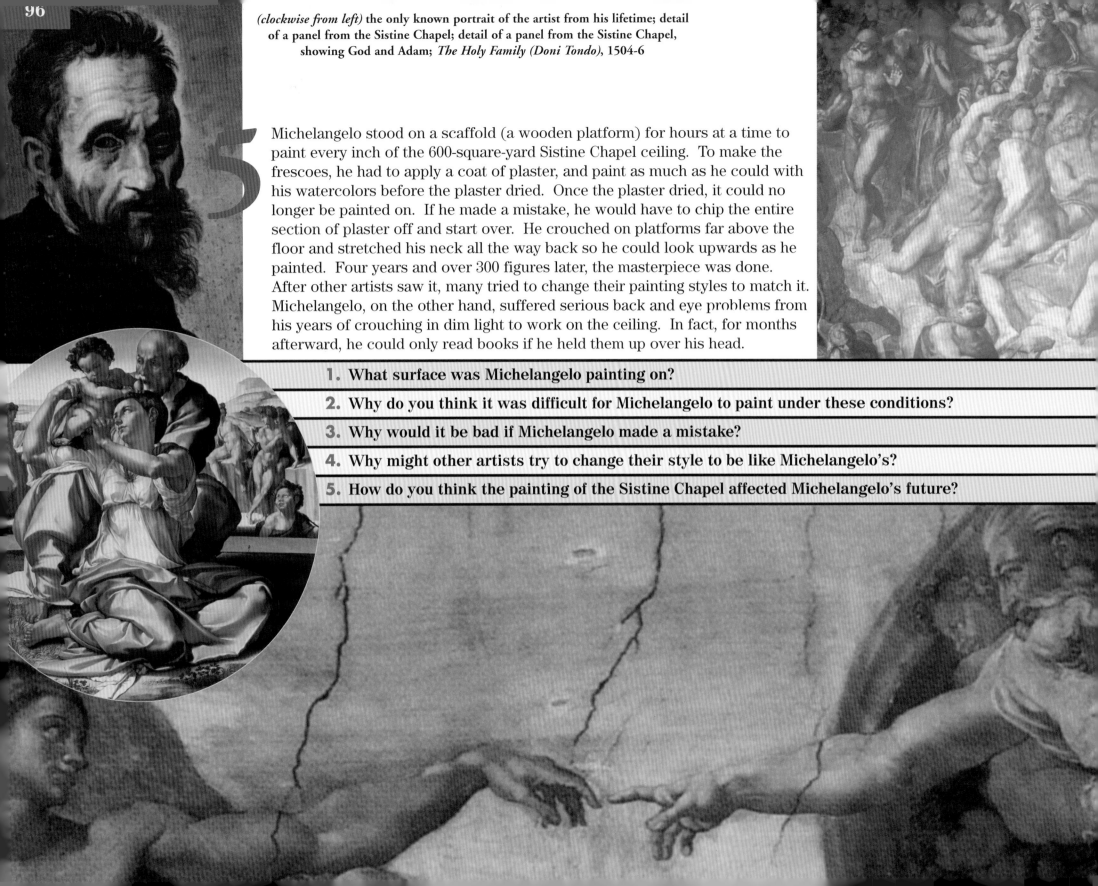

(clockwise from left) **the only known portrait of the artist from his lifetime; detail of a panel from the Sistine Chapel; detail of a panel from the Sistine Chapel, showing God and Adam;** ***The Holy Family (Doni Tondo)*****, 1504-6**

5

Michelangelo stood on a scaffold (a wooden platform) for hours at a time to paint every inch of the 600-square-yard Sistine Chapel ceiling. To make the frescoes, he had to apply a coat of plaster, and paint as much as he could with his watercolors before the plaster dried. Once the plaster dried, it could no longer be painted on. If he made a mistake, he would have to chip the entire section of plaster off and start over. He crouched on platforms far above the floor and stretched his neck all the way back so he could look upwards as he painted. Four years and over 300 figures later, the masterpiece was done. After other artists saw it, many tried to change their painting styles to match it. Michelangelo, on the other hand, suffered serious back and eye problems from his years of crouching in dim light to work on the ceiling. In fact, for months afterward, he could only read books if he held them up over his head.

1. **What surface was Michelangelo painting on?**
2. **Why do you think it was difficult for Michelangelo to paint under these conditions?**
3. **Why would it be bad if Michelangelo made a mistake?**
4. **Why might other artists try to change their style to be like Michelangelo's?**
5. **How do you think the painting of the Sistine Chapel affected Michelangelo's future?**

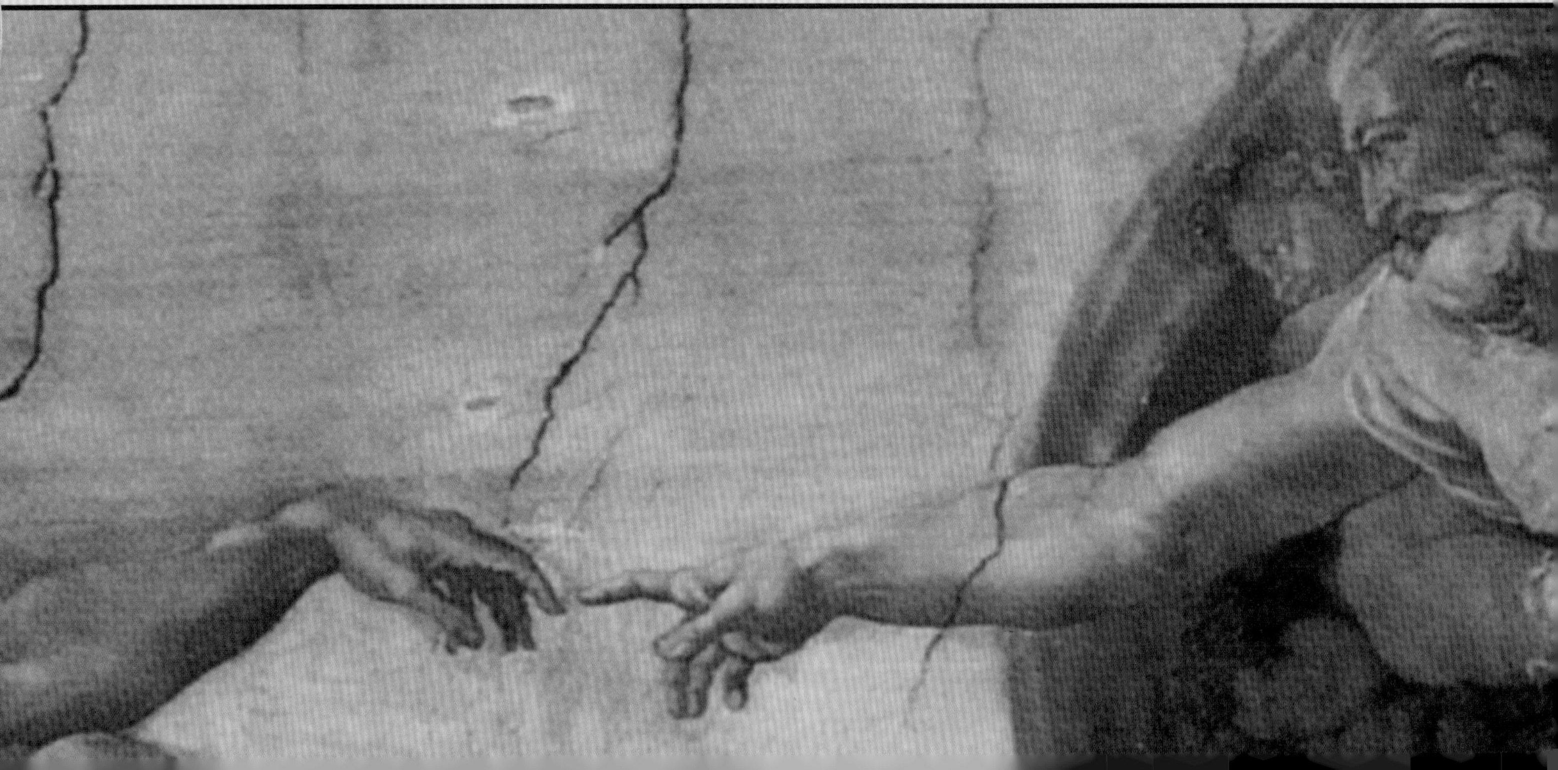

FOOD!

Ivan says—

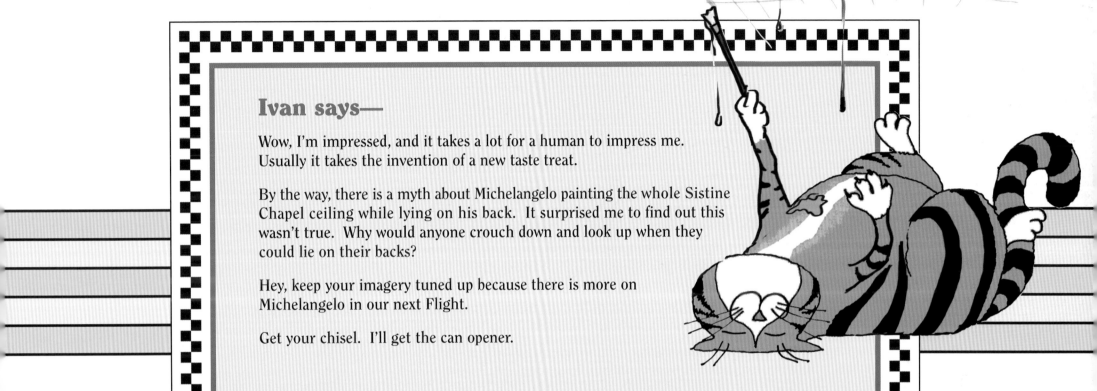

Wow, I'm impressed, and it takes a lot for a human to impress me. Usually it takes the invention of a new taste treat.

By the way, there is a myth about Michelangelo painting the whole Sistine Chapel ceiling while lying on his back. It surprised me to find out this wasn't true. Why would anyone crouch down and look up when they could lie on their backs?

Hey, keep your imagery tuned up because there is more on Michelangelo in our next Flight.

Get your chisel. I'll get the can opener.

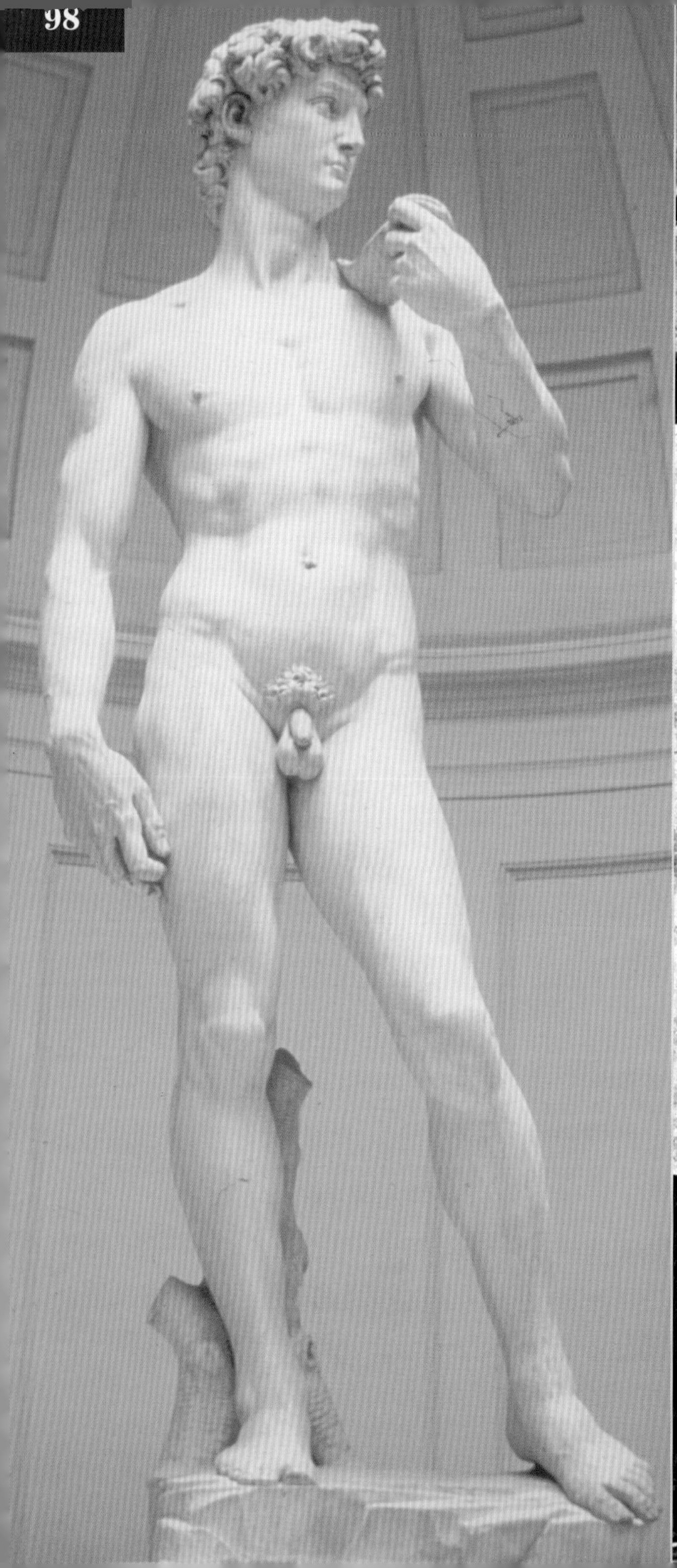

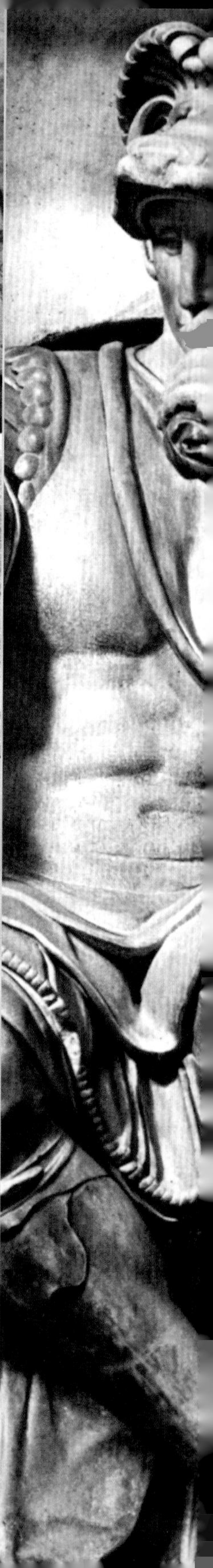

Michelangelo the Sculptor

(*from far left*) *David*, 1501-04, marble, Florence; tomb of Julius II, 1504-45, Rome; statue of Lorenzo de´Medici, from his tomb, 1520-34, Medici Chapel, Florence

Well, Michelangelo found quite a wonderful friend in Pope Julius II. If you're going to have someone in your corner, why not make it the most powerful guy in the known world? Julius, like other popes, appreciated art, especially art made to show the glory of God. Although he and Michelangelo argued like cats and dogs, he was like a second father to the workaholic artist. I'm a workaholic, too. I'm working all the time. Eating.

When Julius II died, Michelangelo was able to show his love and respect through the building of his tomb. In fact, Julius had brought Michelangelo out to Rome in 1506 to begin the great tomb, and at the time of Julius' death, in February, 1513, it wasn't nearly finished. But Michelangelo was determined to finish it. Over the years, he designed and redesigned the tomb, getting approval for his work from the next couple of popes in office. Sometimes Michelangelo fought with them, sometimes he cooperated, and all in all the tomb took almost forty years to finish. But it was really quite a nice tomb.

Michelangelo had such a love of sculpting that it was the focus of his whole life. He said, "I saw the angel in the marble and carved until I set him free." Read and see.

CAT FOOD

1

Michelangelo loved the form of the human body, a marvel of bones, muscles, and skin. He wanted to become an artist and a sculptor to recreate the human form. He spent long hours studying the real thing. He did this secretly in a cold, dark room. He spent hours dissecting human corpses, something that was forbidden by the Church. His close contact with decaying flesh caused him to fall ill several times. But his stubbornness kept him going. In the end, his remarkably life-like sculptures proved that his efforts were not wasted.

1. What did Michelangelo study to learn about the human form?

2. How might dissecting corpses have been helpful to Michelangelo?

3. Why do you think Michelangelo dissected human corpses in secret?

4. Do you think it was a good thing that Michelangelo was stubborn? Explain.

5. How might Michelangelo's sculptures proved that his efforts were not wasted?

2

At only 23, Michelangelo finished *La Pietà* (pg. 102), an amazing larger-than-life-size sculpture of Mary with her dead son, Jesus, draped across her lap. Every fold of Mary's robes was perfect, and her face was pure beauty. The white marble was so smooth that it looked like white glass rather than stone. Michelangelo said that he felt the figures were trapped in the stone, waiting for him to free them. Visiting St. Peter's Church, where the piece was displayed, the proud artist heard a person say that someone else had carved it. Angry, the young man chiseled "Michelangelo Buonarroti made this" across Mary's sash. He soon felt bad about the rash action and vowed never to sign another work of art.

1. Who was draped across Mary's lap?

2. Why do you think *La Pietà* might be considered one of his most amazing works?

3. Why do you think Michelangelo visited St. Peter's Church?

4. Why do you think Michelangelo was upset when someone said another artist carved *La Pietà*?

5. Why do you think he chose to never sign another work of art?

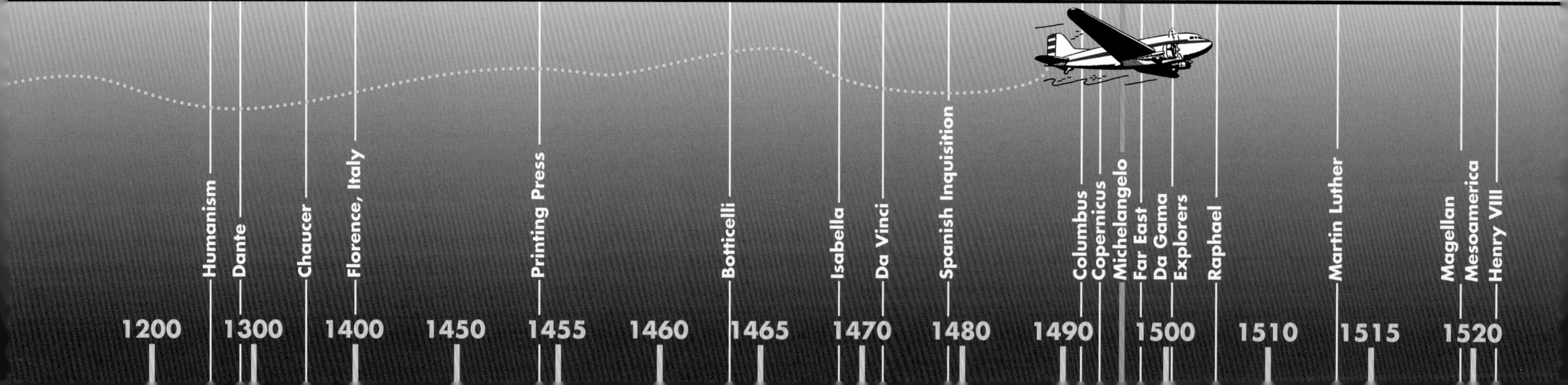
Humanism
Dante
Chaucer
Florence, Italy
Printing Press
Botticelli
Isabella
Da Vinci
Spanish Inquisition
Columbus
Copernicus
Michelangelo
Far East
Da Gama
Explorers
Raphael
Martin Luther
Magellan
Mesoamerica
Henry VIII
1200
1300
1400
1450
1455
1460
1465
1470
1480
1490
1500
1510
1515
1520

3 When he was 26, Michelangelo was hired to carve a statue of David (pg. 98), a hero from the Bible, for a square in Florence. He accepted the task, but was not pleased with the stone he was given to work with. The marble was so full of imperfections that many other artists had already passed on it. So he spent three years chiseling away at the rock in a wooden shack behind a church. Often he would spend long nights just running his hands over the cool white marble. He once said that he was "chipping away everything that wasn't David." The finished piece was a strong, muscled young man with a fiery gaze. People were awed by the amount of life and power the artist had managed to give the sculpture. This led Pope Julius II to ask the artist to work for him in Rome.

1. What did Michelangelo get hired to sculpt?

2. Why do you think Michelangelo was not pleased with the stone he was given?

3. Why do you think he spent so much time running his hands over the marble?

4. Why might the statue have attracted so much attention?

5. Why do you think the Pope asked Michelangelo to work for him in Rome?

4 In the last years of his life, Michelangelo worked as the chief designer for St. Peter's Basilica in Rome. He would work at the church in the day, but often had sleepless nights, pained by a constant ringing in his ears and aching back. He spent his nights alone, carving sculptures by candlelight. People who saw the frail man working were amazed at his strength and speed. One person said that Michelangelo could, in his old age, chip away more rock with his chisel than three young stonecutters could. Another said that he chipped the rock so hard that sparks would fly. His hammering was so precise that if his chisel had gone a hair further into the stone, the entire sculpture would be ruined. He worked through pain and loneliness until his death in 1564, at 88 years old.

1. Where did Michelangelo work as a chief designer in the last years of his life?

2. Why do you think he carved sculptures at night?

3. Why do you think people were amazed when they saw him working?

4. What do you think his mood was as he worked on his sculptures?

5. What do you think of Michelangelo?

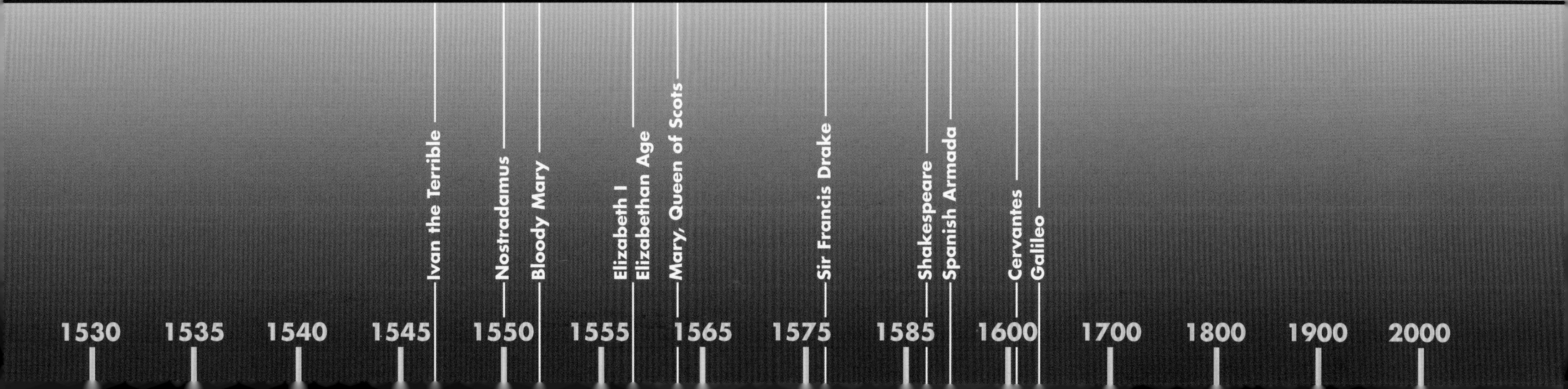
Ivan the Terrible
Nostradamus
Bloody Mary
Elizabeth I
Elizabethan Age
Mary, Queen of Scots
Sir Francis Drake
Shakespeare
Spanish Armada
Cervantes
Galileo
1530
1535
1540
1545
1550
1555
1565
1575
1585
1600
1700
1800
1900
2000

MICHAEL·ÃGELVS·BONAROTVS·FLORENT·FACIEBAT

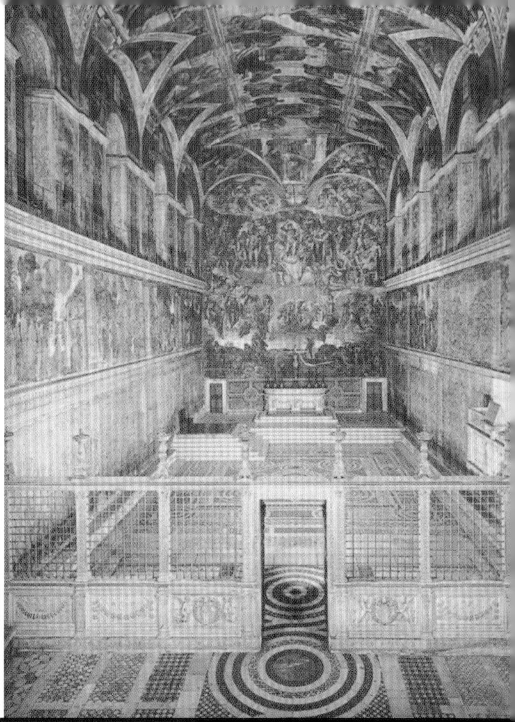

(clockwise from above) **Michelangelo etched this statement on Mary's sash of La Pietà; the Sistine Chapel was more than 600 square yards and rose to a height of 60 feet; Giuliano de'Medici, 1520-34, from his tomb, Medici Chapel, Florence**

5

In his life, Michelangelo devoted so much time to his art that he liked to say that he was married to it. This left no time for a family of his own, though he was close to his brother's children. After his death, his nephew, Leonardo Buonarroti, took care of funeral arrangements. In Florence, where he would be buried, Michelangelo's body was treated as if he were a king. More than 100 of the best artists of the time came to the funeral. Though most who knew Michelangelo disliked his thorny temper, they had a deep respect for his work. When he died, he left behind paintings, drawings, sculptures, and buildings that were far greater than any others. The artists traded stories for hours as they spoke in awe of the man who had been a master of all the arts.

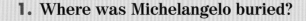

1. **Where was Michelangelo buried?**
2. **Why do you think Michelangelo never married?**
3. **Why do you think his nephew made the funeral arrangements?**
4. **Why do you think Michelangelo's body was treated as if he were a king?**
5. **Why do you think more than 100 artists came to Michelangelo's funeral?**

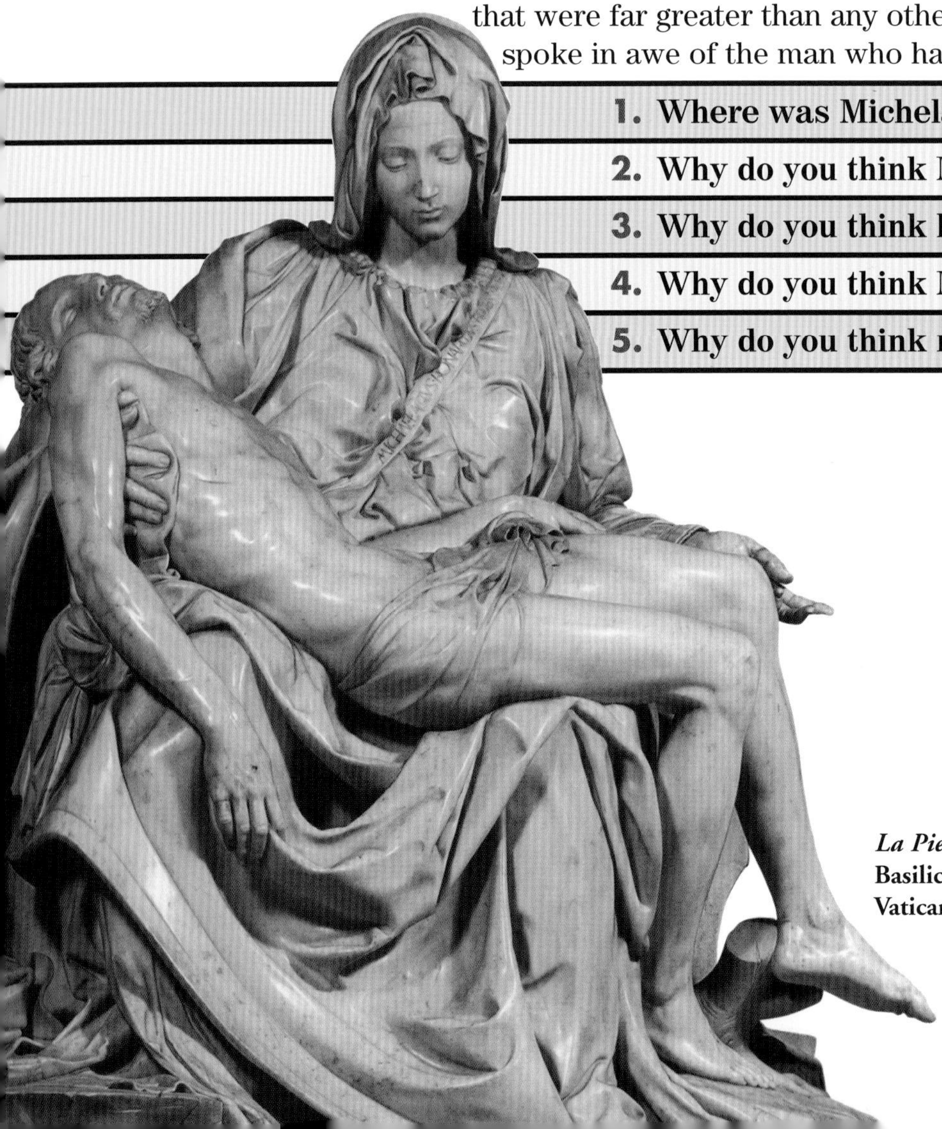

***La Pietà*, 1498-99, marble, Basilica de San Pietro, Vatican, Rome**

Ivan says—

Michelangelo worked as an artist, a sculptor, an architect, a designer...you name it. He made his whole life about art in one form or another. He spent every moment either preparing, doing, or finishing a piece of art. He's the man.

Now we're going to the deep blue sea to meet Magellan. Hey, get this. Magellan sailed around the world. Yep, around the whole world, and that is a long trip. That's a trip that calls for a lot of cans of tuna in the cargo hold, if you know what I mean.

Hop aboard and we'll go on an adventure with Magellan. No. You go. I eat. See you on the other side of the world.

IVAN

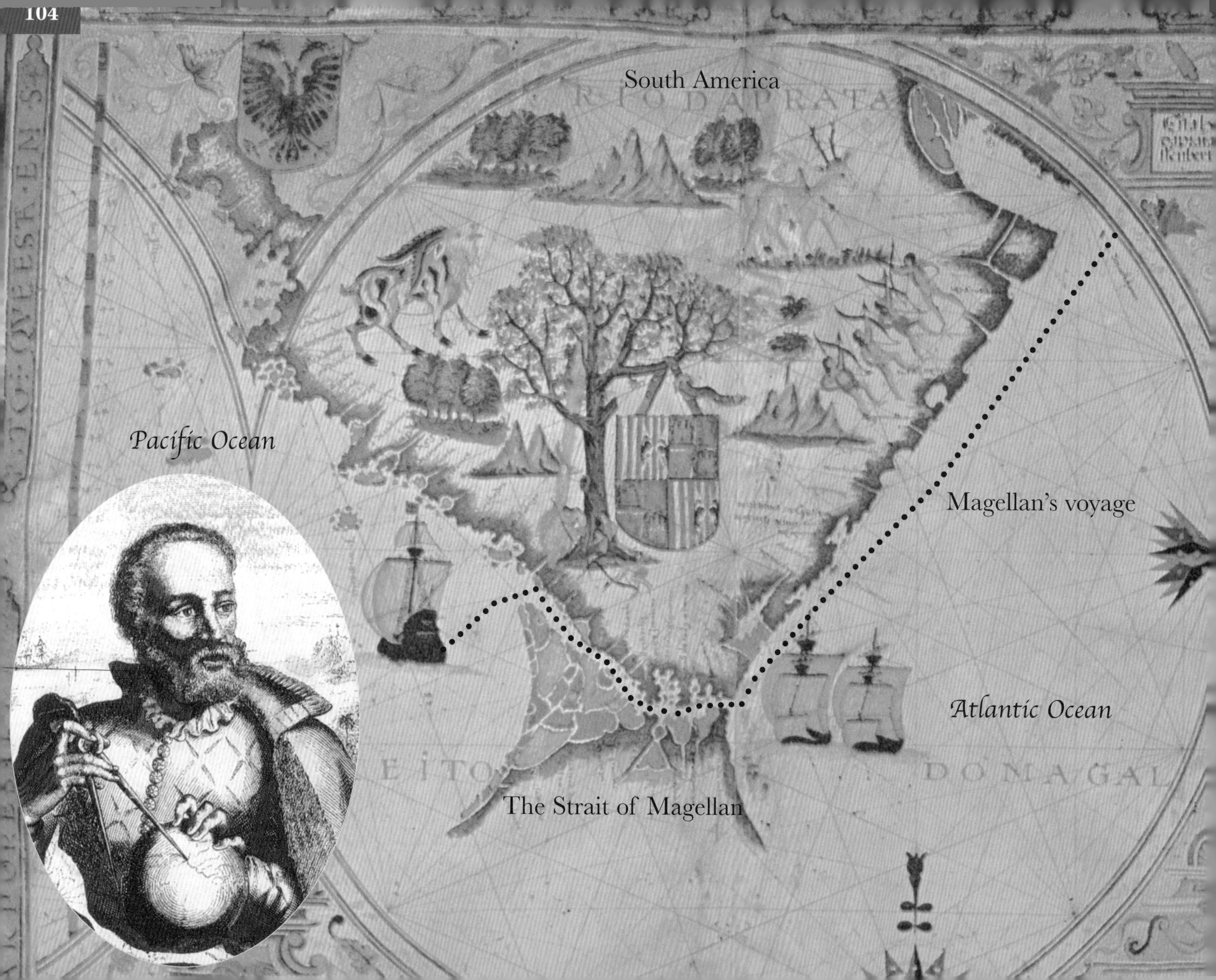
South America
Pacific Ocean
Magellan's voyage
Atlantic Ocean
The Strait of Magellan

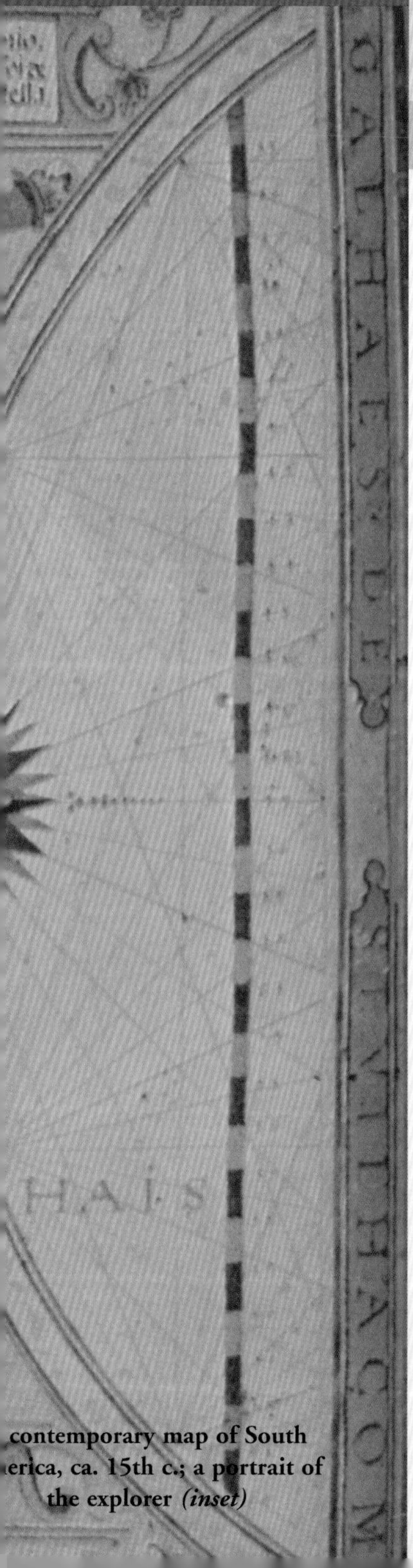

contemporary map of South
erica, ca. 15th c.; a portrait of
the explorer *(inset)*

Magellan

1480-1521

Welcome to the big round planet Earth! Magellan (*Mu-GEL-un*) proved once and for all, without a shadow of a doubt, positively and indubitably, that the world, this planet we call Earth, is round. Nothing better than round, I say. Round tummy, round Dish, round fish, round...

People had known the Earth was round for many years. But no one had ever actually gone around the world to *prove* it. Going all the way around the world is a lot like walking around the block. You start in one direction and keep going. After awhile you arrive at the same exact spot you left. Of course, the world is bigger than a block. A lot bigger. And you can't walk the whole way, especially not with those big oceans out there. So Magellan did it by sailing. He actually sailed around the entire world!

Other guys, like Columbus, certainly tried to get to the other side of the world. But Magellan's expedition, launched from Spain, was the first one to make the full circle. So, I give you Magellan, the original globetrotter. Visualize away. I'm heading for a round cheese and sardine pizza.

1

Ferdinand Magellan was born to wealthy parents in Portugal in 1480. He was raised in the royal court and schooled by the best teachers. His favorite subject was nautical (ships and sailing) science. He loved to hear of the voyages of the explorers, and he longed to go to sea. When he was 25, he got his wish and spent the next 13 years sailing on eastern trade routes to India, the Spice Islands, and Africa. After sailing so much, Magellan decided that the route he was taking to the Spice Islands was not the best way. He wanted to go west instead. He asked King Manuel to fund a voyage to the west, the direction Columbus had sailed. The King refused and so Magellan, angry and dishonored by this action, gave up his citizenship in Portugal.

1. What country was Magellan from?

2. Why do you think Magellan might have wanted to go to sea instead of stay at the royal court?

3. How do you think Magellan came up with the idea for a western sea route to the Spice Islands?

4. Why do you think Magellan got so angry when King Manuel refused to fund his voyage?

5. What do you think happened next?

2

Magellan went to Spain to ask the new 18-year-old King Charles for funds for his voyage. King Charles gave Magellan the money to sail west around the tip of South America to try to reach the Spice Islands. Magellan set sail in 1519, at age 39, with five ships and about 260 men. He made his way south to search for a water passage west through the New World. No passage could be found. During the bitter winter, while the ships sat out the cold weather in a South American port, some members of the scared and hungry crew tried to mutiny (rebel against the person in charge). Magellan had two of his captains executed and left a third captain and his men on the shores of South America. Once the summer arrived, the journey continued.

1. In what direction did Magellan sail?

2. Why might some of the crew have tried to mutiny?

3. Why do you think the crew members were scared?

4. Why do you think Magellan left crew members on shore?

5. What might have happened to the crew members who were left in South America?

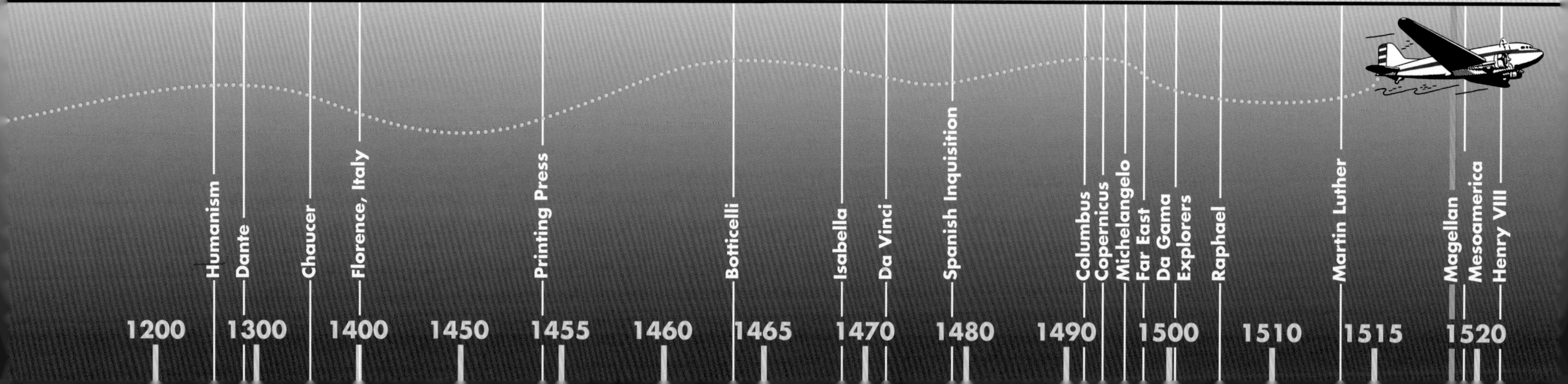
Humanism
Dante
Chaucer
Florence, Italy
Printing Press
Botticelli
Isabella
Da Vinci
Spanish Inquisition
Columbus
Copernicus
Michelangelo
Far East
Da Gama
Explorers
Raphael
Martin Luther
Magellan
Mesoamerica
Henry VIII
1200
1300
1400
1450
1455
1460
1465
1470
1480
1490
1500
1510
1515
1520

3

Finally, Magellan found a narrow passage at the bottom of South America. He was down to four ships now. They sailed for 38 days through the dangerous, winding waterway. One ship, the *San Antonio*, secretly deserted in the night with a large amount of the expedition's food. Now Magellan had only three ships and little food. In November 1520, the ships entered a calm ocean that Magellan named *Mar Pacifico* (Pacific Ocean). Magellan was thrilled and thought they would now reach the Spice Islands in only a few days, but he was wrong. They sailed on and on, but found nothing but water. They ran out of food, eating rats and sawdust to survive. Nineteen men died in the 98 days they wandered, lost in the Pacific. Finally, they reached an island of friendly natives, giving the men a much needed rest.

1. How long did it take Magellan to sail through the passage?

2. Why do you think the *San Antonio* deserted?

3. Why might Magellan have been wrong about when they would reach the Spice Islands?

4. What might be one of the reasons the remaining ships ran out of food?

5. How do you think the crew members felt when they reached the island?

4

Among friendly and kind natives, Magellan was able to get enough food and water stocked in his holds to sail on. He went on to the Philippines. The people there were also very friendly and again the crew rested for many weeks. Magellan converted many of the natives to his own religion, Christianity. He developed a friendship with one of the local tribal leaders. In gratitude for the tribe's kindness towards his men, Magellan agreed to help fight against their enemies. The battle cost Magellan his life. It is said he died by a poison arrow.

1. Where did the expedition sail to after stocking the holds with food and water?

2. Why do you think Magellan and his crew stayed in the Philippines so long?

3. Why do you think Magellan converted some natives to Christianity?

4. Why might the local tribal leader and Magellan have become friends?

5. Why do you think Magellan felt he should help the local tribe fight against their enemies?

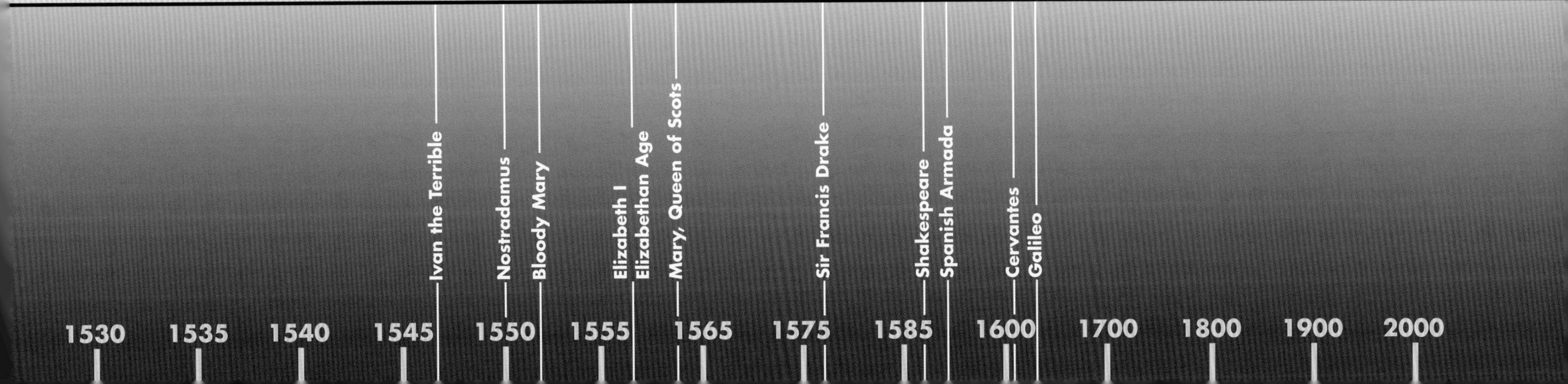
Ivan the Terrible
Nostradamus
Bloody Mary
Elizabeth I
Elizabethan Age
Mary, Queen of Scots
Sir Francis Drake
Shakespeare
Spanish Armada
Cervantes
Galileo
1530
1535
1540
1545
1550
1555
1565
1575
1585
1600
1700
1800
1900
2000

Mare antiliarum.
America
Brasilis.
Quinta orbis pars.
Mundus nouus.
Terra Incognita

(clockwise from left) **a map of South America; a portrait of Magellan; The Victoria, Juan Sebastian del Cano's ship, the first to sail around the world; an engraving from the 1800's illustrates Magellan's death.**

5

After Magellan's sudden death, his second in command, Juan del Cano, took over the three ships. It was April of 1521 when they once again set out, and there weren't many sailors left. Del Cano burned one ship and they once again headed west, sailing for a year and five months. Finally they reached the Spice Islands, where the ships were loaded with fragrant cloves, pepper, and other spices. Del Cano's ship continued west while he sent the other ship east, with the hope that one of them would someday make it back to Spain. It was del Cano who arrived in Spain on September 6, 1522, three years after they had set out. The other ship had met a bad end. Of the 260 original crew, only 18 men survived the trip around the world.

1. Who took command after Magellan's death?

2. Why do you think del Cano burned one of the ships?

3. How do you think del Cano and his men felt when they finally reached the Spice Islands?

4. Why do you think only 18 men survived the trip?

5. Would you consider Magellan's voyage a success? Why or why not?

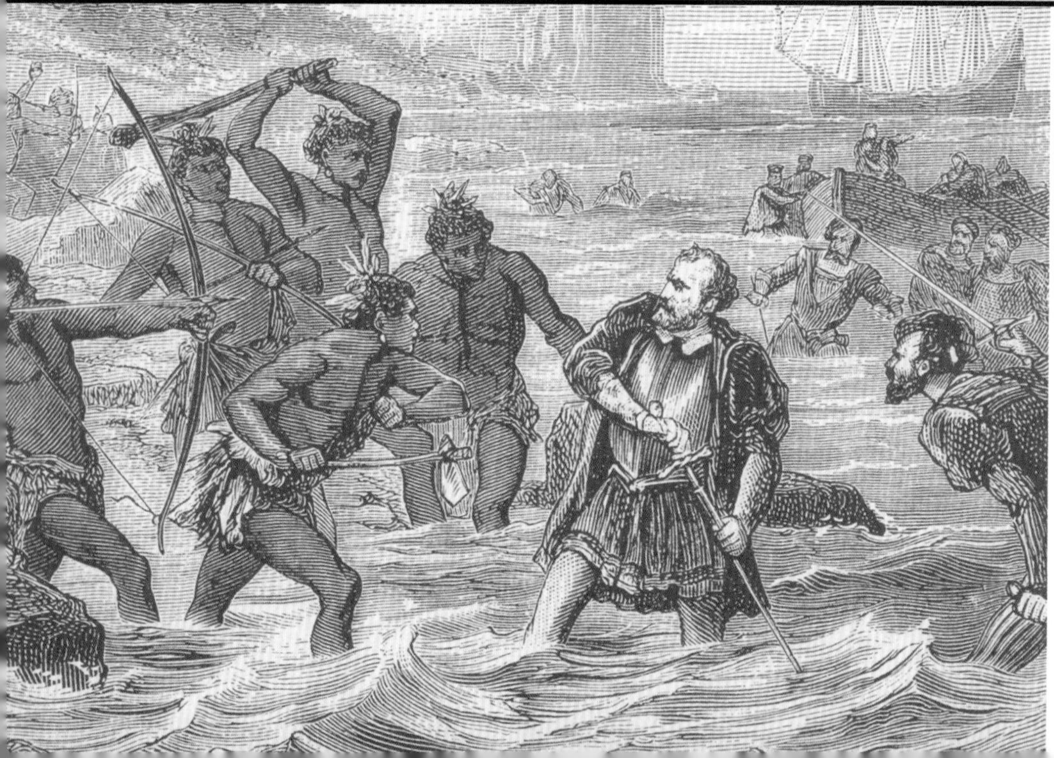

Ivan says—

Tough journey. Although Magellan died before completing the trip, he is still considered the first man to sail around the world.

While del Cano made it home, the other ship didn't. Del Cano was named a hero on his return, and kings and queens started laying claim to the southern lands and islands the expedition had found. Many wanted to convert native people to their religion, but most wanted new foods, trade goods, foods, riches, and foods.

The next Flight is full of beauty. In fact, the artist Raphael, who we are flying to Italy to meet, created some of the most beautiful paintings of all time. He was younger than those other greats of his time, Leonardo da Vinci and Michelangelo, but he studied their work and even met them.

You read and visualize. I'll be sailing around the fish tank.

I'd Rather
Be Sailing

Flight 19

(clockwise from left) *The Transfiguration*, 1518-20; *Bacco vane*; *The Sistine Madonna*, 1513-14; e Julius II, 1512, detail of a fresco at the Vatican; detail of a study for *donna col Figlio e S. Giovannino*; *St. orge and the Dragon*; *The Madonna of the Chair*, 1513-14 *(center)*

Raphael

1483-1520

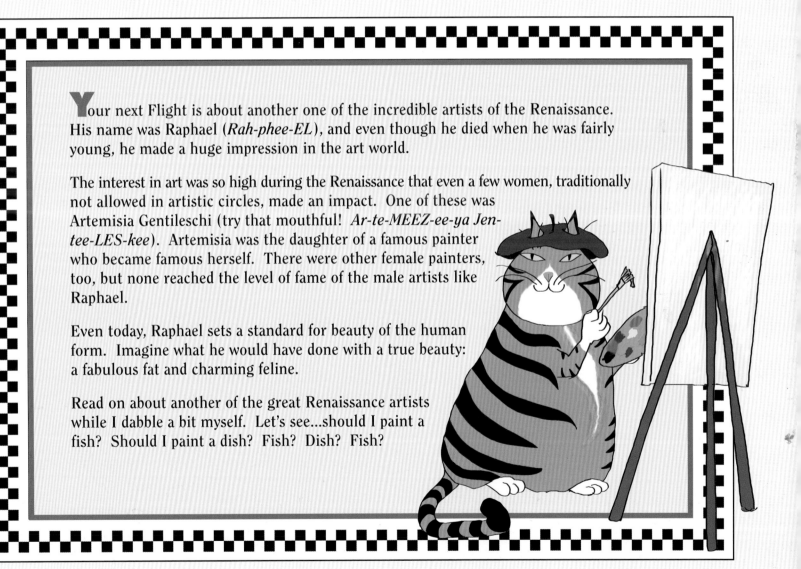

Your next Flight is about another one of the incredible artists of the Renaissance. His name was Raphael (*Rah-phee-EL*), and even though he died when he was fairly young, he made a huge impression in the art world.

The interest in art was so high during the Renaissance that even a few women, traditionally not allowed in artistic circles, made an impact. One of these was Artemisia Gentileschi (try that mouthful! *Ar-te-MEEZ-ee-ya Jen-tee-LES-kee*). Artemisia was the daughter of a famous painter who became famous herself. There were other female painters, too, but none reached the level of fame of the male artists like Raphael.

Even today, Raphael sets a standard for beauty of the human form. Imagine what he would have done with a true beauty: a fabulous fat and charming feline.

Read on about another of the great Renaissance artists while I dabble a bit myself. Let's see...should I paint a fish? Should I paint a dish? Fish? Dish? Fish?

1

Raphael Santi was the son of an artist in Urbino, Italy. His father had worked as an art collector, so Raphael grew up among art lovers and intellectuals. From an early age, he was drawing and painting, and showed amazing talent. Sadly, his parents died and the young boy became a poor orphan. Raphael's art training did not end, however. When he was 11 years old, he was sent by an uncle to study with a famed artist, and later as a teenager went to work for Perugino, one of the most famous painters in central Italy. Unlike other students, Perugino had Raphael clean the studio and run errands. He provided the boy with a room and food, and taught him all he knew. Raphael later became the head of the studio.

1. **Who did Raphael go to work for as a teenager?**
2. **Why might Raphael have drawn and painted from an early age?**
3. **Why do you think Raphael's art training did not end when his parents died?**
4. **Why do you think Raphael had to work at the studio and not just learn?**
5. **What does being sent to study with the most famous painter in central Italy tell you about Raphael's talent?**

2

Perugino influenced the young artist's style and Raphael often imitated him. By the time he was 22, his talent surpassed that of his teacher. He moved to Florence, the center of art and culture, for four years. There he began to study the works of local legends Michelangelo and Leonardo da Vinci. Raphael idolized (adored) the two famed artists, who were known as rivals. Soon Raphael became known all over Italy for the beauty and delicacy of his own work, especially the many Madonnas (Mary, the mother of Jesus) that he did while in Florence. Each time he painted a Madonna, he tried new colors and styles in a search for perfection, so that each one would be uniquely beautiful.

1. **How old was Raphael when he moved to Florence?**
2. **Why do you think Raphael moved to Florence instead of continuing to work for Perugino?**
3. **Why might Raphael have wanted to study the works of Michelangelo and da Vinci?**
4. **Why do you think Raphael painted so many Madonnas?**
5. **Why might Raphael have wanted to perfect his style?**

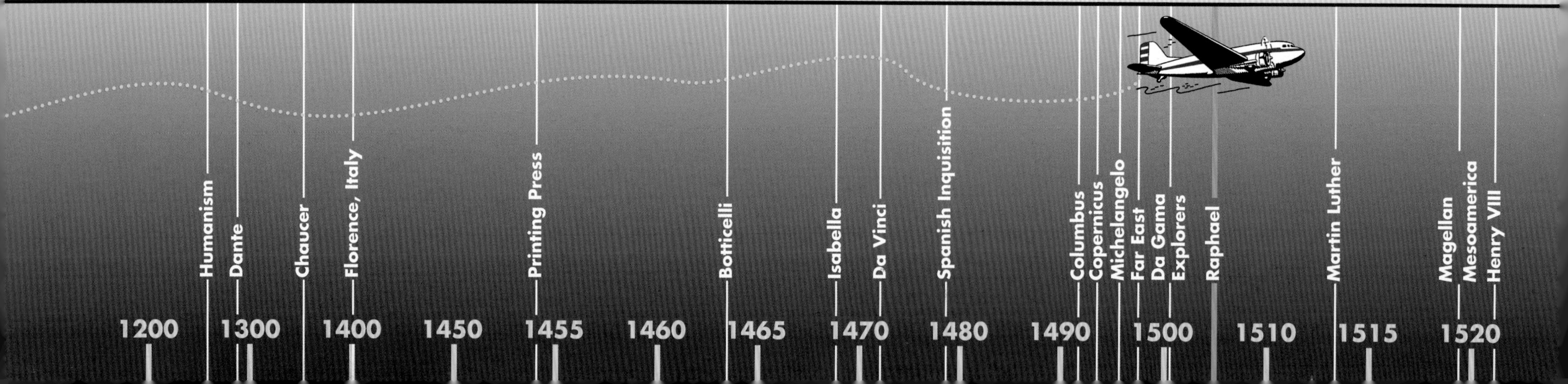
Humanism
Dante
Chaucer
Florence, Italy
Printing Press
Botticelli
Isabella
Da Vinci
Spanish Inquisition
Columbus
Copernicus
Michelangelo
Far East
Da Gama
Explorers
Raphael
Martin Luther
Magellan
Mesoamerica
Henry VIII
1200
1300
1400
1450
1455
1460
1465
1470
1480
1490
1500
1510
1515
1520

3

In 1508, Pope Julius II called the modest 25-year-old artist to Rome to paint the walls of his private rooms. Under the Pope's financial support and friendship, Raphael blossomed into a genius of painting. He created some of his most famous works, including *The School of Athens* (pg. 114). The painting shows classical thinkers Plato and Aristotle talking as they walk through a forum in ancient Greece. Raphael also painted himself, Michelangelo, and da Vinci as characters in the picture. The painting has a soft, rounded, realistic style that quickly became hugely popular. His other work included portraits of the Pope, like *Mass of Bolsena* (pg. 110), considered a masterpiece, that is stunning in its color and drama.

1. **Who gave Raphael financial support while he was in Rome?**
2. **Why do you think the Pope asked Raphael to paint the walls of his private rooms?**
3. **Why might Raphael have blossomed under the Pope's support?**
4. **Why might Raphael have painted portraits of the Pope?**
5. **What is the main idea of all this imagery?**

4

Raphael was at the height of his fame before he was even 30. However, at this time Michelangelo unveiled his paintings on the ceiling of the Sistine Chapel. The masterpiece humbled Raphael and his self-confidence was shattered. He wrote to a friend about a *fresco* (a painting on wet plaster), "If this idea possesses any perfection I do not know it, though this is what I endeavor to attain." He even avoided painting for a while, working in other artistic areas. He designed beautiful *tapestries* (rugs with pictures), which were much loved by the next Pope, Leo X. But despite his fears, he was still in huge popular demand. Soon he had to rely more and more on his assistants to help him complete the great amount of painting he was asked to do. Incredibly polite and kind, he could not say no to any job, and so he suffered from exhaustion.

1. **What did Raphael do artistically instead of paint?**
2. **Do you think Raphael was too hard on himself? Explain.**
3. **Why might Raphael have gone back to painting?**
4. **Why might it have been bad for Raphael to take on so many jobs?**
5. **What problems might have resulted from relying on his assistants for much of his work?**

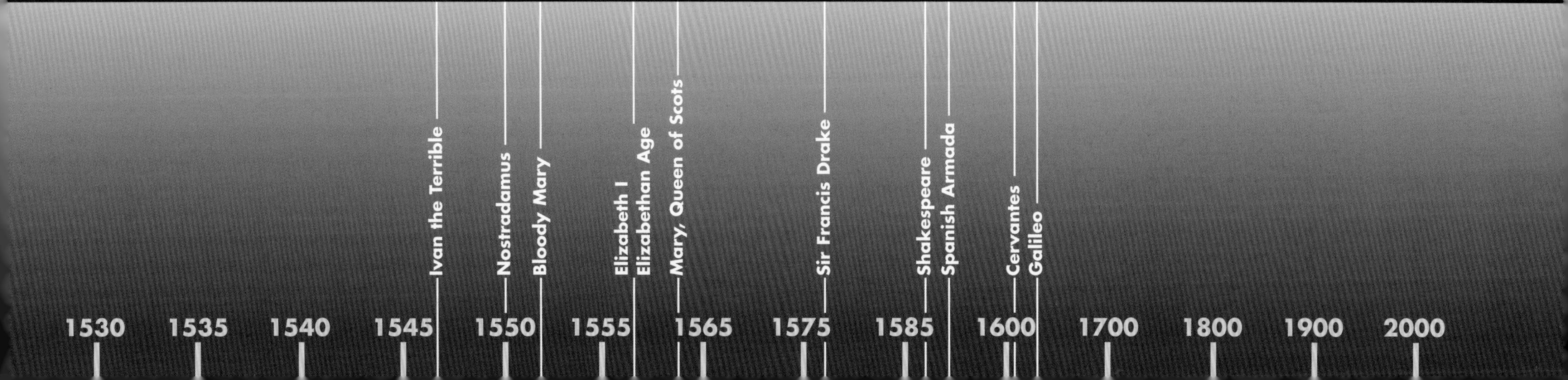
Ivan the Terrible
Nostradamus
Bloody Mary
Elizabeth I
Elizabethan Age
Mary, Queen of Scots
Sir Francis Drake
Shakespeare
Spanish Armada
Cervantes
Galileo
1530
1535
1540
1545
1550
1555
1565
1575
1585
1600
1700
1800
1900
2000

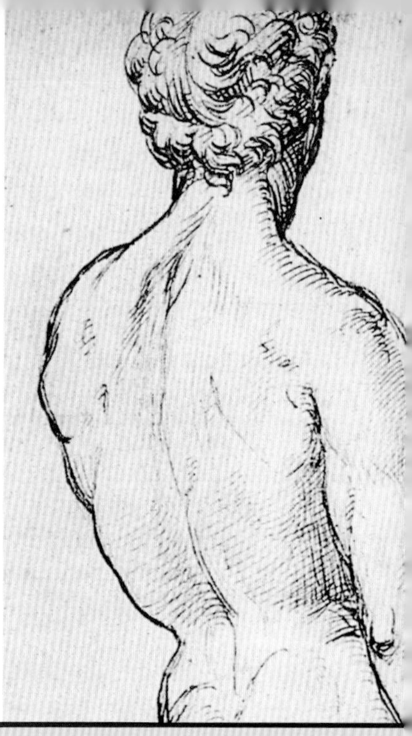

5 Raphael never married, though he was engaged to a patron's daughter for years. But his true love was a poor model he used for many paintings. He had a workshop full of students, but none of them could paint as well as he could. After ten straight days of painting while sick with a high fever, he died on his 37th birthday. His body was found next to his unfinished painting, *The Transfiguration* (pg. 110). His best pupil finished the painting to honor him and it stood at his funeral. The Pope wept openly at the funeral for the loss of such a great and yet modest talent and friend.

1. How old was Raphael when he died?

2. Why do you think Raphael never married?

3. Do you think Raphael trusted his students to do his work? Explain.

4. Why do you think his body was found next to his painting?

5. Why do you think his final painting stood at his funeral?

Detail of *La Velata*, 1515-16 *(top left)*; Raphael's self-portrait with his fencing master, who is on the right *(bottom left)*; study of a nude *(top right)*; *The School of Athens*, 1509-11, is the centerpiece for the Stanza della Segnatura at the Palazzi Vaticani *(bottom right)*

Ivan says—

What a great and sad story. It's too bad Raphael died so young. Who knows what great art he might have given the world had he lived as long as da Vinci or Michelangelo, who each lived nearly 50 years longer than Raphael.

Raphael's paintings were designed to look pleasing and inviting. He used a technique picked up from Leonardo called *sfumato,* in which the edges of figures are blurred so they fade into the background. Makes them warm and fuzzy.

Buckle up. We're turning the airplane toward Germany next. We're about to learn how Europe went from one Christian religion to two religions. Martin Luther had a problem with rules, and he did something about it.

You do as I say. Turn the page, read, and picture...and I'll do as I say. Nap, Ivan, nap.

Flight 20

Martin Luther

1483-1546

We're landing in Germany, start swallowing your tongue and speaking in short bursts of air. Kidding. It's time to learn again how one person can make change happen. This Flight is about Martin Luther, a man who took on a giant called the Catholic Church.

A long time ago in the Roman Catholic Church some of the leaders were great, but some weren't always honest and good. Some Catholic leaders had more power than kings and they lived lavish (rich) lifestyles. To build up the Church bank, they sold coupons, called indulgences, that people were told would rid them of their sins. Some indulgences were fancy for the rich, while those for the poor were simple slips of paper.

COUPON

Martin Luther, a monk in Germany, didn't like this, and tried to point out some of the ways the Church had gone astray from its real purpose. In the end, he divided the Church into two churches. Because of him, the Protestant Church was born. This change in religion is called the Reformation—all started by Martin Luther.

Hmmm. Speaking of reform, I think I'll use my coupon and re-form a little bigger by adding some food to my tummy. You read. I eat. That's good.

Martin Luther, painted by Cranach the Elder, 1533 *(left)*; Pope Leo X, painted by Raphael, 1517-1519 *(right)*

1

Martin Luther was born in Germany in 1483. His father beat Luther as much as 15 times in one morning. He insisted his son enter college at 18 to become a lawyer and make good money. But Luther went against his father's wishes and quit school after an event in 1505 changed his life. When he was 22 years old, while he was traveling, a severe thunderstorm filled the skies. Lightning threw him to the ground, and is said to have killed his companion. Fearing for his life, he promised God that he would become a priest if he survived. In a later letter, Luther wrote to his friend, "When I was terror-stricken and overwhelmed by the fear of impending death, I made an involuntary and forced vow."

1. What happened to Luther that made him become a priest?

2. Why do you think Luther was afraid for his life?

3. Why do you think Luther promised God that he would become a priest instead of a lawyer?

4. What do you think Luther's father thought of him becoming a priest?

5. How do you think Luther felt about becoming a priest?

2

Luther was happy and fulfilled living in a monastery and studying the Bible. He became an expert on religion and began to teach at a German university. Around 1511, at age 28, Luther went to Rome and observed firsthand the lifestyle of the Church leaders. He returned to teaching in Germany, but his attitude was changed. He refused to eat or drink, locked himself in his room, and suffered from severe insomnia (lack of sleep). He was appalled, and ashamed of his superiors in the Church. In 1513, two years later, the Church began selling *indulgences* to raise money. These were pieces of paper that said the purchaser would be forgiven for sins on Earth and would go straight to Heaven when he or she died. Luther became even more upset.

1. What did Church sell to raise money?

2. Why do you think Luther's attitude changed after his visit to Rome?

3. Why might people have wanted to buy indulgences?

4. Do you think the selling of indulgences raised a lot of money? Explain.

5. Why do you think Luther was appalled and upset?

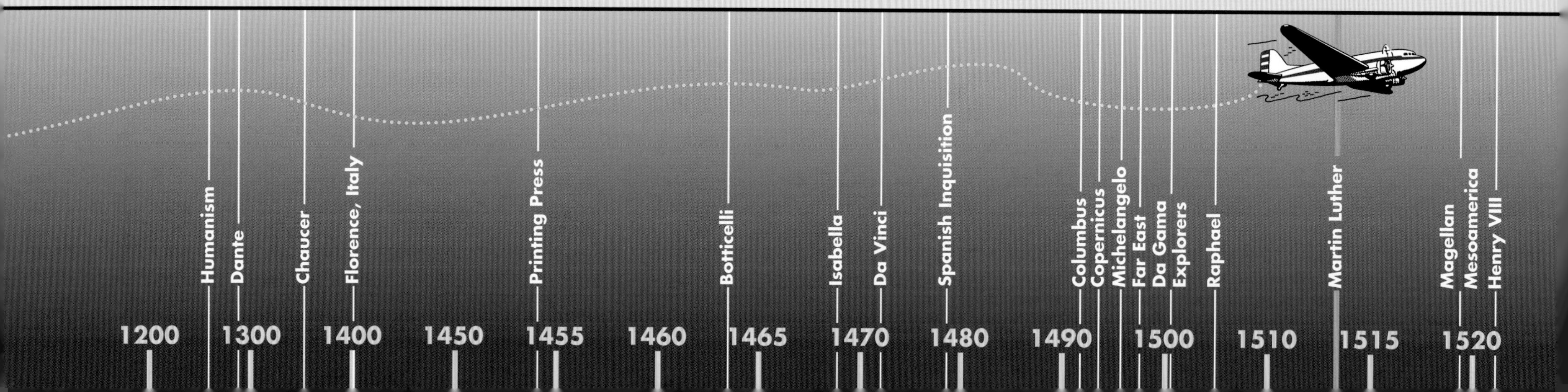
Humanism
Dante
Chaucer
Florence, Italy
Printing Press
Botticelli
Isabella
Da Vinci
Spanish Inquisition
Columbus
Copernicus
Michelangelo
Far East
Da Gama
Explorers
Raphael
Martin Luther
Magellan
Mesoamerica
Henry VIII
1200
1300
1400
1450
1455
1460
1465
1470
1480
1490
1500
1510
1515
1520

3

Luther thought the Church was bringing dishonor to God, and that faith was the only true path to Heaven. He believed that a man's salvation was based on his faith in God, not on what he could afford to purchase. Luther also was concerned about the lavish lifestyles of some Church officials. He wrote a paper called the *Ninety-five Theses.* He posted this list of objections and criticisms on the church door, where people would place papers for public reading and debate. Some people translated Luther's ideas from Latin to German, making them even more available to the everyday folk. *Ninety-five Theses* was printed and quickly spread throughout the country, generating excitement and anger. In one case, a seller was mobbed by religious students, who burned 800 copies in a bonfire at the center of town.

1. What was the name of Luther's paper?

2. Do you think Luther wanted people to know about his objections and criticisms regarding the Church?

3. Why do you think Luther wanted people to read and debate his paper?

4. How do you think the public reacted to Luther's ideas?

5. Why do you think the religious students burned copies of Luther's paper?

4

As farmers and shopkeepers read the *Ninety-five Theses*, many found themselves nodding in agreement with Luther. They could see the Church leaders living in luxury while they suffered. They also knew that the rich were getting special treatment from the Church. Debates about the Church took place all over Europe, sometimes even leading to riots. The Church leaders became very upset and kicked Luther out of the Church. Luther had only hoped to change some of the practices of the Church with the *Ninety-five Theses.* Instead, as people took sides for Luther's ideas or for the Church, it began to divide into two churches. Luther became a fugitive on the run, and, though absent, was put on trial for *heresy*. Church leaders called him the "child of iniquity (evil or sin)."

1. What had Luther hoped to do with his *Ninety-five Theses*?

2. Why do you think many people agreed with Luther?

3. How might debates about the Church have led to riots?

4. How might Luther have felt about the Church dividing?

5. Why do you think Luther had become a fugitive?

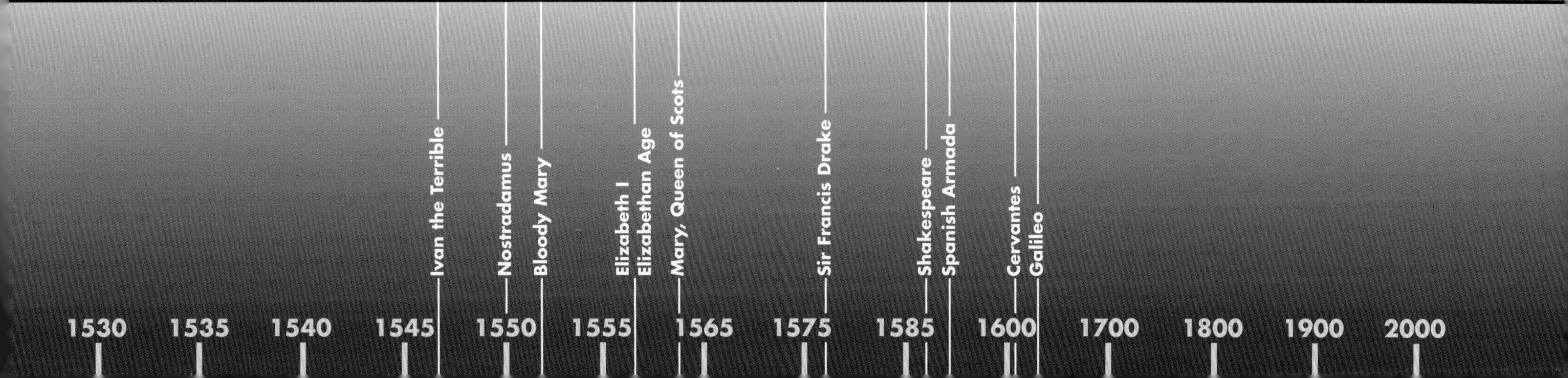
Ivan the Terrible
Nostradamus
Bloody Mary
Elizabeth I
Elizabethan Age
Mary, Queen of Scots
Sir Francis Drake
Shakespeare
Spanish Armada
Cervantes
Galileo
1530
1535
1540
1545
1550
1555
1565
1575
1585
1600
1700
1800
1900
2000

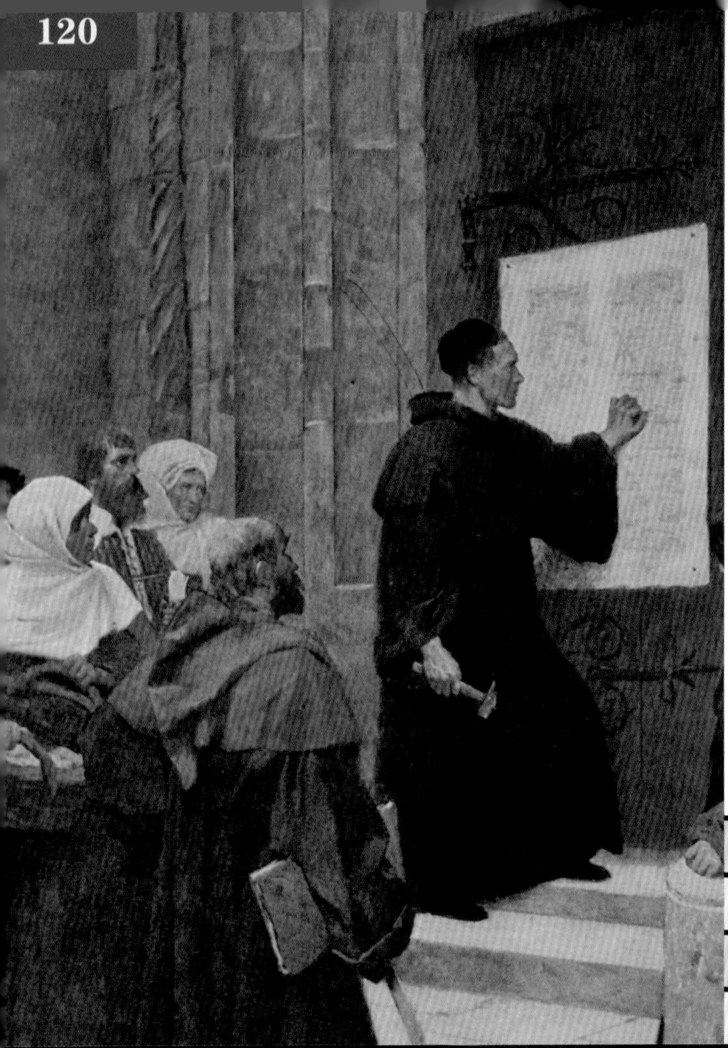

Luther posts the *Ninety-five Theses* on the church door *(left)*; the frontispiece of Luther's Bible *(right)*

5

Luther was named an outlaw by his country's Emperor, Charles V. He was excommunicated (exiled) from the Catholic Church. In fear for his life, his supporters hid him in an isolated dreary castle. During the miserable year he stayed there, Luther translated the Latin Bible into common German. Luther's stand against the powerful and corrupt Church made him a hero to the common people. He returned to his home in Germany on the one-year anniversary of his posting of the *Ninety-five Theses*. He agreed to a truce with his enemies, although he claimed, "It was never my intention to revolt." He spent the last 20 years of his life fighting the Catholic Church and developing what would become the basis for the new Protestant Church.

1. How long did Luther hide in the isolated castle?

2. Why do you think Luther's supporters feared for his life?

3. Why might Luther have translated the Bible into German?

4. Why do you think Luther returned home to Germany?

5. Why might Luther have decided to start the Protestant Church?

The selling of indulgences *(left)*; Emperor Charles V *(right)*

Ivan says—

Pretty interesting and brave. Well, here is some more to visualize about the Reformation. In 1573, Philip II, the King of Spain, a Catholic, was persecuting (harassing) Protestants (members of the new Lutheran-style church) in the Low Countries. The Low Countries lay on the coast between France and Germany. The land is very low, below sea level, in fact, hence the name Low Countries.

Well, the people built dikes to hold back the sea so it would not flood their farms. Spain had a strong army and they had won a lot of battles against those Protestants. But now the Spanish Army surrounded one of the Low Countries' cities. The people refused to surrender. Instead they held out for months. Many people starved and died, until finally a few brave men snuck out and opened the dikes. Then the Protestants' ships, called the Sea Beggars, were able to sail in from the open sea, across the flooded farmland. They drove the Spanish off, saving the city.

Your next Flight covers the Tudors. No, they weren't teachers. That would be tutors. The Tudors were a family of English rulers. No, they didn't go around measuring things. They were the "Off with her head!" type of rulers.

First meet King Henry VIII. Hang onto your head while I sing a catchy tune: *Henry the 8th I am, I am*...Now. I like you read and I eat better.

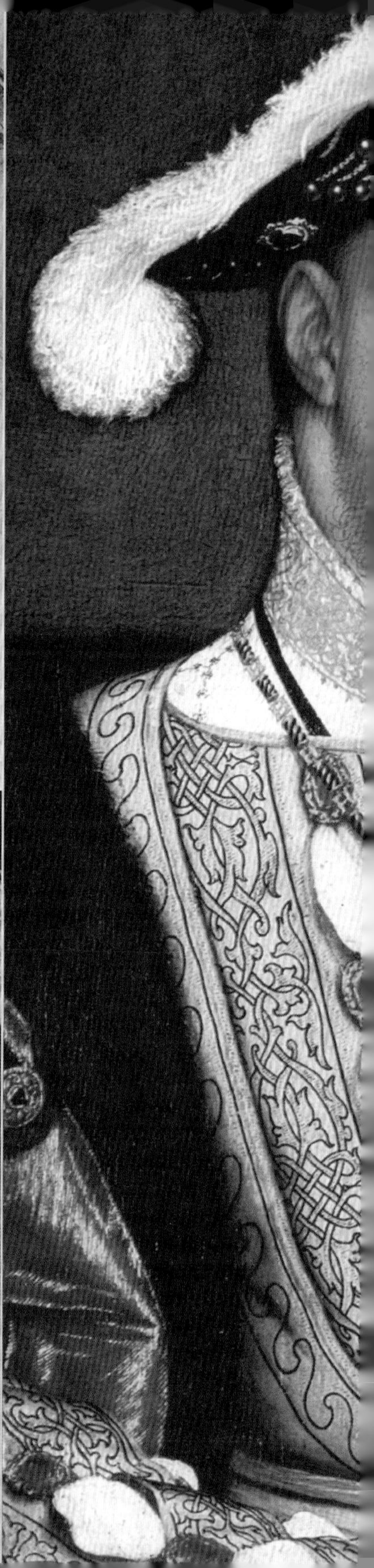

KATHARINE PARRE

Henry VIII

1491-1547

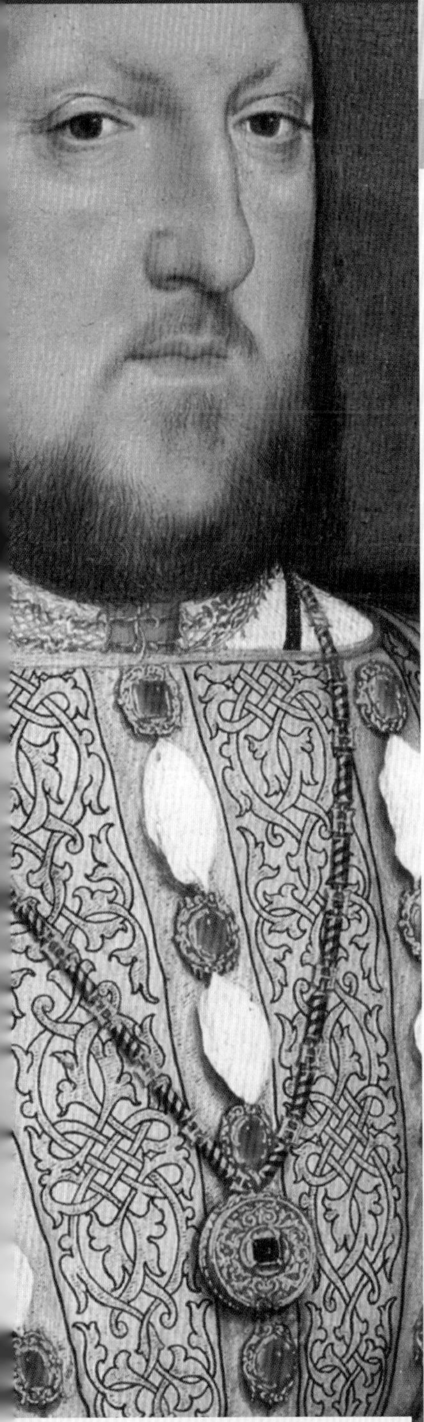

Hang on to your hats—er, heads. We're in England. It is the big King Henry VIII—and he liked to see heads roll.

King Henry VIII feasted on meals that took hours to eat. He hunted, fished, and rode big horses. He loved to wrestle, played tennis, and liked telling jokes. When he sang, he had a big voice like a big angel. Oh, yes, Henry did all things in a big way. For example, in 1520, there was a meeting between Henry VIII and France's King Francis I. Francis wanted Henry's support in a war. He didn't get it, but the meeting was a chance for Henry to show off. So he had the huge grassy field they were to meet on covered with a big cloth made of gold.

He also had more wives than you could count on one hand and had two of them executed. He had a bad habit of getting rid of anyone who didn't agree with him.

You spend some time getting to know King Henry VIII (but don't marry him) and I'll go sit in my big chair and take a big nap. I know this guy already and my neck hurts if I visualize too much of this stuff.

lockwise from top left) Catherine of ragón; Anne Boleyn; Jane Seymour; enry VIII; Catherine Parr; Catherine Howard; Anne of Cleves

1

Henry VIII did not expect to be King of England because he was the second son of King Henry VII. But when he was 11, his older brother Arthur died, and he became next in line to be the king. Prince Henry was a good student who could speak five languages. He spent most of his days outdoors, playing sports and hunting. He was also a talented singer and musician. Then, when Henry was 17, his father died and Henry became the king. He came to power when England was a stable nation with a lot of money in the treasury.

1. **How old was Henry VIII when he became the King of England?**

2. **Do you think Henry VIII had a good childhood?**

3. **Why might it have been important for a king to learn several languages?**

4. **Do you think Henry was prepared to be the king? Why or why not?**

5. **Why might having a healthy treasury be good for a nation?**

2

At first, the teenage Henry spent little time running England. Instead, he left the daily government duties to advisors like Cardinal Wolsey. Henry preferred to spend his days hunting, singing, or reading. But under Wolsey's advice, Henry went to war against France, and he liked the danger and excitement. So Henry increased the size of the English Navy from five ships to 53, and went to war often to fight over territory with France and Spain. He only won small areas of land, but his people loved him for it anyway. The English were very proud of their country and their fighting king.

1. **What country did Henry go to war with?**

2. **Why do you think Henry left the daily government duties to his advisors?**

3. **Why might it have been important to increase the size of the English Navy?**

4. **Why do you think Henry's small victories were popular with the English people?**

5. **What is the main idea of all this imagery?**

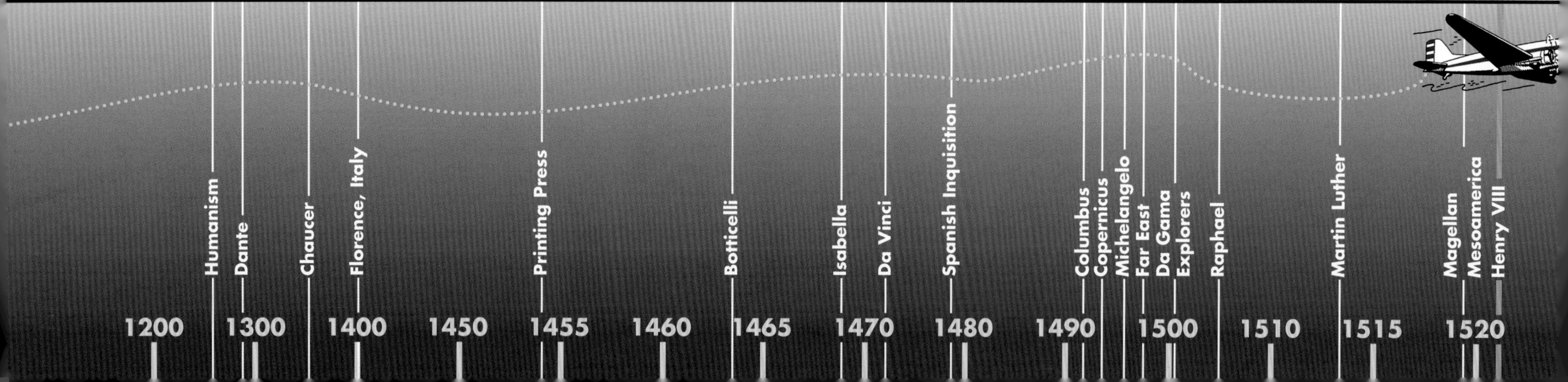
Humanism
Dante
Chaucer
Florence, Italy
Printing Press
Botticelli
Isabella
Da Vinci
Spanish Inquisition
Columbus
Copernicus
Michelangelo
Far East
Da Gama
Explorers
Raphael
Martin Luther
Magellan
Mesoamerica
Henry VIII
1200
1300
1400
1450
1455
1460
1465
1470
1480
1490
1500
1510
1515
1520

3

At first, Henry was a good ruler, but soon his personal life would come close to tearing the country apart. The trouble began with his marriage to Catherine of Aragón, the daughter of King Ferdinand and Queen Isabella of Spain. Henry, 18, had married her to strengthen his alliance with Spain, and she had been his late brother's wife. Catherine gave birth at least six times, but only a daughter named Mary survived. Henry wanted a son to be his heir, so he decided to end his marriage and marry young, pretty Anne Boleyn. But the Catholic Church would not allow divorce, even for a king. Henry got so angry that he created a new church called the Church of England and made himself the head of it. He then took all of the Catholic Church's money and land in England.

1. What was the name of Henry's child that survived?

2. Why might marrying the daughter of the King and Queen of Spain be a good idea?

3. Why do you think Henry wanted to marry Anne Boleyn?

4. Why do you think Henry started his own church?

5. Why do you think Henry took all the land and money from the Catholic Church?

4

Attacking the Catholic Church was risky, and Henry was warned by his advisor Wolsey not to make a rash decision. But anyone questioning Henry, a big man prone to fits of rage, was charged with treason. Wolsey was ruined by the scandal, leaving the headstrong young king to rule by himself. Henry divorced Catherine and married Anne Boleyn. Anne gave birth to a girl, Elizabeth, but she miscarried two boys. Rather than deal with another divorce, Henry had Anne arrested and tried on charges of adultery and witchcraft. He then had her beheaded. Just eleven days later, Henry married his third wife, Jane Seymour. She gave him the son he long desired, but she died after giving birth.

1. What was the name of Henry's second wife?

2. Why do you think no one stopped Henry from divorcing Catherine?

3. Do you think it was wise for Wolsey to warn Henry about attacking the Catholic Church? Why or why not?

4. Do you think that Anne was really guilty and deserved beheading? Explain.

5. Who do you think was King Henry VIII's favorite wife? Explain.

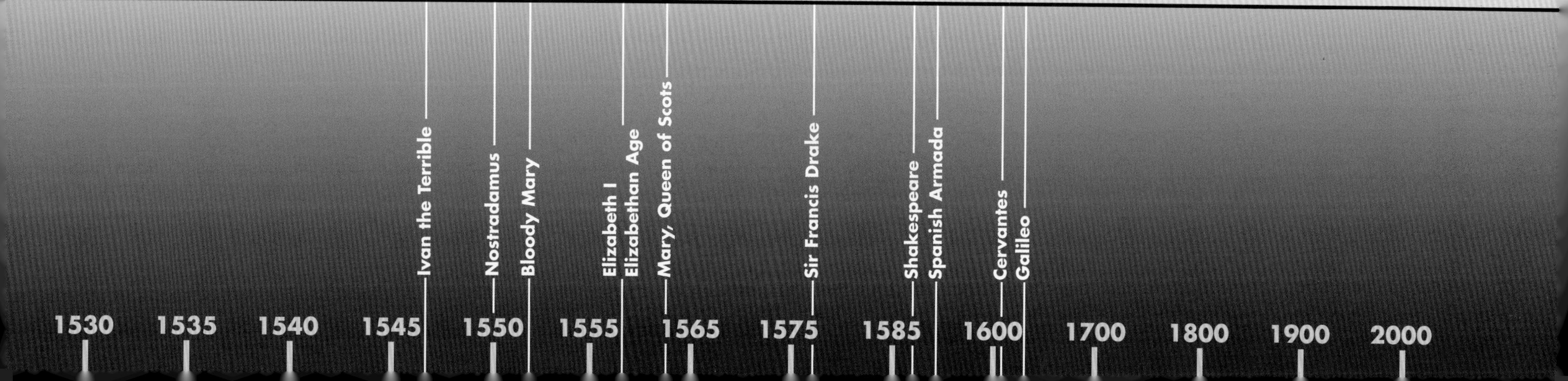
Ivan the Terrible
Nostradamus
Bloody Mary
Elizabeth I
Elizabethan Age
Mary, Queen of Scots
Sir Francis Drake
Shakespeare
Spanish Armada
Cervantes
Galileo
1530
1535
1540
1545
1550
1555
1565
1575
1585
1600
1700
1800
1900
2000

A portrait of Henry VIII, one of many done by Hans Holbein, 1540

5

Henry was devastated by Jane's death, as she was perhaps the only wife he truly loved. It was more than two years before Henry married again. In fact, Henry married three more times. He divorced Anne of Cleves because he deemed her too ugly. He beheaded Catherine Howard for adultery, though in this case she was actually guilty. Only one wife, the smart and kind Catherine Parr, survived her husband, and she was a loving stepmother as well. After all this marrying, Henry had a single living son, sickly Edward VI, who was crowned King at age nine after Henry's death. Weak Edward, no real replacement for his strong and brave father, inherited a country that was now deeply divided between Catholics and members of the new Protestant Church of England.

1. **What was the name of Henry's last wife?**
2. **Why do you think women kept agreeing to marry Henry?**
3. **Why do you think Edward was no real replacement for his father?**
4. **What problems might Edward have as King of England?**
5. **Why do you think the Church of England survived after Henry's death?**

Edward VI, Henry's heir and only son, ruled from 1547 to 1553 *(left)*; Hampton Court Palace, built by Cardinal Wolsey and gifted by him to Henry VIII in 1526 *(right)*

Ivan says—

Henry VIII was the first person to have the Bible translated into English, which made it accessible to a lot more people. Oh yes, he used the same Bible the old Church had used. The new church was a lot like the old church, but with a few of Martin Luther's ideas thrown in.

Here is some creepy news about old Henry VIII. When his wife Anne was being beheaded, Henry was said to be enjoying a hearty game of tennis. He was a big guy. When his many royal portraits were painted (and several of them by the same artist, Hans Holbein), the artists pared down the immense size of their royal subject to please him with a thinner likeness.

Enough of that heavy stuff—and what's wrong with heavy anyhow? We're flying to meet a mysterious man—Nostradamus. Practice saying Nostradamus (*Nose-tra-DA-mus*) with me. Tongue up, tongue up, tongue up, lips together, then hiss. Nostradamus.

Aries. leo. sagittarius. sunt calida et sicca collerica masculina. Orientalia.
Taurus. virgo. capricornus. sunt frigida et sicca melancolica feminina. Occidentalia.
Gemini. aquarius. libra. sunt calida et humida masculina sanguinea. Meridionalia.
Cancer. scorpius. pisces. sunt frigida et humida flemmatica feminina. Septentrionalia.

An early 15th century manuscript illumination of the Zodiac *(left)*; Nostradamus, from an 18th century engraving *(right)*

Nostradamus

1503-1566

We've landed in France. Unbuckle carefully and slip quietly from your seat to disembark. It's Nostradamus time—tongue up, tongue up, tongue up, lips together, then hiss. He was convinced he could see the future. He had visions. Say, I have visions myself. Ah, another time.

Nostradamus wrote down all his visions, but he didn't exactly write things out clearly. He didn't say that this guy would do this thing on this day. Instead, he wrote them in rhyme, something called a quatrain, and he combined four different languages—making it all a big riddle. Pretty smart of the guy, right? Now no one can be absolutely sure what he meant. Hey, I could do that. No mystery.

Speaking of mysteries, why am I still awake? Bye, bye. Remember, you read. I sleep.

1

Nostradamus was a French physician and *astrologer* (person who uses the stars to predict the future). He was very talented and traveled throughout France treating people sick with the *Black Death* (the plague). He was said to be able to cure even the most seriously ill patients, but this led some people to suggest he was using magic. Yet, the doctor's own wife and two sons all died of the plague, with him unable to save them. After their deaths, Nostradamus left home, partly out of grief and partly on the run from the Inquisition, which pursued him for witchcraft. He spent six years wandering around Italy and France, never staying in one place for very long.

1. What was Nostradamus' occupation?

2. Why do you think Nostradamus chose to treat people who had the plague?

3. Why might Nostradamus have thought he could save his family?

4. Do you think Nostradamus was using magic to cure people? Explain.

5. Why do you think Nostradamus never stayed in one place for very long?

2

Lonely Nostradamus eventually returned home to France, remarried, and had several more children. The chubby, balding man with the long gray-black beard continued to gain notice for his ability to work miracles with the sick. But he became famous throughout Europe for another reason. Around 1550, when he was 47 years old, Nostradamus began writing about the future and the end of the world. He said he had visions that came to him while he was in a trance. They were visions of events that would happen during the next 2,000 years. Nostradamus wrote down his predictions and published them in a popular book, called *Centuries*.

1. When did Nostradamus begin to write about the future?

2. Why do you think Nostradamus remarried?

3. Why do you think he wrote down his visions?

4. Why might he have decided to publish his predictions?

5. Why might his book have been popular?

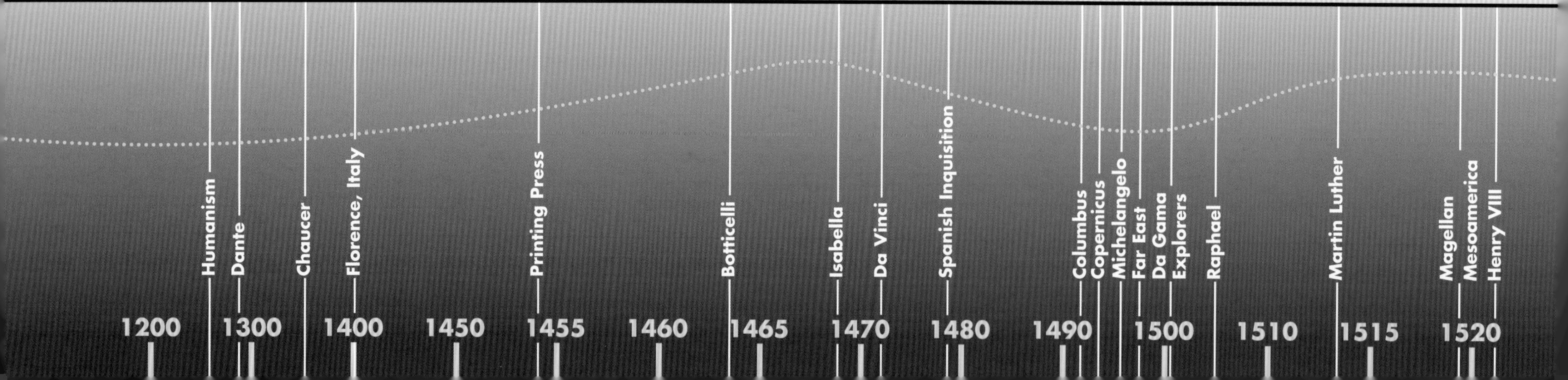
Humanism
Dante
Chaucer
Florence, Italy
Printing Press
Botticelli
Isabella
Da Vinci
Spanish Inquisition
Columbus
Copernicus
Michelangelo
Far East
Da Gama
Explorers
Raphael
Martin Luther
Magellan
Mesoamerica
Henry VIII
1200
1300
1400
1450
1455
1460
1465
1470
1480
1490
1500
1510
1515
1520

3

Despite its popularity, Nostradamus' book was not easy to read. He wrote it in a combination of four languages. He also wrote it in a rhyming verse. Further, all the quatrains (four-line poems) were filled with imagery and symbols that no one but Nostradamus understood. But he did not share the meaning with anyone. This may have been done to confuse the priests and judges of the Inquisition and make it difficult for them to arrest and charge him with heresy. His words could be seen as speaking against the Church, or even as witchcraft. Because his book was written in such a confusing manner, no one could be sure exactly what he predicted.

1. **How many languages did Nostradamus use to write his book?**
2. **How do you think using four languages combined would make it hard to read?**
3. **Why do you think Nostradamus would publish a book that was difficult to understand?**
4. **Why might the Inquisition not have arrested or charged Nostradamus?**
5. **What might be a problem with trusting Nostradamus' predictions?**

4

Many people read Nostradamus' book and believed his predictions. They were certain that his forebodings would come true. His fame even gained him entry to the court of King Charles IX of France. Catherine de Medicis, the mother of the French king and a huge Nostradamus fan, gave him a job as an advisor. She also gave Nostradamus riches and invited him to parties where she introduced him to important people. She was devoted to her astrologer and hardly made a decision without his advice. Nostradamus rarely gave her bad news, predicting that her sons would all be kings. But many people were still afraid of Nostradamus. He was seen by some as a witch or a servant of the devil.

1. **To whom did Nostradamus become an advisor?**
2. **Why do you think Nostradamus was given a job in King Charles IX's court?**
3. **Why might it be good for Nostradamus to rarely give Catherine bad news?**
4. **Do you think Nostradamus liked being Catherine's advisor? Explain.**
5. **Why might some people have been afraid of Nostradamus?**

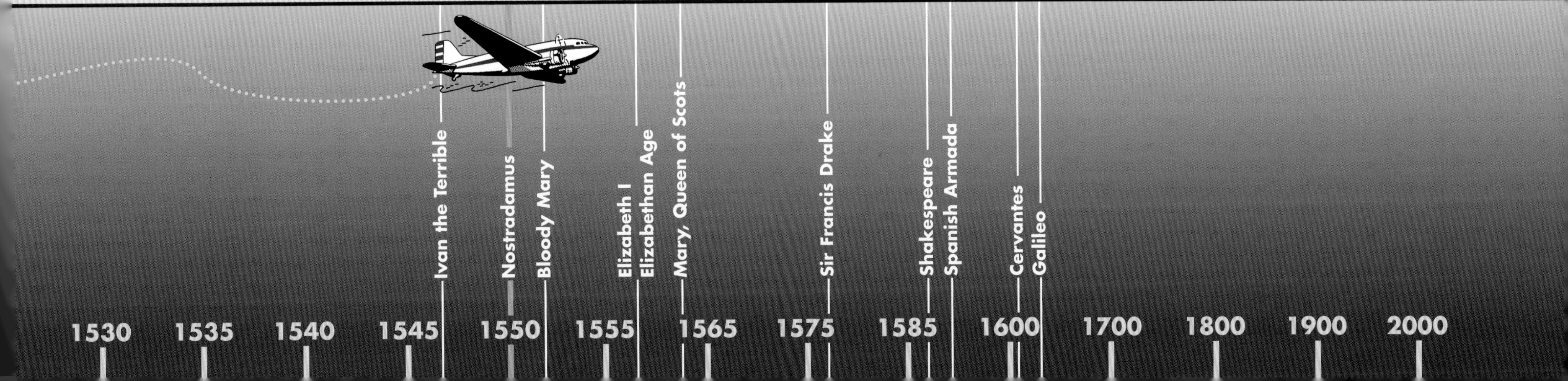
Ivan the Terrible
Nostradamus
Bloody Mary
Elizabeth I
Elizabethan Age
Mary, Queen of Scots
Sir Francis Drake
Shakespeare
Spanish Armada
Cervantes
Galileo
1530
1535
1540
1545
1550
1555
1565
1575
1585
1600
1700
1800
1900
2000

LES VRAYES CENTURIES
et
PROPHETIES
de Maiftre
MICHEL NOSTRADAMUS
A Amfterdam Chez Iean Ianßon à Waesberge et la
Vefve du Feu Elizée Weyerftraet. l'An 1668.

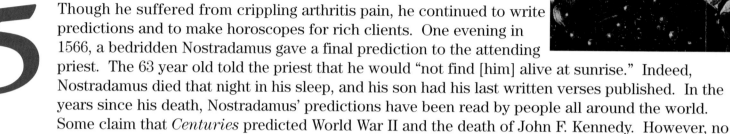

(clockwise from left) the frontispiece of the 1668 printed version of the *Centuries*; Catherine de Medicis, the rich and powerful patron of Nostradamus *(right)*; Nostradamus, an etching from a portrait bust by his son César *(lower right)*

5

Though he suffered from crippling arthritis pain, he continued to write predictions and to make horoscopes for rich clients. One evening in 1566, a bedridden Nostradamus gave a final prediction to the attending priest. The 63 year old told the priest that he would “not find [him] alive at sunrise.” Indeed, Nostradamus died that night in his sleep, and his son had his last written verses published. In the years since his death, Nostradamus’ predictions have been read by people all around the world. Some claim that *Centuries* predicted World War II and the death of John F. Kennedy. However, no one will ever be certain if he really could tell the future. Even so, his writings are just as popular today as they were in the 1500’s.

1. **What was Nostradamus’ final prediction?**

2. **Why do you think people continue to read his predictions?**

3. **Why might no one ever be able to tell if Nostradamus could really tell the future?**

4. **Why might his predictions be as popular today as they were when he published them?**

5. **What do you think of Nostradamus?**

Ivan says—

Nostradamus did find love again after his first wife and sons died from the plague, marrying Anne Gemelle in 1554 and together they had six children. He settled in Salon, France, where he wrote 10 separate books called *Centuries*, each filled with his mysterious quatrains. Here's an example of one, translated for you:

From the human flock nine will be sent away,

Separated from judgment and counsel:

Their fate will be sealed on departure

Kappa, Thita, Lambda the banished dead err (I.81)

No, I don't understand it either. Hey, he also wrote a cookbook! Now that's something I can understand.

Hmmmm. Let's see, we're off for a cocktail. Serve me a Bloody Mary, please. Oh, sorry. Read on. I'll see you in England!

LATE RENAISSANCE

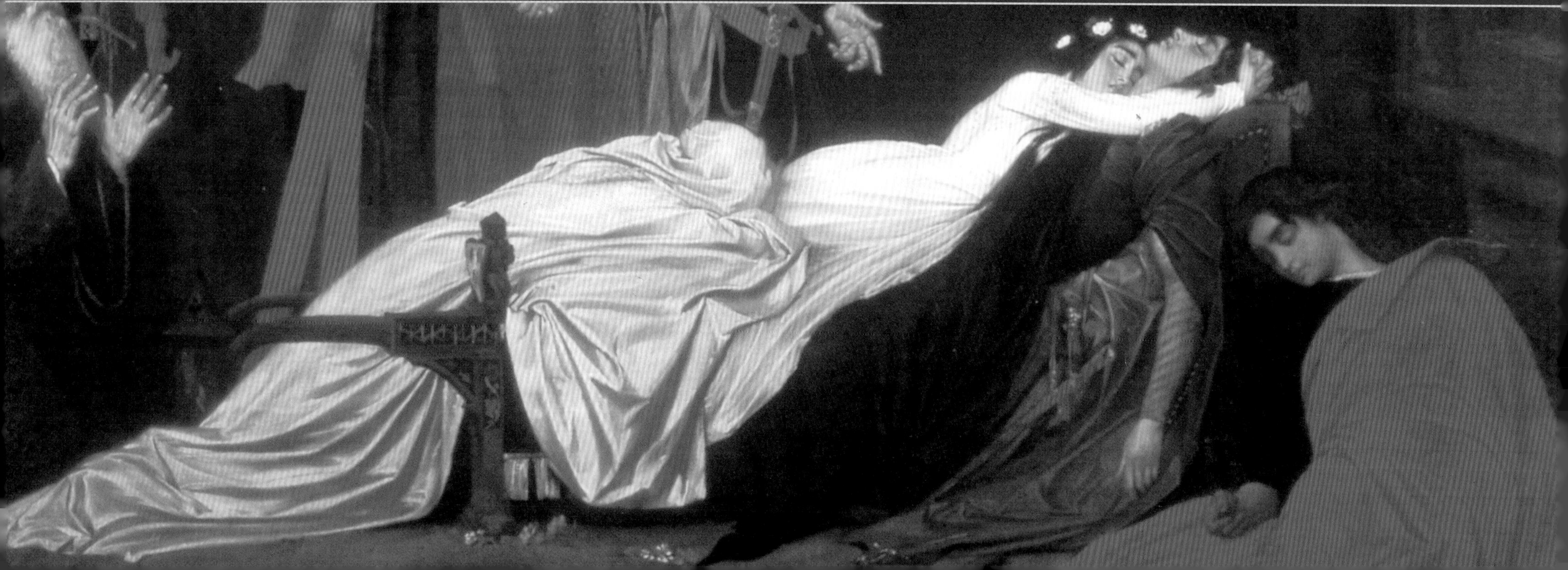

Bloody Mary

1516-1558

Leeds Castle, one of Mary's Royal residences, is known as the most beautiful castle in the world.

This is a pretty interesting Flight that only sounds like a late night horror movie. Yep! We're back in merry old England. For you fans of the weird, remember Henry VIII? Well, Henry VIII's oldest daughter, Mary I, became known as Bloody Mary. She ruled for a few years after Henry's death, and the death of his only son Edward. No predictions, but lots of actions.

The first thing Mary I did was drop the whole Church of England thing that her dad had started. Then she started executing anyone who didn't want to go back to the Catholic Church. Hence, Bloody Mary.

The next queen after her, her younger sister Elizabeth, wouldn't have lived to get the job if Mary hadn't decided, after some weeks of thought, not to chop her head off.

On to a round of Bloody Mary for you and a trip to the refrigerator for me. For the faint of heart, I'll gas up the plane and be waiting to rescue you at the end.

Bandages

1

Mary Tudor was born in 1516, the only child of England's King Henry VIII and his first wife, Catherine of Aragón. Mary was pampered and treated like a princess for the first 15 years of her life. Her happiness was marred by one tragic problem. When her mother failed to have a son who lived past infancy, Henry divorced Catherine and married another woman. He was determined to have a son to inherit his crown. The divorce made the formerly beloved princess and her Queen Mother social outcasts, and they went off to live in quiet isolation. Because of the divorce, the nobles called Mary illegitimate.

1. **Who was Mary Tudor's father?**
2. **Why might Mary have enjoyed growing up as the daughter of Henry VIII?**
3. **How do you think Mary felt when Henry divorced her mother?**
4. **Do you think Mary was pampered anymore after the divorce? Why or why not?**
5. **How do you think Mary's life might have been different if one of her brothers had lived?**

2

The divorce had a huge effect on Mary because she suddenly lost her title of Princess and had to leave the royal court. Her stepmother, Anne Boleyn, hated her. There were rumors that Anne might have Mary and her mother killed, but Anne soon lost her own head instead. Mary was not allowed to practice her Catholic faith. She lived a quiet modest life in the country away from court, practicing her skill as a musician. Her father wed a total of four more times and had a second daughter, Elizabeth, and finally a son, Edward. Some of Henry's wives were nice to Mary, but it was her half-sister, Elizabeth, who was considered the only legitimate princess by the nobles. Mary and Elizabeth were both older than Edward, but he became King when Henry died.

1. **What religion was Mary?**
2. **Why do you think Mary was sent away from court?**
3. **How might all of her father's marriages have made Mary feel?**
4. **Do you think Mary had a better life in the country than she would have had at court? Explain.**
5. **How do you think Mary felt when Edward became King?**

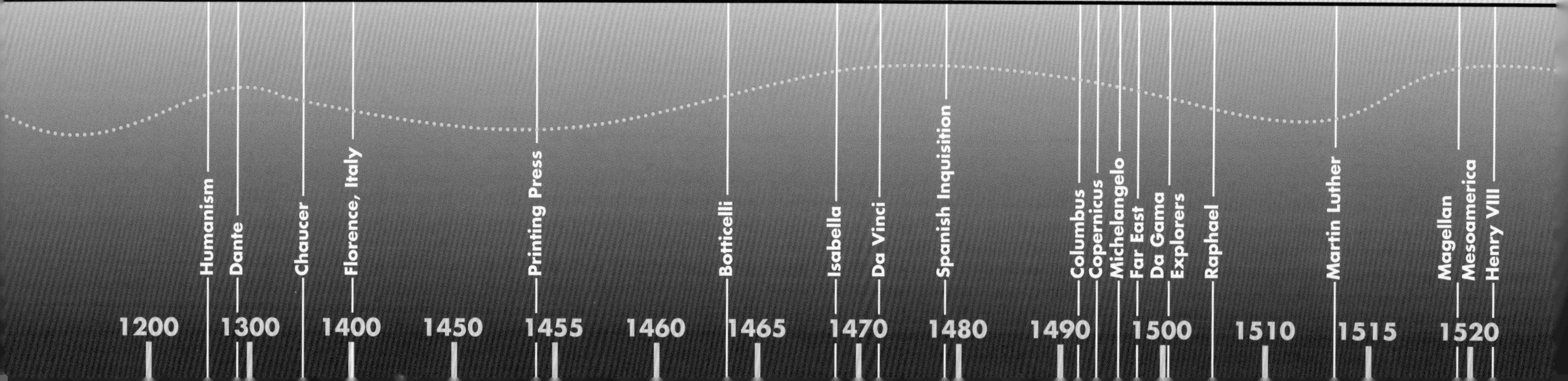
Humanism
Dante
Chaucer
Florence, Italy
Printing Press
Botticelli
Isabella
Da Vinci
Spanish Inquisition
Columbus
Copernicus
Michelangelo
Far East
Da Gama
Explorers
Raphael
Martin Luther
Magellan
Mesoamerica
Henry VIII
1200
1300
1400
1450
1455
1460
1465
1470
1480
1490
1500
1510
1515
1520

3

Edward VI was only nine years old when he became the King of England. He was a very sickly child and only ruled for a few years. After he died at age 16, Mary, 37 years old, was now recognized by the nobles as the true heir to the throne. She became the first woman to rule England. Mostly mild mannered and kind, Mary had a stubborn devotion to her mother's religion. For years, Mary had secretly been a Catholic, suffering and praying in the silence of her room. Now it seemed her prayers had been answered, and she quickly restored the Catholic Church as the official church of England. Around 300 people were tried and put to death for heresy during her reign. This is why the public gave the Queen the nickname, "Bloody Mary."

1. How old was Mary when she became the Queen of England?

2. How might it have been difficult to be the first woman to rule England?

3. Why might Mary have wanted to restore the Catholic Church?

4. Why do you think Mary tried people for heresy?

5. Do you think "Bloody Mary" was a good nickname for her? Explain.

4

Mary knew that if she did not have children, the throne would pass to her younger half-sister Elizabeth, a Protestant whom she hated. To stop that from happening, she decided to marry Prince Philip II of Spain, also a Catholic. But Philip was one of the most powerful men in Europe, so many nobles worried about his influence in England's affairs. Mary's popularity continued to fall, but she married Philip anyway, and genuinely loved him, though he paid no attention to her. To make matters worse, Mary never became pregnant, and Philip soon left the troubled Queen and returned to Spain.

1. Who did Mary wed?

2. Why might Mary not have wanted the throne to pass to Elizabeth?

3. Why do you think the nobles were worried about having Mary wed Prince Philip?

4. Why do you think Mary became less popular with the people of England?

5. Why might Mary not having a child be a problem for the people of England?

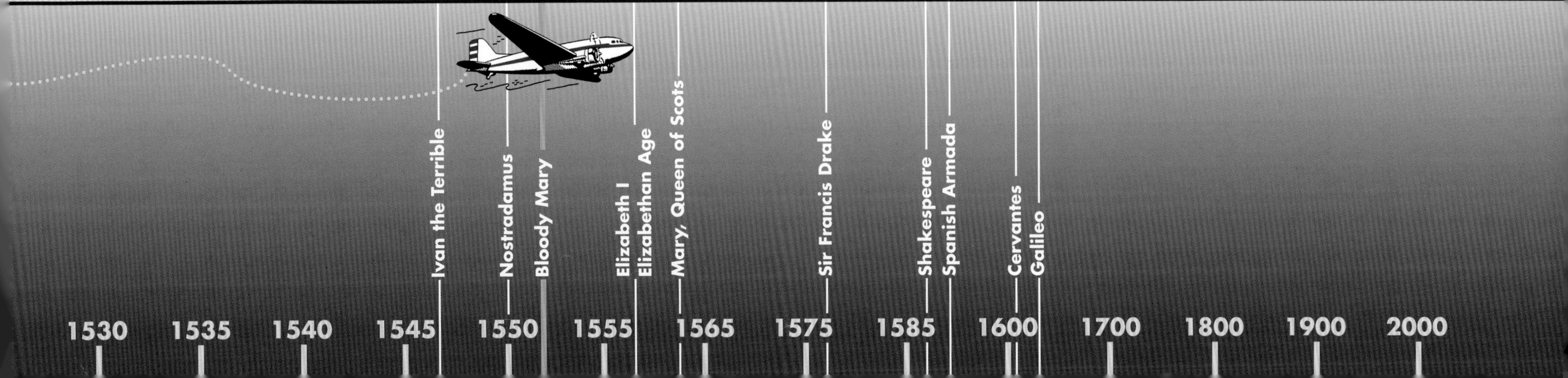
Ivan the Terrible
Nostradamus
Bloody Mary
Elizabeth I
Elizabethan Age
Mary, Queen of Scots
Sir Francis Drake
Shakespeare
Spanish Armada
Cervantes
Galileo
1530
1535
1540
1545
1550
1555
1565
1575
1585
1600
1700
1800
1900
2000

The ominous Tower of London, where Mary once imprisoned her sister Elizabeth *(right)*

Philip never saw his wife again after he returned to Spain. She was left sad and lonely, suffering from dropsy, a sickness in which the the body swells hugely both inside and out. For a short time, she may have believed that she was finally pregnant, but her swollen belly was from the sickness. Within months of Philip leaving, Mary got worse and sank into depression, ignoring her royal duties. Mary I died while praying alone in her room, at age 42. She had ruled England for only five years. Despite all of her efforts, the throne passed to Mary's Protestant half-sister, Elizabeth. All of Mary's attempts to change England back to a Catholic nation were wasted.

1. What disease did Mary suffer from?

2. Why do you think Mary was depressed?

3. Do you think Philip leaving her had anything to do with Mary's death? Explain.

4. Why might Mary's attempts to change England back to a Catholic nation have been wasted?

5. What do you think happened next?

Queen Mary I, near the end of her life, holding a Tudor rose *(top left)*; Mary and her husband Philip of Spain *(right)*

Ivan says—

Well, that was a pleasant little slice of history, wasn't it? Here's more. Queen Mary, though she hated Elizabeth, overturned a decision by Henry VIII that had made Elizabeth's birth illegitimate, just as Henry had made Mary illegitimate when she was younger. Neither of them were illegitimate, really, but with all those divorces, it was confusing. Elizabeth did not return the favor when she was made queen.

The night before Mary and Philip were to wed, his father, the Holy Roman Emperor Charles V gave him Sicily and Milan so that he would have the title of King, and not be beneath Mary in status. And he got them a nice toaster, too.

Enough of all these kings and queens, I can't keep them straight. Let's head to the tropics. All up and down the New World, explorers were finding native people already living there. Some people lived in highly civilized societies. No matter, the explorers had better weapons. They took over the New World in the worst way possible and sometimes whole civilizations were wiped out. Not pretty. I just want to remind you that we cats never do anything like that. I ask you, who is more humane?

Aztec
Inca
South and Central America
North America

Flight 24

Conquest of Mesoamerica

1519-1532

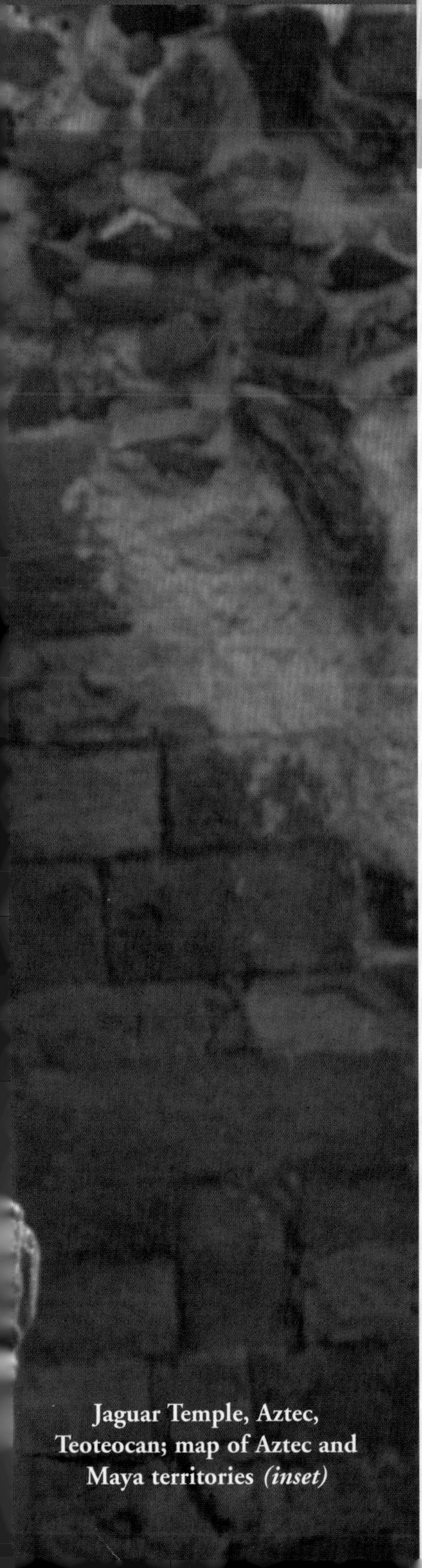

Jaguar Temple, Aztec, Teoteocan; map of Aztec and Maya territories *(inset)*

We're off to Mesoamerica—the New World, the home of the Aztecs and Incas. They had amazing societies and cities.

The Aztecs believed in some incredible gods. There were gods for every natural element and creature. Some of their gods looked like a crab with a human head and legs, a jaguar, a sugar cane, a crocodile, and a snake with an elephant's trunk.

Then there were the Incas who believed in lots of strange serpent gods and scary-looking warrior kings that they carved into all their fabulous pyramids. Both the Aztecs and the Incas worshiped gods who demanded a lot, even death. On one single day, the Aztecs sacrificed 20,000 people to their scary gods. Real civilized.

And then along came the Spanish conquistadors, who really showed the Aztecs and Incas what scary was. They conquered these two great societies of the world.

Hmmm. Conquering. Oh, yes. It is time. Fish tank, here I come.

1

When Columbus first set foot on the sandy beaches of the New World, he did not find an empty land. He claimed the land, rich with gold, for Spain, but millions of native people were already there. Many natives were members of large and well-developed civilizations which had already existed for hundreds of years. They had made great advances in science, astronomy, and engineering. Two of these great Mesoamerican peoples, the Aztecs and the Incas, had large cities that rivaled the greatest cities of Europe. Both were wiped out by Spanish explorers and their crew, who followed Columbus' footsteps 40 years later. They were the tragic victims of greed, superior weapons, and deadly disease.

1. **What were the names of two of the greatest civilizations in the New World?**
2. **Why do you think Columbus claimed the land for Spain when people were already there?**
3. **Why do you think the Spanish wiped out the Aztecs and Incas?**
4. **How do you think the civilizations were destroyed so quickly?**
5. **What do you think "they were the tragic victims of greed" means?**

2

The Aztecs were the powerful rulers of central Mexico. Their capital was a gleaming white city built in an area that was once swampland. The Aztecs drained the swamps and built large islands and canals. They also built giant pyramids with enormous stairways and temples on the top restricted to elite (top-ranking, special) priests. Captives from enemy tribes were often sacrificed to the gods at the top of the pyramids. The deeply religious Aztecs believed human sacrifices would keep their gods happy and their crops healthy. Other captives became slaves and kept the stone city walls and tiles clean and white.

1. **Where did the Aztecs rule?**
2. **Why do you think they built giant pyramids?**
3. **Why do you think the temples were at the top of the giant pyramids?**
4. **Why might the Aztecs have sacrificed captive enemies?**
5. **Why might it have been important to the Aztecs that their gods were kept happy?**

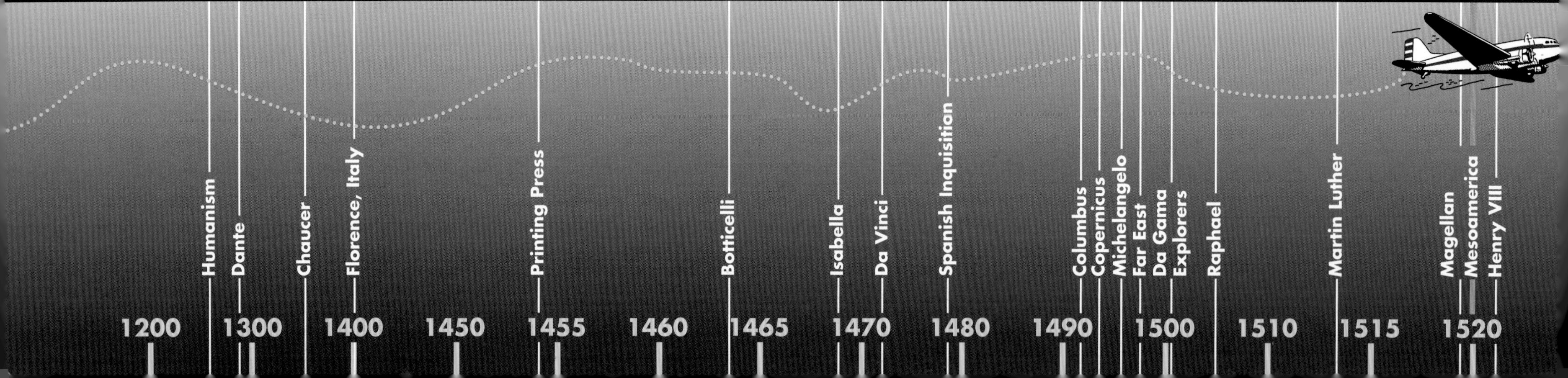
Humanism
Dante
Chaucer
Florence, Italy
Printing Press
Botticelli
Isabella
Da Vinci
Spanish Inquisition
Columbus
Copernicus
Michelangelo
Far East
Da Gama
Explorers
Raphael
Martin Luther
Magellan
Mesoamerica
Henry VIII
1200
1300
1400
1450
1455
1460
1465
1470
1480
1490
1500
1510
1515
1520

3

The Aztecs ruled until a Spanish *conquistador* (exploring soldier), Cortés, arrived in 1519. The Aztecs were kind and welcomed the Spanish, thinking they were gods. Montezuma, the Aztec king, gave the Spanish lavish gifts of gold and silver. But Cortés was unsatisfied and greedy. Cortés and his men kidnapped Montezuma. They killed him, which left the Aztecs in fear and confusion. The Spanish took all of the Aztecs' gold and jewels. They nearly destroyed their society, killing most of the natives and making others into slaves for their use. They brought new germs that led to sickness, and since the Aztecs had never been around these illnesses before, most grew very ill and died. Huge numbers of people died, not knowing or understanding how to treat their sickness.

1. **In what year did Cortés arrive?**
2. **Why might the Aztecs have thought the Spanish were gods?**
3. **Why might Cortés have been unsatisfied with the Aztec gifts?**
4. **Why do you think Cortés kidnapped the Aztec king?**
5. **What are the ways the Spanish destroyed Aztec society?**

4

The Incas were the largest Mesoamerican society. They lived mostly in the tall mountains of Peru. They had cities, fortresses, roads, trading, religion, and art. Their stonework was so precise that each block fit exactly with those around it, so much so that not even a sheet of paper could slide between the stones. They had a strict class system, with kings and priests at the top and slaves at the bottom. Some of the citizens fixed the great network of cobblestone roads that snaked through the high mountains, while others served in the army. Others built step-like terraces into the sides of mountains to farm, with irrigation canals. Gold was so common, it was everywhere.

1. **Name one of the two types of people who were at the top of the Incan class system?**
2. **Why do you think they needed great cobblestone roads?**
3. **Why might the cobblestone roads have been difficult to build?**
4. **Why do you think the Incas built terraces for farming?**
5. **What might the Incas have that others would want?**

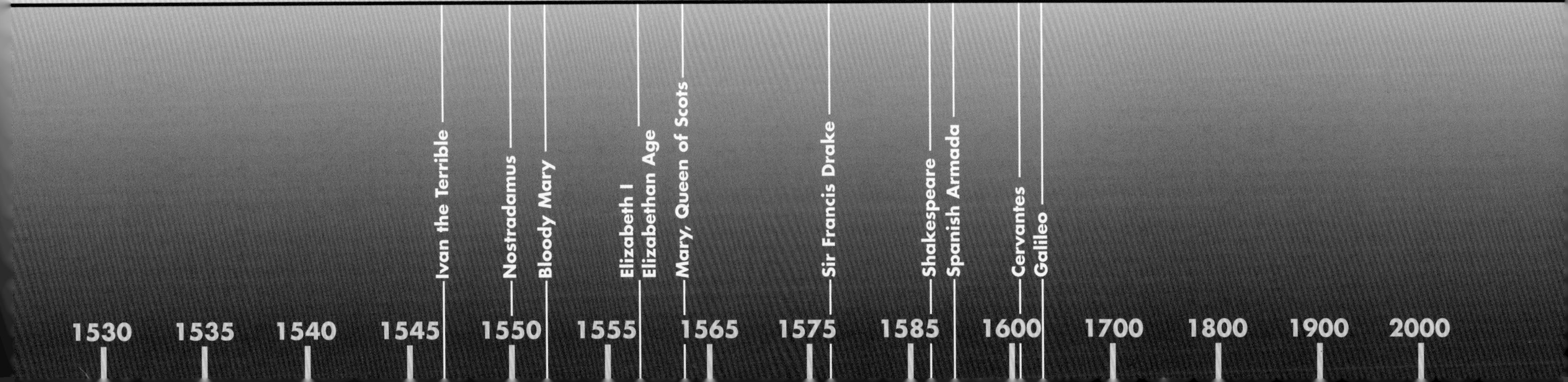
Ivan the Terrible
Nostradamus
Bloody Mary
Elizabeth I
Elizabethan Age
Mary, Queen of Scots
Sir Francis Drake
Shakespeare
Spanish Armada
Cervantes
Galileo
1530
1535
1540
1545
1550
1555
1565
1575
1585
1600
1700
1800
1900
2000

(*clockwise from left*) the death of Montezuma, from the *Codex Mendoza*; an Incan mask of silver; a gold mask from Quimbaya in Columbia; *Pizarro seizing the Inca of Peru* by Millais, 1846; a human skull with an inlaid Aztec mosaic; 16th century Spanish armor

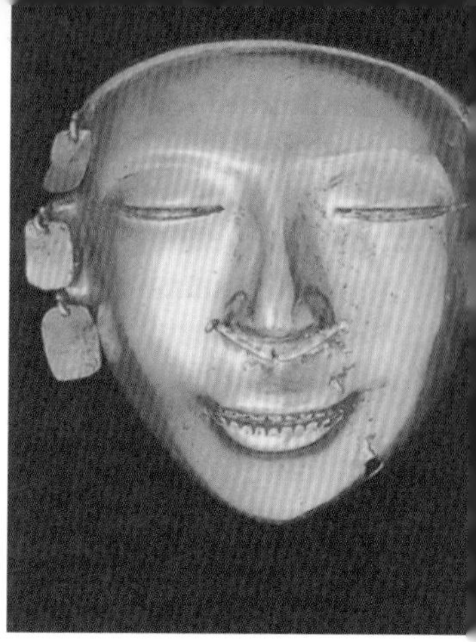

5

In the early 16th century, European diseases brought by exploring conquistadors had weakened the Incan people greatly, killing off much of their population. Then a Spaniard named Francisco Pizarro arrived with a small army. He was searching for the famed Incan gold. Pizarro kidnapped the Incan ruler, Atahuallpa, and demanded a huge ransom. The people paid it, but Pizarro still killed their king. The Incas fought back, but their knives and clubs were no match for the Spanish guns and swords. They lost 8,000 warriors in one attack alone. The Incan Empire fell in 1532.

1. **What weakened the Incan people?**
2. **Why do you think Pizarro brought an army with him to the Incan Empire?**
3. **Why do you think Pizarro kidnapped Atahuallpa?**
4. **Why do you think Pizarro killed Atahuallpa after he received the ransom?**
5. **Why do you think the Spanish were able to kill over 8,000 Incas in a single attack?**

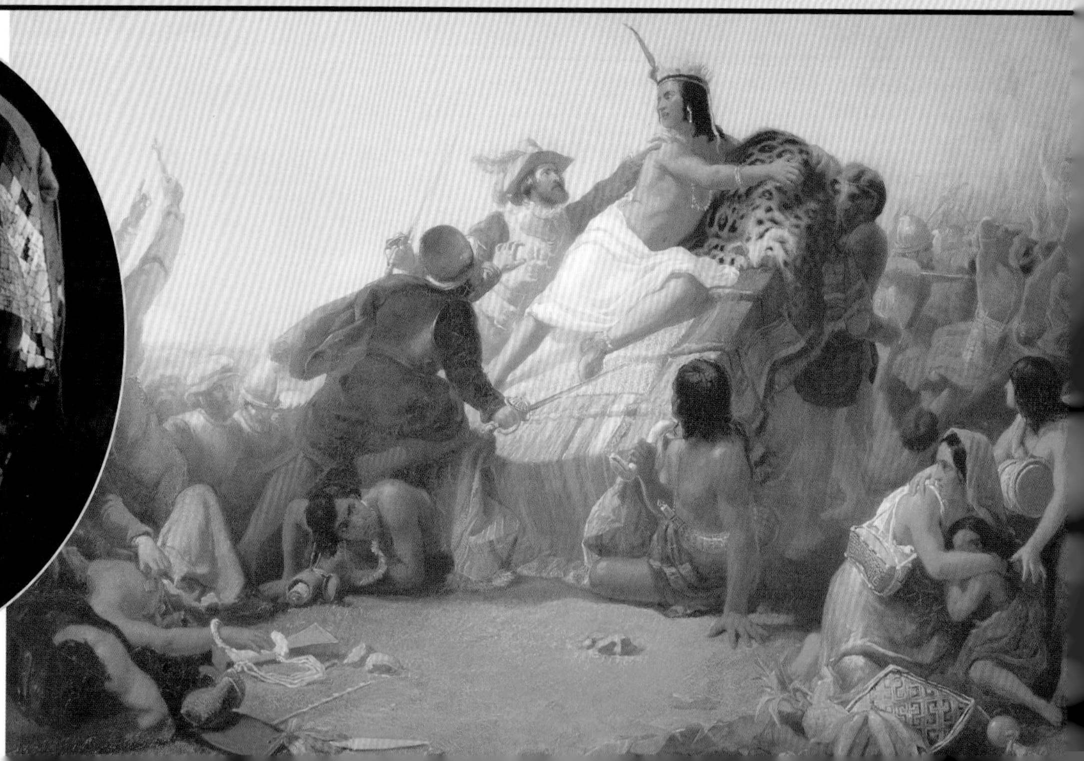

Ivan says—

Here's more imagery for you: historians have figured out that the ransom Pizarro was paid for Atahuallpa would have added up to over 250 million dollars in today's money. And that still wasn't enough for Pizarro?

When the New World was first settled by Europeans, the American Indians living there were forced into hard labor. The harsh working conditions and diseases the settlers brought with them killed millions of Indians. Slaves from Africa became the new workforce. Soon the call for slaves was so great that a busy shipping system, called the triangular trade, was set up. Slave traders branded Africans with red-hot irons and chained them together for the 90-day voyage. Men, women, and children were forced to lie crammed in the ships' hulls. Many died during the journey. The slave trade rapidly grew into a terrible but successful business.

Enough of that imagery. Terrible. Terrible. Now let's fly to the Late Renaissance, and all the way to the barren and harsh land of Russia, where the only thing colder than the weather was their ruler.

Ivan the Terrible

1530-1584

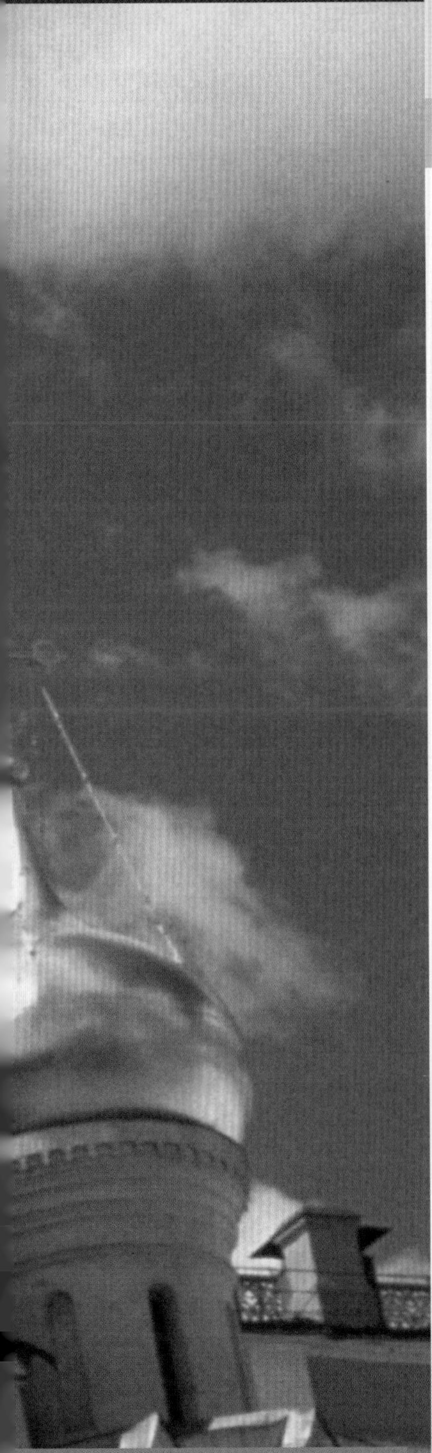

The Cathedral of the Annunciation, built in the 14th c., was the site for the coronation of Ivan in 1547.

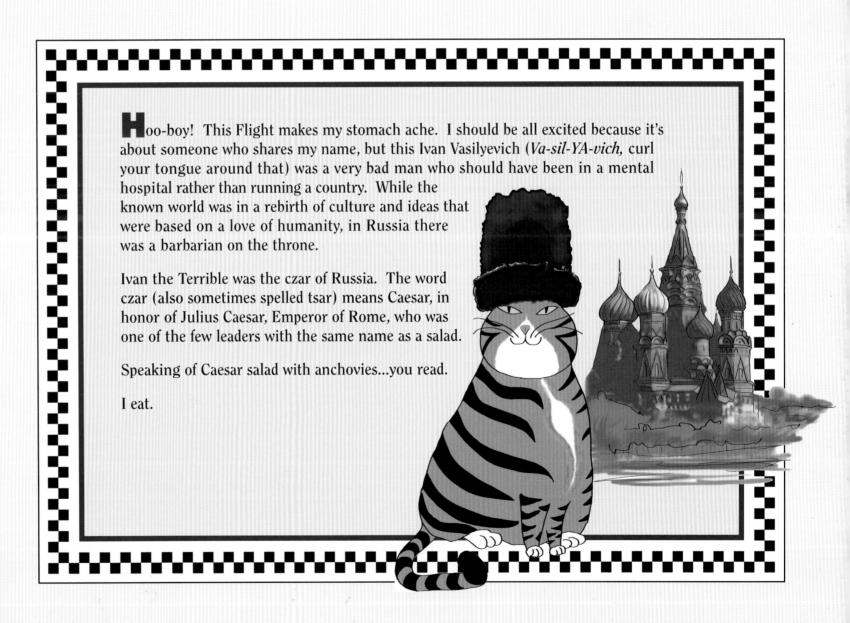

Hoo-boy! This Flight makes my stomach ache. I should be all excited because it's about someone who shares my name, but this Ivan Vasilyevich (*Va-sil-YA-vich,* curl your tongue around that) was a very bad man who should have been in a mental hospital rather than running a country. While the known world was in a rebirth of culture and ideas that were based on a love of humanity, in Russia there was a barbarian on the throne.

Ivan the Terrible was the czar of Russia. The word czar (also sometimes spelled tsar) means Caesar, in honor of Julius Caesar, Emperor of Rome, who was one of the few leaders with the same name as a salad.

Speaking of Caesar salad with anchovies...you read.

I eat.

1

Ivan Vasilyevich was the first *czar* of Russia, a title he came up with himself based on the great reign of Julius Caesar. He inherited the throne from his father, Vasily III, when he was just three years old. Because Ivan was too young, his mother ruled in his place, but the *boyars* (nobles) constantly challenged her authority. Then, when Ivan was just eight years old, his mother was poisoned. Her death left the boyars free to control Russia, and no one to protect or guide Ivan.

1. How old was Ivan when he inherited the throne?

2. Why do you think the boyars constantly challenged the authority of Ivan's mother?

3. Who do you think poisoned Ivan's mother?

4. Why do you think Ivan wasn't killed?

5. Why do you think Ivan may have needed someone to protect or guide him?

2

Ivan was abused and neglected by his advisors. He often went hungry and had to beg at the palace kitchen for food to feed himself and his little brother. They wandered the huge palace, with no one to watch over them, living like wild animals amidst the glamour and riches of the Russian throne. As Ivan grew older and began to take control of his life, he treated others the same mean and cruel way that he had been raised. He flew into fits of rage and attacked the servants. He sometimes appeared to feel bad about his harsh actions and even spent hours praying in the chapel for forgiveness. But he would quickly change moods and become mean and cruel again. Soon he became known by all as "Ivan Grozny," which translates to "Ivan the Terrible."

1. Who abused Ivan?

2. Why do you think he was hungry?

3. Why might Ivan have been cruel to others?

4. Why might Ivan have had to spend a lot of time praying?

5. Why do you think he became known as "Ivan the Terrible?"

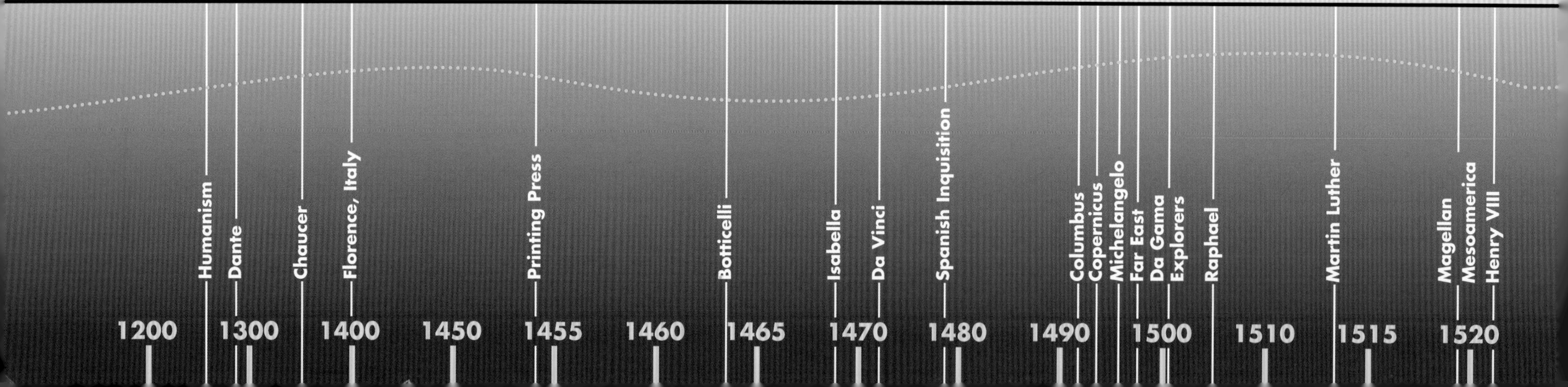
Humanism
Dante
Chaucer
Florence, Italy
Printing Press
Botticelli
Isabella
Da Vinci
Spanish Inquisition
Columbus
Copernicus
Michelangelo
Far East
Da Gama
Explorers
Raphael
Martin Luther
Magellan
Mesoamerica
Henry VIII
1200
1300
1400
1450
1455
1460
1465
1470
1480
1490
1500
1510
1515
1520

3

Ivan began to actively rule Russia when he was 17 and he then married the beautiful Anastasia Romanov. His first years as Czar were relatively quiet and he and his wife were happy. He ended government corruption, wrote laws, and increased the size of the country with border wars. But with the death of his wife in 1560, when he was 30, Ivan suffered a mental collapse. He became paranoid (extreme fear and distrust) and suspicious. He created a group of black-clothed, secret soldiers, the *oprichniki* (*O-preech-nee-kee*) During this time, Ivan and his soldiers killed thousands of innocent people as well as genuine plotters. Many were tortured, drowned, or hanged. The oprichniki had no law to follow except Ivan, and he was crazy, lashing out at anyone who he even suspected of working against him.

1. How old was Ivan when he began to actively rule Russia?

2. Why do you think his first years as Czar were relatively quiet?

3. Why might the death of his wife have caused Ivan to have a mental collapse?

4. Why do you think Ivan created the oprichniki?

5. Why do you think the soldiers were able to get away with torturing and killing people?

4

Ivan tried twice to give up the throne, feeling he was a failure as a leader, but the boyars and the people of Russia begged him to return. Everyone was terrified of his madness, but felt they needed him because he was a strong ruler who came from a long line of kings. Because Ivan was of royal blood, he was allowed to act as he pleased. Even his children were not safe from his bad temper. After an argument with his oldest son, the heir to the throne, Ivan angrily struck the young man on the head with his heavy staff. His son lay in a coma for several days, while Ivan prayed for his son's healing and begged for forgiveness from God night and day. Despite Ivan's prayers, his son and heir to the throne died without waking up. Once again, Ivan lost his sanity in his grief.

1. Who did Ivan strike with his staff?

2. Why do you think everyone was terrified of Ivan?

3. Why do you think the boyars and people wanted Ivan to return to the throne?

4. How do you think Ivan felt after he accidentally killed his son?

5. What do you think of Ivan?

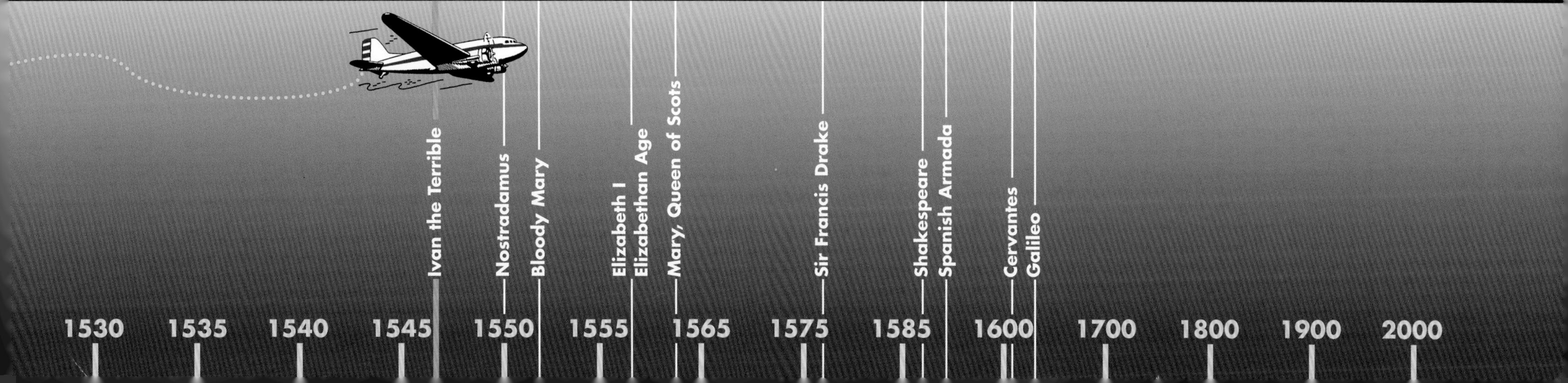
Ivan the Terrible
Nostradamus
Bloody Mary
Elizabeth I
Elizabethan Age
Mary, Queen of Scots
Sir Francis Drake
Shakespeare
Spanish Armada
Cervantes
Galileo
1530
1535
1540
1545
1550
1555
1565
1575
1585
1600
1700
1800
1900
2000

(*clockwise from left*) **Ivan, by Ilya Repin; Ivan was devastated after striking a mortal blow to his own son; St. Basil's Cathedral, built by Ivan**

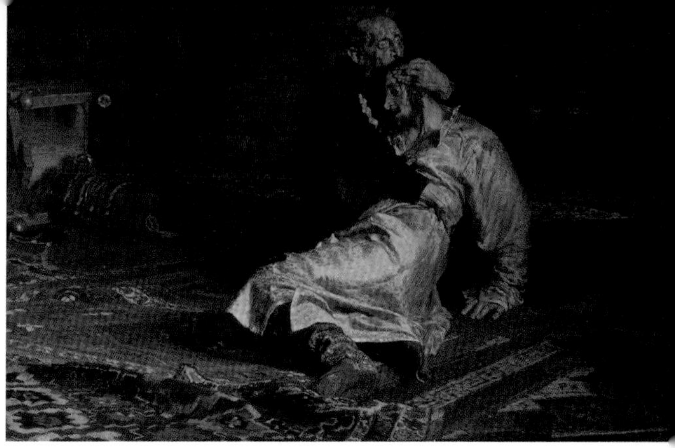

The rest of Ivan's life was spent seesawing between madness and regret. He even became a monk for a while to try to gain forgiveness for his many sins. However, to the end of his life, he was still a violent and moody man, always looking over his shoulder and suspecting everyone around him of treason. When Ivan died in 1584, at the age of 54, he was buried in his brown monk's robes. The only heir left alive was his mentally-handicapped son, and the greedy boyars fell into fighting with each other over control of Russia. The empire began to crumble with no strong leader to control. Ivan had left a bloody mark on Russia that would take years to remove.

1. **What was Ivan buried in?**
2. **Why do you think Ivan felt he needed forgiveness?**
3. **Why might Ivan have been always looking over his shoulder?**
4. **Why might the empire have crumbled with no strong leader?**
5. **Why do you think the greedy nobles were able to take control of Russia after Ivan died?**

Ivan says—

Drats. Ivan the Terrible was terrible. Couldn't he have had the name Bill? Or Egor? There we go. Egor the Terrible. Much better.

One reason for Ivan's strange behavior might have been that he drank deadly mercury every day as medicine. In addition to poisoning himself, it's also believed he had a bunch of diseases, some of which were capable of driving a person insane.

Russia was largely left out of the Renaissance because Ivan kept the country isolated from Europe. While other countries were creating art and discovering new things, Russia fell into a sort of Dark Age of its own. Russia didn't really catch up with the rest of Europe for about one hundred years.

We're now going to leave Russia and fly back to England to meet one of the most famous Queens in history: Elizabeth I. She was tough and truthful—and loved going to the theater.

Speaking of truth—here's the truth. While you read and image, I'll be drinking a little ale.

(clockwise from far left) **The many faces of the Queen: Elizabeth I in a portrait commissione Bess of Hardwick; Elizabeth's coronation portrait; a portrait celebrating the defeat of the Spa Armada; Elizabeth painted in her favorite garden at Wanstead; Elizabeth attends a weddi procession carried by courtiers; the Rainbow portrait of Elizabeth**

Elizabeth I

1533-1603

Tally ho! We've landed in England to visualize a unique chapter in your history. It was a wild and fun time when Queen Elizabeth I ran England. She was on the throne for 45 years, and she was as smart as she was strong. All the noblemen around her tried to tell her what to do, but she did things her own way. She was, as she herself said, her father's daughter, that father being the very stubborn Henry VIII. Unlike King Henry VIII, Elizabeth didn't produce an heir. She never married either, which was something of a scandal. She was the only queen to insist on staying kingless.

Elizabeth I was supposed to be a great ruler, but I heard that she hated mice. She couldn't stand them at all. Silly woman. She should have tried them with barbeque sauce. She had a habit of waiting until the very last minute to make important decisions, and she was very fair in asking for and listening to the advice of everyone in her council of advisors. She listened and then she did what she wanted.

"Good Queen Bess," as the people called her, loved to dress up and surrounded herself with the finest in luxury and the latest in gadgets. She never lost a love for learning that had been fed by long hours alone as a child, motherless, reading books.

You go visualize the English court and I'll eat. Mice. Lovely little things.

1

Elizabeth I was the red-headed daughter of King Henry VIII and his second wife, Anne Bolcyn. Her mother was beheaded for adultery when Elizabeth was just two years old. For many years, Henry largely ignored his daughter, while making sure she had the best education and care that money could buy. She spent most of her childhood away from the royal court, not even recognized by some nobles as a legitimate princess because her mother was Henry's second wife. But Elizabeth's quick mind kept her reading and learning to fill empty hours alone. Like her father, Elizabeth had a talent for music and writing. She spoke several languages and read everything.

1. **How old was Elizabeth when her mother was beheaded?**
2. **Why might Elizabeth have had a tough childhood?**
3. **Why do you think Henry ignored his daughter?**
4. **Why do you think Henry still made sure his daughter had the best education and care?**
5. **Why do you think Elizabeth read so much?**

2

When Elizabeth was thirteen, her father died. For a few short years, her younger half-brother Edward was King. When he died, her older sister Mary, the daughter of Henry's first wife, came to power. Mary hated Elizabeth and kept her imprisoned in the Tower of London for years. Elizabeth spent those years learning about politics and diplomacy (relations between countries), unusual for a woman of that time. She learned about the many nobles and their petty fights and deals over land and power. Then Queen Mary died and since she had no children, Elizabeth ascended to the throne. So, at the age of 25, Elizabeth, once unwanted and looked down on as illegitimate by many nobles, became Queen of England. Even though she was very young, she was ready. She began to make some changes that would help England become the most powerful country in the world.

1. **How old was Elizabeth when she became Queen of England?**
2. **Do you think Elizabeth ever thought that she might become Queen? Why or why not?**
3. **Why might it have been important for Elizabeth to learn about politics and diplomacy?**
4. **Why do you think Elizabeth learned about the nobles?**
5. **How might Elizabeth have been ready to become Queen?**

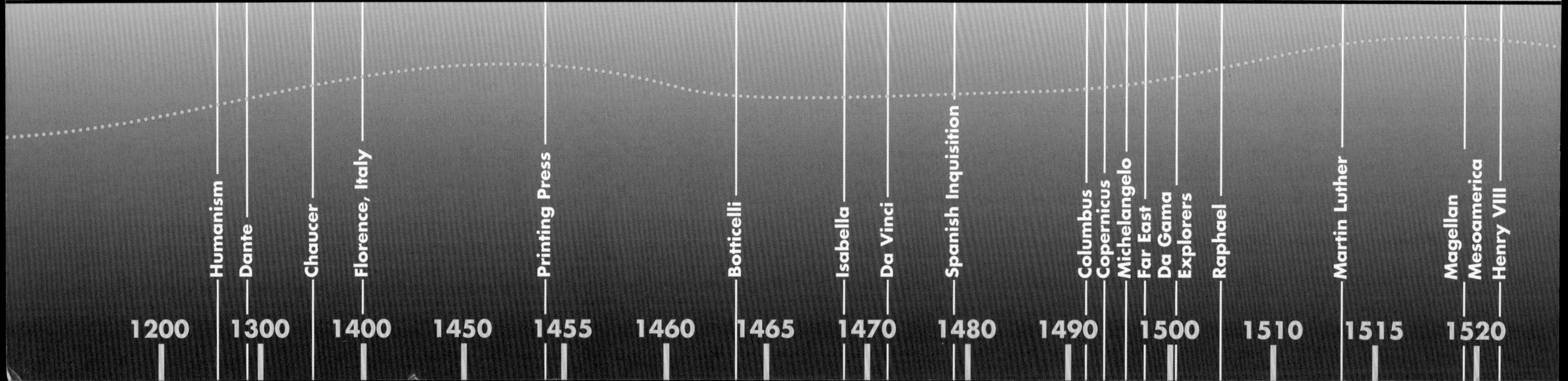
Humanism
Dante
Chaucer
Florence, Italy
Printing Press
Botticelli
Isabella
Da Vinci
Spanish Inquisition
Columbus
Copernicus
Michelangelo
Far East
Da Gama
Explorers
Raphael
Martin Luther
Magellan
Mesoamerica
Henry VIII
1200
1300
1400
1450
1455
1460
1465
1470
1480
1490
1500
1510
1515
1520

3

The young Queen Elizabeth immediately made some changes in the way England was run, shutting down the Catholic Church Mary had set up and replacing it with her father's Church of England. It quickly became clear to the nobles that she would not be pushed around. Elizabeth understood that it was important that she look and act like a Queen so people would respect her power. She dressed lavishly (richly) in the finest fabrics and jewels, and teased her red hair high with pins and pearls in it. She painted her face white and made her lips dark red. She made certain there was plenty of ceremony around the court, and she was excellent at making speeches. All this awe-inspiring spectacle made her people love Good Queen Bess more.

1. **What was the name of Elizabeth's chosen church?**
2. **Why do you think Queen Elizabeth wanted to make changes in England?**
3. **Why do you think Elizabeth wanted people to respect her power?**
4. **Why do you think Elizabeth dressed in lavish clothes and jewels?**
5. **Do you think lavish clothes and jewels made people respect her? Explain.**

4

The young Queen made Protestantism the official religion of England, angering the Catholics. Elizabeth also encouraged trade, as well as exploration and expansion to the New World. She saw that adding more land to England's territory would strengthen her country, and that the New World would bring resources and wealth to her. This caused special problems with Spain, who thought the New World belonged to them only. Elizabeth had a navy built of faster and smaller ships that could outrun the mighty galleons (large three-masted ships) of the past. She also secretly supported pirates who attacked and harassed the Spanish ships as they brought back wealth from the New World. Many nobles attempted to knock Elizabeth out of power or even kill her, but her network of spies was very good, and she escaped every time.

1. **What religion did Elizabeth make the official one for England?**
2. **Why do you think Elizabeth was interested in the New World?**
3. **Why do you think it was important for England to have fast ships?**
4. **Why might Elizabeth have secretly supported pirates?**
5. **Why might it have been important for Elizabeth to have a good spy network?**

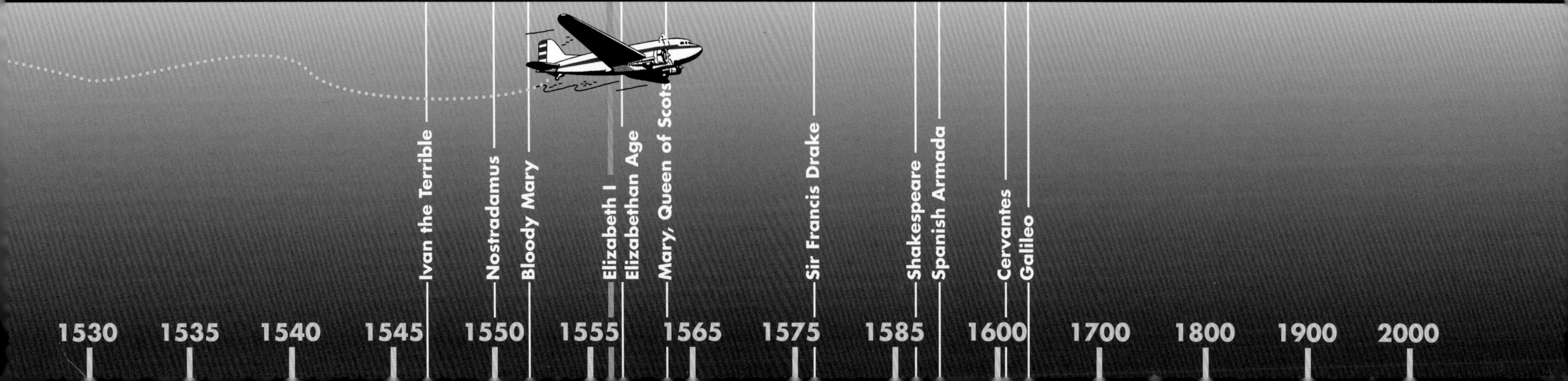
Ivan the Terrible
Nostradamus
Bloody Mary
Elizabeth I
Elizabethan Age
Mary, Queen of Scots
Sir Francis Drake
Shakespeare
Spanish Armada
Cervantes
Galileo
1530
1535
1540
1545
1550
1555
1565
1575
1585
1600
1700
1800
1900
2000

Sir Francis Drake, Elizabeth's favorite pirate *(left)*; Windsor Castle, a home to the royalty since the 12th century *(right)*; London, from an engraving ca. 1800's, by William H. Bartlett *(bottom left)*; Elizabeth's realm *(bottom right)*

Elizabeth brought more than just economic prosperity to her people. She loved the arts and education that were flourishing in England, as they had in Italy years before. Writers, artists, and scholars were always welcome in her court. She built a theater and often attended plays. This Golden Age brought about the works of some of England's greatest writers. At her death, the respected English historian John Stow noted, "There was such a general sighing, groaning, and weeping as the like hath not been seen or known in the memory of man."

1. **Who was always welcome in Elizabeth's court?**
2. **Why do you think the arts and education flourished during this time?**
3. **How might more arts and education have benefited the people of England?**
4. **Why do you think this period became known as the Golden Age?**
5. **Why do you think there was great mourning among the people when Elizabeth died?**

NORTHE
E R
LANDE
FLANDER

Ivan says—

Elizabeth liked to make up her face chalky white. She wore towering red wigs with gold pins and jewels in them. She also wore brightly-colored, heavily-decorated clothes.

The truth of the matter is that Elizabeth did much to improve the quality of life while she was in charge. She did stuff like give money to dancers and writers and artists. She went to the theater with all the regular folk instead of having the plays come to her. She was a great hunter and was known to spit and curse.

Hey, here's something really cool about Elizabeth. She supported the goings on of a known pirate, even knighting him later in his career. He was Sir Francis Drake—part rogue and part pirate and part gentleman. Let's meet him next for a high seas adventure.

Speaking of high seas, I hear some splashing in the fish tank.

Greenland
North America
Atlantic Ocean
Pacific Ocean
South America
Europe
Asia
Africa
Indian Ocean
Australia
N

Voyage of Francis Drake

Flight 27

Queen Elizabeth I knights Francis Drake on board the *Golden Hind*; map of Drake's voyage *(inset)*

Sir Francis Drake

1540-1596

Ahoy there, matey! Take a pirate, throw in a dash of naval officer, and you've got the second man to sail around the world.

Sir Francis Drake was one of the most hated and honored men in British history. For the British, he was a national hero. To many others, he was a criminal. Some say that Elizabeth I was secretly in love with the dashing sea dog, but no one knows for sure.

Ship captains were often called "sea dogs" at that time, but I don't think I will call him that. Now, don't get me wrong, I like Sir Francis Drake. He was a bold buccaneer. I just don't like to mention dogs.

When Drake returned from one of his pirate raids, he came back to a crisis. Spain's King had demanded Drake's head be sent to him as proof of punishment. Upon hearing that Drake had returned, Queen Elizabeth called for a sword and strode down to the ship, in her gown and jewels. As she stood on the deck, Drake kneeled before her. But instead of killing him, she knighted him!

So instead of losing his head, he gained a title. Much better deal. I'll see you after your adventure with Francis Drake.

1

Francis Drake was born around 1540, and grew up on the coast of England. As a youth, Francis watched the ships sailing in and out of port and dreamed of going to sea. In 1566, when Drake was 26, his cousin, John Hawkins, gave the young man the chance. Hawkins invited Drake to assist on two daring slave-trading voyages to the Spanish-controlled West Indies. While Drake and Hawkins were on their second trip at sea, Spanish ships attacked them. Although Drake and Hawkins managed to escape on their fast ships, several other slave-trading ships were sunk. Drake stopped working the slave routes, but he vowed to get revenge on the Spanish.

1. Where did Francis Drake grow up?

2. Why do you think Drake dreamed of going to sea?

3. Why do you think Spanish ships attacked Drake and Hawkins?

4. Why do you think Drake stopped working the slave routes?

5. Why do you think Drake vowed to get revenge on the Spanish?

2

In 1570, at age 30, Drake became a *privateer* (a type of pirate) captain and began to attack Spanish ships and settlements in the New World. The Spanish were using slave labor to mine gold and silver from the hills of South America. American Indian slaves brought the treasure from mines to a port on the backs of llamas (camel-like animals without humps). Then the Spanish sailed the treasure back home to Spain by ship. Drake decided not to attack the ships, but instead he attacked the unguarded llama trains. Drake and his men hid in the jungle for several months. With the help of some escaped slaves, Drake captured a llama train and then took all the riches. Drake returned to England a very rich man and the greatest enemy of Spain.

1. Where did Drake and his men hide for several months?

2. Why do you think the Spanish had ships and settlements in the New World?

3. Why might Drake have chosen to attack the llama trains instead of the ships?

4. Why do you think the escaped slaves helped Drake? Do you think they got any treasure? Explain.

5. Why do you think the Spanish considered Drake their greatest enemy?

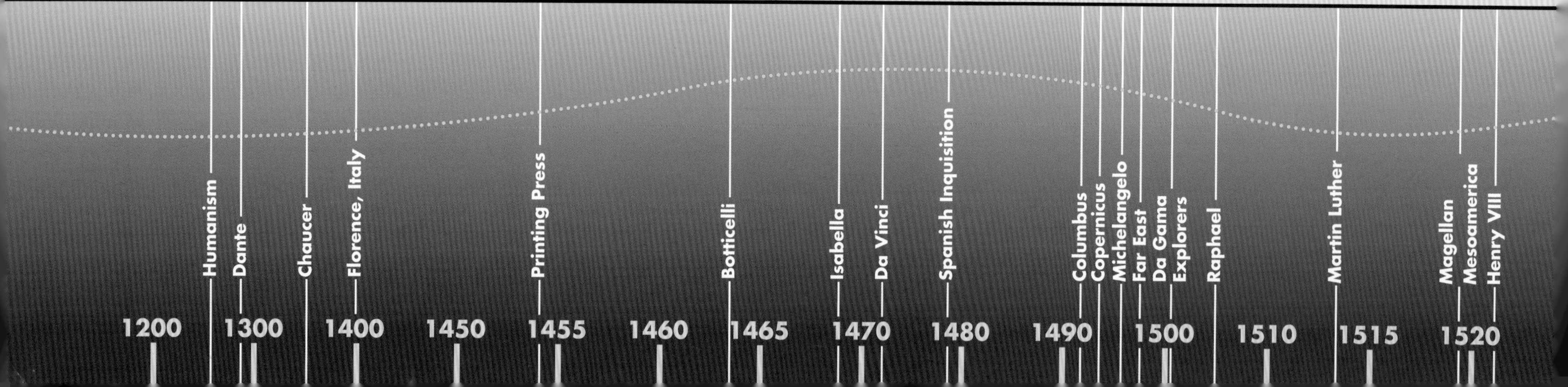
Humanism
Dante
Chaucer
Florence, Italy
Printing Press
Botticelli
Isabella
Da Vinci
Spanish Inquisition
Columbus
Copernicus
Michelangelo
Far East
Da Gama
Explorers
Raphael
Martin Luther
Magellan
Mesoamerica
Henry VIII
1200
1300
1400
1450
1455
1460
1465
1470
1480
1490
1500
1510
1515
1520

3

Queen Elizabeth I of England approved of Drake's actions against Spain. The relations between Spain and England were tense at the time, so Elizabeth supported Drake in secret. She gave him the money for what would become his greatest voyage. When he was 37, Drake set out for the New World with five ships and more than 160 men, in December, 1577. They sailed to South America, where they were hit by fierce storms. Three of the ships were destroyed in the storms and one ship, blown far off course, decided to return to England. Only Drake's lead ship, the *Golden Hind*, reached the Pacific Ocean.

1. Where was Drake sailing to in 1577?

2. Why do you think Elizabeth I approved of Drake's actions against Spain?

3. Why do you think Elizabeth gave Drake money for his voyage?

4. Why do you think one ship decided to return to England?

5. What do you think is the main idea of all this imagery?

4

Drake sailed up the west coast of the Americas, the first English ship to do so. Along the way, he raided the unguarded Spanish ports along the western coast of South America. He also attacked Spanish ships and stole their maps and treasure. He kept going and hugged the coast of America as he sailed north, but he found no way through the land back to the Atlantic Ocean. Finally, he began the long trip west across the Pacific, around Africa to England. Drake and his tired crew docked in England in the fall of 1580, three years after they had set out. Drake and his crew had become the first Englishmen to sail around the world. They returned home with spices, treasure, newly-claimed lands, and wild stories of adventure.

1. What did Drake steal from the Spanish ships?

2. Why might the Spanish ports in South America have been unguarded?

3. Why do you think Drake stole maps from the Spanish ships?

4. Why do you think Drake wanted to find a way through the land instead of sailing back down the coast?

5. Why might Drake and his crew have had wild stories of adventure?

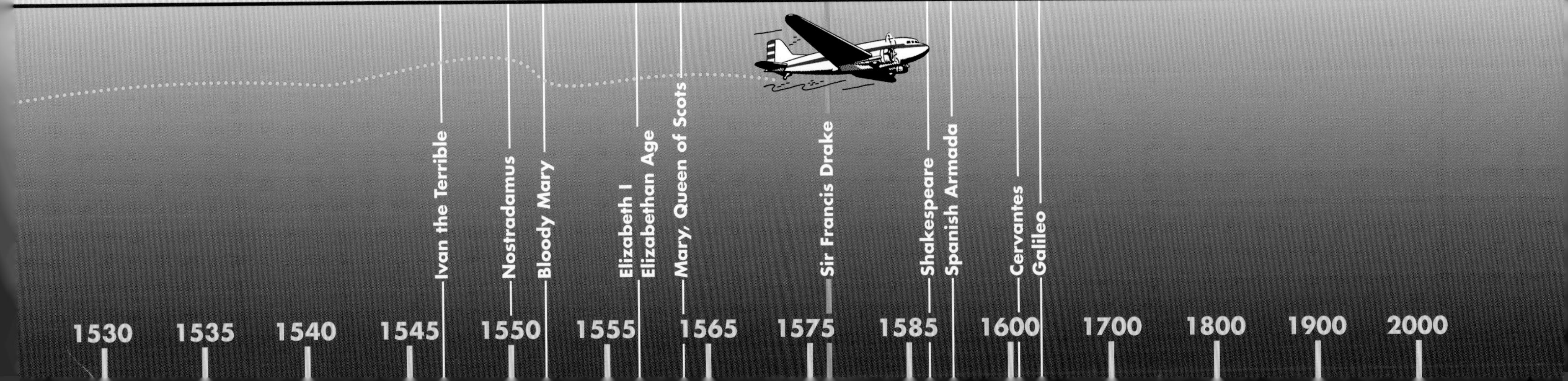
Ivan the Terrible
Nostradamus
Bloody Mary
Elizabeth I
Elizabethan Age
Mary, Queen of Scots
Sir Francis Drake
Shakespeare
Spanish Armada
Cervantes
Galileo
1530
1535
1540
1545
1550
1555
1565
1575
1585
1600
1700
1800
1900
2000

The silver cup Elizabeth awarded to Drake, which encases a coconut he brought back from his voyage to the Pacific *(left)*; a portrait of Drake *(right)*

5 King Philip II of Spain was very angry about Drake's attacks and demanded that the Queen of England punish him, by death. Instead, Elizabeth I made Drake a knight and an admiral in the English Navy. He became Sir Francis Drake. Furious, King Philip ordered his navy, the Spanish Armada, to prepare for an invasion of England. The Queen learned of the plan, and she gave Drake orders to stop the Spanish. Drake and his fleet of small quick ships surprised the Spanish as they were readying ships in their harbor. Drake's men used fire to destroy the fleet. Drake faced the Spanish again and again, and always came out the victor. In his 50's, still harassing Spanish trading ships in the West Indies, the brave man became ill and died. He was buried at sea, and Elizabeth openly mourned the loss of her dear friend.

1. **Who knighted Drake?**
2. **Why do you think Elizabeth made Drake a knight?**
3. **Why do you think King Philip II became furious?**
4. **Why do you think Drake's ships attacked the Spanish ships while they were in the harbor, not out at sea?**
5. **Why do you think Drake was buried at sea?**

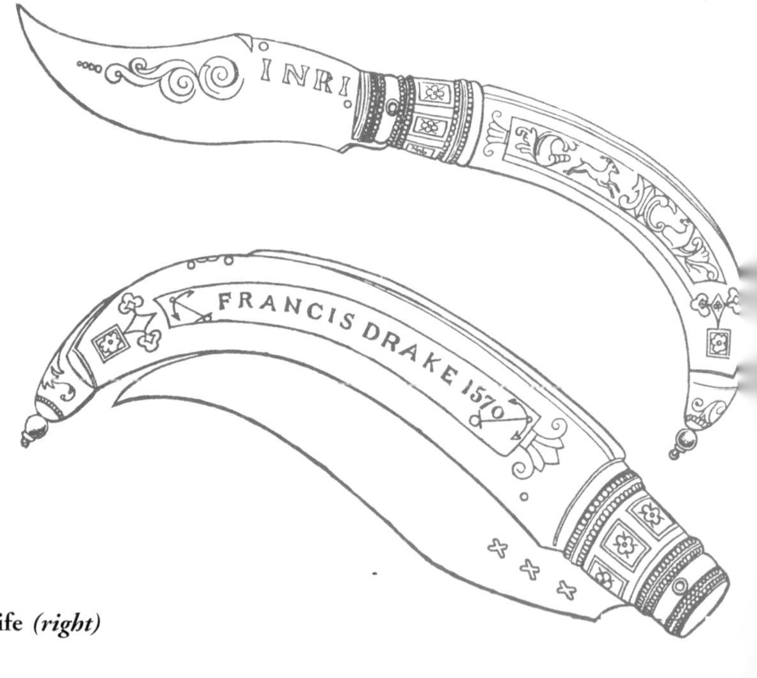
INRI
FRANCIS DRAKE 1570

The *Golden Hind (left)*; a sketch of Drake's knife *(right)*

Ivan says—

Legend tells that Sir Francis Drake was enjoying a game of lawn bowling with some friends when news came that the Spanish Armada had been sighted. Drake is said to have casually remarked that there was plenty of time to finish the game and beat the Spanish, too.

Drake made quite an impression on the American Indians of North America when he and his crew rested there for some months during his around-the-world voyage. He was one of the few explorers who treated the natives of the New World with respect. While his crew rested, they traded and shared knowledge with the natives, and built a fort. However, no one knows where exactly Drake stopped. Wherever it was that Drake stopped, he named the area Nova Albion, noting that the natives were "free from guile or treachery."

Everyone wants their ultimate moment of glory, and that's what the next Flight is all about: The defeat of the Spanish Navy, called the Armada. The Spanish Armada was the greatest navy in the world. Unsinkable. Hmmm. Read on, and let loose the dogs of war! Let them loose and let them run off. See you at sea.

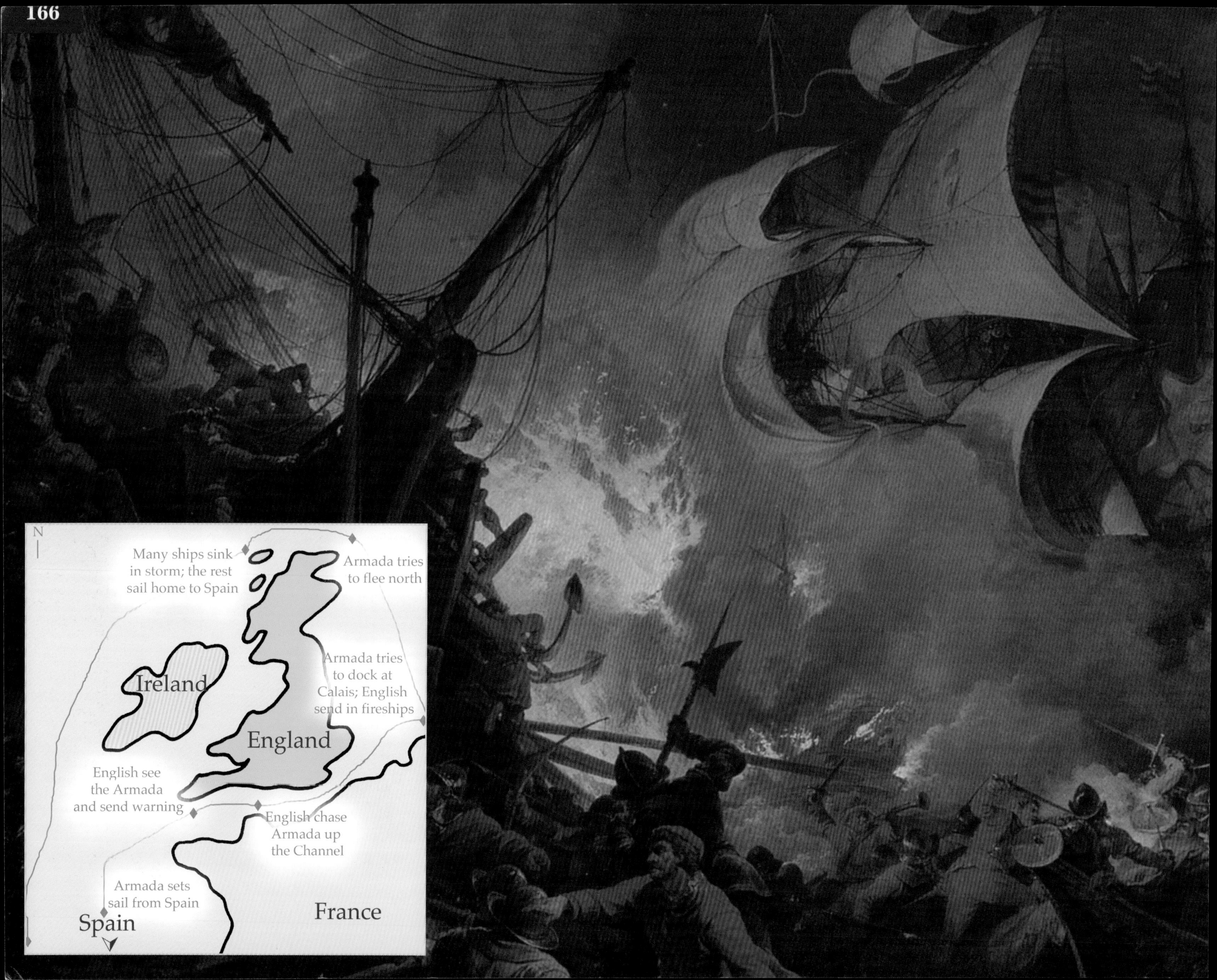
N
Many ships sink
in storm; the rest
sail home to Spain
Armada tries
to flee north
Armada tries
to dock at
Calais; English
send in fireships
Ireland
England
English see
the Armada
and send warning
English chase
Armada up
the Channel
Armada sets
sail from Spain
Spain
France

Flight 28

Spanish Armada

1588

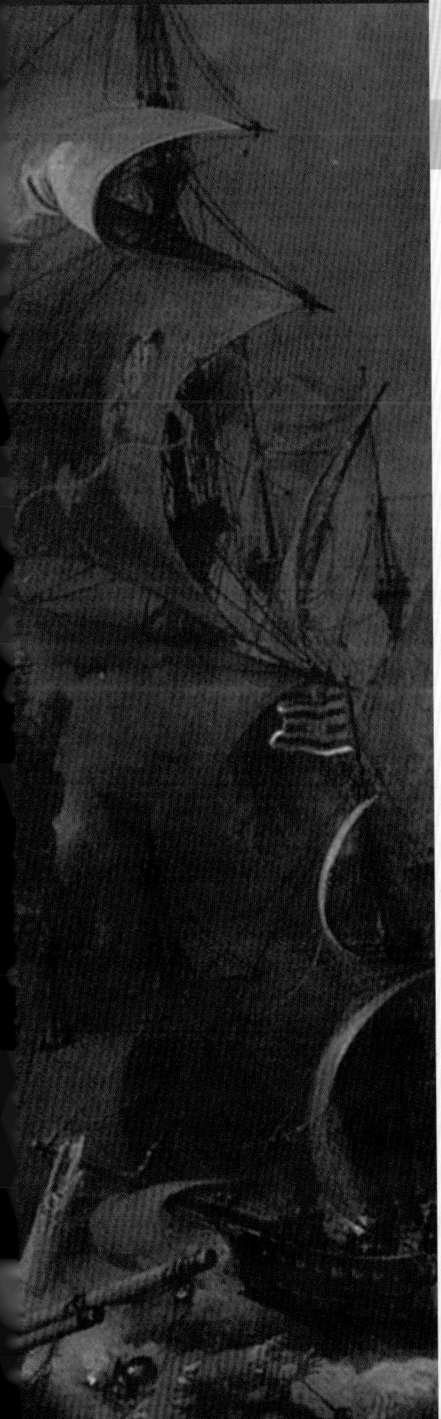

The Defeat of the Armada, by P.J. de Loutherbourg, 1796; map of the battle *(inset)*

Waves crashing fiercely across slippery wooden decks. Wild winds tossing the ships around on the sea like toys. Huge cannonballs smashing thick wood timbers into splinters. Why, oh why would anyone want to go to sea? Crazy. Too much water.

The Spanish got mad at England and sent their massive navy, the Armada, across the English Channel to crush their enemies. Spain had built this incredible fleet of ships with all the money from gold and silver they plundered from the New World.

England sent out its own navy of swift, smaller ships into the choppy waters of the Channel. They set up a pretty clever pre-telephone, early warning system. They used some fancy maneuvering, led by our friend Sir Francis Drake. The fat lady sang, the other shoe dropped, and the Armada sank.

I could've told them. You've got ships built with money gleaned from haunted gold, and you're choosing to fight on water, of all surfaces. Mistake. You read and swim. I'll eat.

1

In the 16th century, Spain was the richest and most powerful country in Europe. Ships crammed with gold and silver from the New World sailed into its home ports. Their mighty navy, the Armada, controlled the seas. But there was tension between Spain and England. For years, English pirates had attacked and raided Spanish ships and towns. The English Queen, Elizabeth I, received a large share of the stolen Spanish wealth. She did nothing to stop the raids. Religious differences caused problems, too. Spain's King Philip II swore that he would return Catholicism to England by marrying Elizabeth, but she insulted him with her refusal. The stage was set for a great battle.

1. **Who was the ruler of Spain?**
2. **Why do you think Spain was the most powerful country in Europe?**
3. **Why do you think there was tension between Spain and England?**
4. **Why do you think pirates raided Spanish ships?**
5. **Why do you think Elizabeth I did not stop the raids?**

2

In 1586, King Philip II of Spain began to prepare for the invasion of England. He ordered many new warships to be built and tons of supplies to be gathered. But problems soon started. In 1587, the English pirate Sir Francis Drake sailed into Cadiz harbor where the ships were being built. He led a surprise attack on the navy and destroyed 30 ships, most of the Armada, as they sat in the harbor. He also ruined much of the Spanish supplies before he sailed away. Now the invasion would have to wait for another year.

1. **In what year did King Philip II begin to prepare for invasion?**
2. **Why do you think King Philip II wanted many new warships to be built?**
3. **Why do you think Sir Francis Drake attacked the ships at Cadiz harbor?**
4. **Why do you think Drake destroyed the Spanish supplies as well as the ships?**
5. **Why do you think the invasion had to wait another year?**

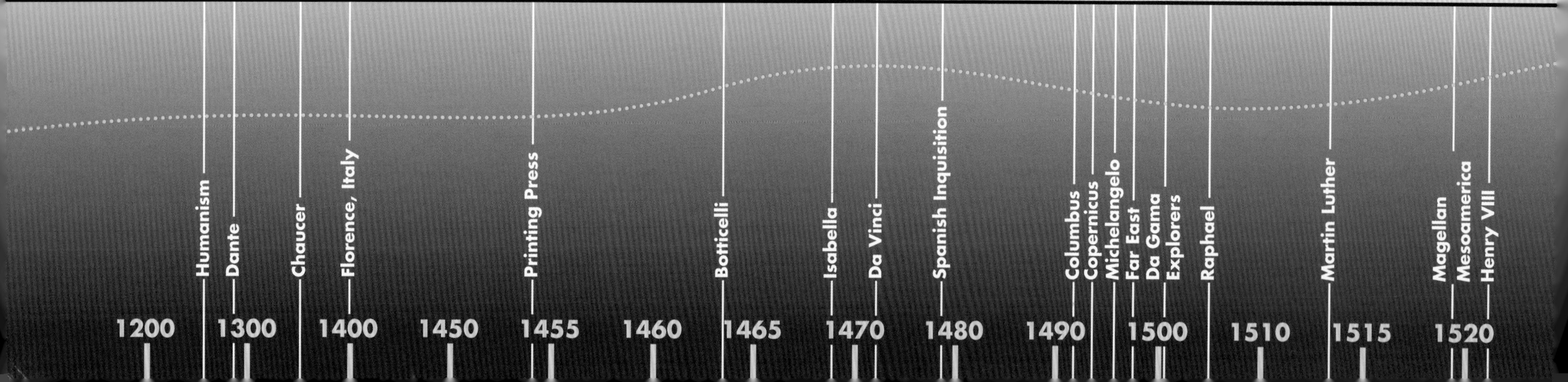
Humanism
Dante
Chaucer
Florence, Italy
Printing Press
Botticelli
Isabella
Da Vinci
Spanish Inquisition
Columbus
Copernicus
Michelangelo
Far East
Da Gama
Explorers
Raphael
Martin Luther
Magellan
Mesoamerica
Henry VIII
1200
1300
1400
1450
1455
1460
1465
1470
1480
1490
1500
1510
1515
1520

3

In 1588, the Spanish Armada was finally ready. A massive fleet of 130 Spanish ships set sail for England with 29,000 men. But the English were waiting to outfox them, having set up an early warning system of bonfires to communicate. The English met the Spanish in the rough waters of the English Channel, which was known as a difficult passage to sail due to bad weather and choppy seas. The large galleons were no match for the swift small ships of the English. The Spanish Armada tried to get away. They wanted to get more Spanish troops before attempting to land and invade England again.

1. **How many Spanish men sailed to England?**
2. **Why do you think the Spanish Armada sailed with so many ships?**
3. **Why do you think the English were able to outfox the Spanish?**
4. **How do you think the English used bonfires to communicate?**
5. **How do you think the English ships were better in the Channel than the Spanish ships?**

4

The ships of the Spanish Armada dropped their anchors at Calais, a French port, to reorganize. But the English Navy had chased them and now filled eight of their old ships with tar and gunpowder. Then they set the ships on fire and launched them at the Spanish fleet. The Spanish panicked and cut the ropes holding their anchors, scrambling to get away. The Spanish were on the run again. In the deadly cold waters of the Channel, the English swarmed over the Spanish. With their small, fast ships, the English were able to outmaneuver the large, heavy Spanish boats. The English could also fire their cannons more rapidly. The Spanish were not prepared for this new style of shoot-and-run battle strategy. In this fight, the English had the advantage.

1. **Where did the ships of the Spanish Armada drop their anchors to reorganize?**
2. **Why do you think the English Navy launched eight ships filled with gunpowder at the Spanish fleet?**
3. **Why do you think the Spanish cut their anchors instead of pulling them up?**
4. **How do you think the "shoot-and-run" strategy helped the English win?**
5. **Why do you think the English had the advantage over the Spanish?**

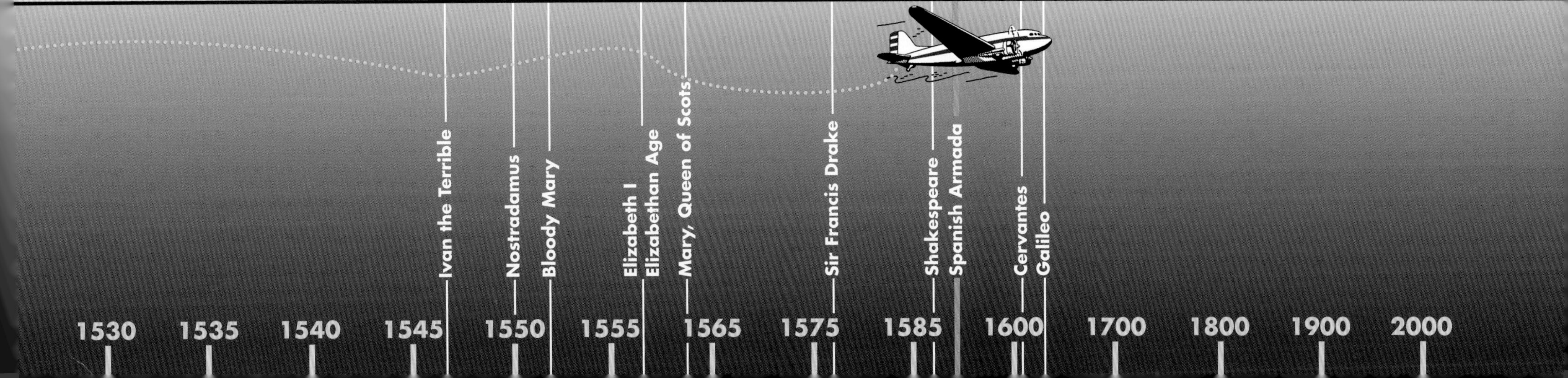
Ivan the Terrible
Nostradamus
Bloody Mary
Elizabeth I
Elizabethan Age
Mary, Queen of Scots
Sir Francis Drake
Shakespeare
Spanish Armada
Cervantes
Galileo
1530
1535
1540
1545
1550
1555
1565
1575
1585
1600
1700
1800
1900
2000

(clockwise from left) **the Armada battles England's navy; a map shows the English fire signaling system along the cliffs; English fireships in the harbor**

5 The Spanish steered to sail out of the English Channel into the North Sea and escape the English attack. Suddenly, the wind shifted directions. The Spanish ships, without their anchors, were at the mercy of the violent winds. The winds forced them to sail away from home, putting them far off course. Storms pounded the fleet the whole time and many ships were lost. Of the 130 ships that had left Spain, only half were ablc to return home. More than 15,000 Spanish men died.

1. **How many Spanish men died?**
2. **Why might the change in wind direction have been a problem for the Spanish ships?**
3. **Why do you think it was a problem for the Spanish ships to be without their anchors?**
4. **What do you think was the mood of the Spanish?**
5. **Why do you think so many Spanish men died?**

Ivan says—

Things would have gone better for Spain if the reserve fleet hadn't been a couple of days late. But still, the Spanish lost and never regained their glorious position of power. England, meanwhile, got more powerful. Elizabeth declared that goose be served for dinner at Christmas all over England because that was what she ate just before her victory over the Spanish Armada.

I can't disagree with a lady who orders me to eat goose. In fact, I'm off to find a goose for dinner. You go on without me.

Oops, back to my job for a minute as your history professor. Besides King Philip II of Spain, next is someone in England that Elizabeth wasn't so fond of: her cousin, Mary, Queen of Scots. Mary was an unfortunate girl; she fell for all the wrong guys and made the mistake of scheming against her Queen. Read on!

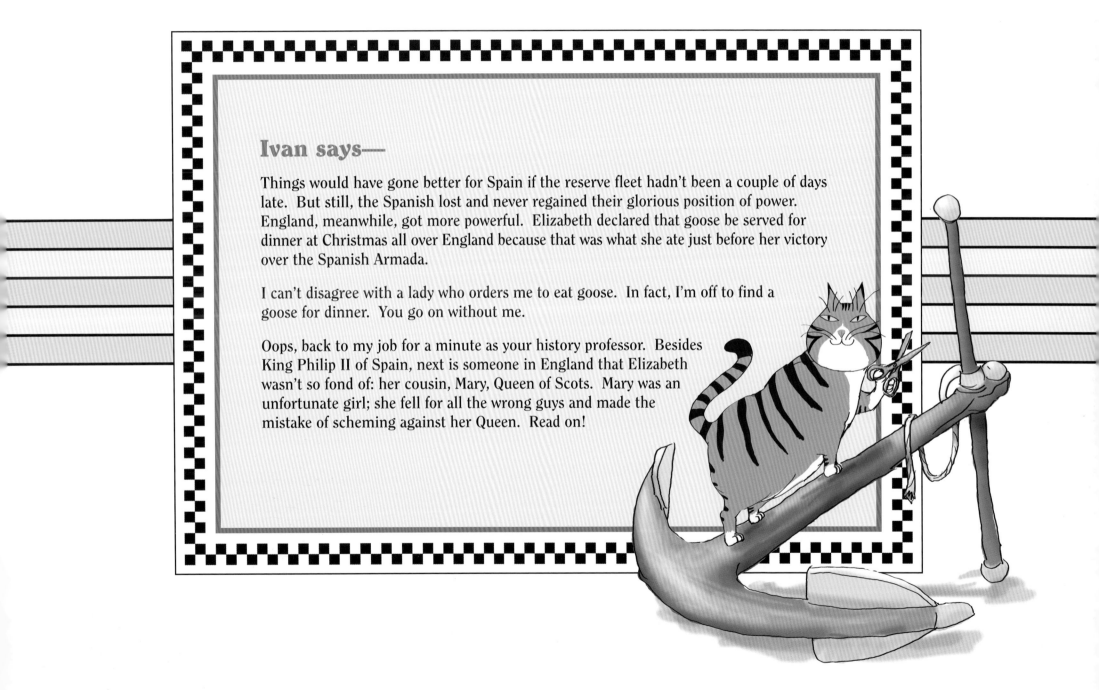

Flight 29

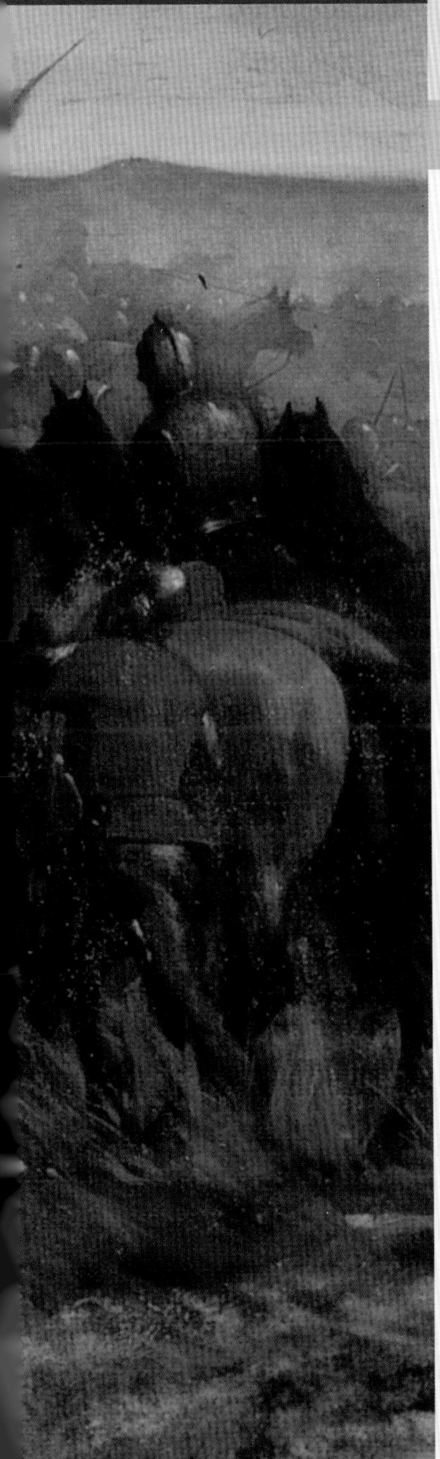

Mary, Queen of Scots, surrenders after the Battle of Langside, fought to regain the Scottish crown

Mary, Queen of Scots

1542-1587

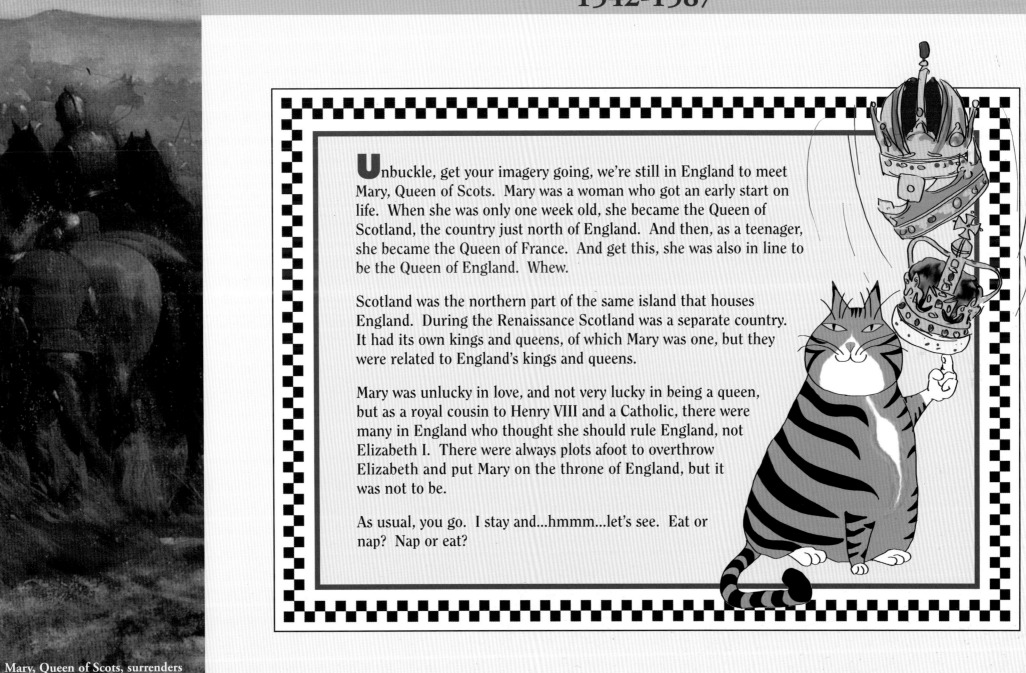

Unbuckle, get your imagery going, we're still in England to meet Mary, Queen of Scots. Mary was a woman who got an early start on life. When she was only one week old, she became the Queen of Scotland, the country just north of England. And then, as a teenager, she became the Queen of France. And get this, she was also in line to be the Queen of England. Whew.

Scotland was the northern part of the same island that houses England. During the Renaissance Scotland was a separate country. It had its own kings and queens, of which Mary was one, but they were related to England's kings and queens.

Mary was unlucky in love, and not very lucky in being a queen, but as a royal cousin to Henry VIII and a Catholic, there were many in England who thought she should rule England, not Elizabeth I. There were always plots afoot to overthrow Elizabeth and put Mary on the throne of England, but it was not to be.

As usual, you go. I stay and...hmmm...let's see. Eat or nap? Nap or eat?

1

Mary Stuart was the daughter of Scottish King James V and his French wife, Mary of Guise. When little Mary was only one week old, her father died and she became the Queen of Scotland. Since she was much too young to rule, her mother ruled in her place. To ensure her safety from power-hungry nobles, the young girl was sent to France when she was five. There she lived as part of the French royal family and was given a first-class education. She married Prince Francis II of France, as arranged, when she was fifteen. When he came to power a year later, the tall shy beauty became the Queen of both Scotland and France.

1. How old was Mary when she wed Prince Francis II of France?

2. Why do you think it was important to keep Mary safe?

3. Do you think Mary had a good childhood in France? Why or why not?

4. Why do you think Mary was given a first-class education?

5. What might be some problems with being the Queen of two countries?

2

Just 17 months after he became King, Mary's sickly husband Francis II died and she returned to Scotland, now 17 years old. She was beautiful, with red hair and a charming nature. She hated leaving France, the only home she had known, although the Scots welcomed her back as their Queen. But Scotland was now in the middle of religious conflict and economic troubles, partly because of its many wars with England. It soon became obvious that the young, emotional, and impulsive Mary was not up to the challenge of ruling a country. Although she tried hard to be a good queen, she was nervous, unsure, and out of touch with her own people. Because she had been raised in France, her people complained she seemed more French than Scottish.

1. How old was Mary when she returned to Scotland?

2. Why do you think Mary hated leaving France?

3. Why do you think the Scots people welcomed Mary back?

4. Why do you think Mary might have had trouble ruling a country?

5. How might being raised in France have affected Mary to be Queen of Scotland?

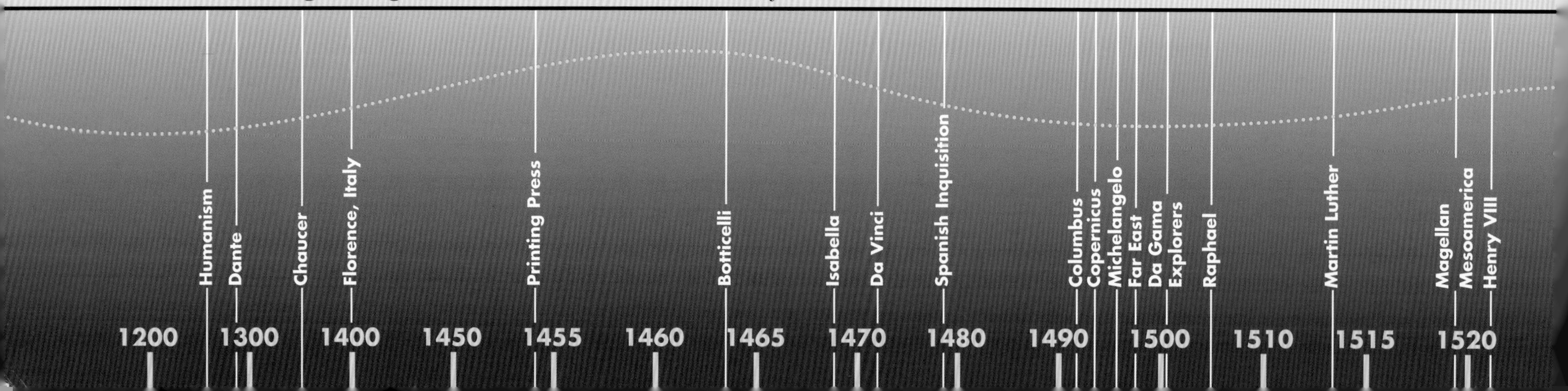
Humanism
Dante
Chaucer
Florence, Italy
Printing Press
Botticelli
Isabella
Da Vinci
Spanish Inquisition
Columbus
Copernicus
Michelangelo
Far East
Da Gama
Explorers
Raphael
Martin Luther
Magellan
Mesoamerica
Henry VIII
1200
1300
1400
1450
1455
1460
1465
1470
1480
1490
1500
1510
1515
1520

3

In 1565, Mary married Henry Stuart, the Lord of Darnley. To Henry, it was a dream come true because he had planned this marriage so that he would someday be King. But soon after their marriage, the Queen realized the man she loved was greedy and married her just to become King. Mary, pregnant at the time, refused to give him any kingly power, and he resented her. He then turned his rage toward Mary's secretary and trusted friend, David Rizzio. In front of the Queen, Henry and a group of men dragged Rizzio into a hallway and killed him as the poor man begged Mary to save his life. Mary was horrified and left her husband within days.

1. **What was the name of Mary's husband?**
2. **Why do you think Mary refused to give Henry any power?**
3. **Why do you think Henry resented Mary?**
4. **Why do you think Henry killed David in front of the Queen?**
5. **Why do you think Mary left her husband?**

4

Shortly after Mary's son James was born, her former husband, Henry, plotted against her to seize the throne. But he didn't live long enough to do it. Henry fell ill, and Mary helped him settle into a house called Kirk o'Field, near her palace. That night, a huge explosion shook the grounds at two in the morning. The house had been blown up and Henry was dead. A Scottish nobleman, James Hepburn, was accused of the crime, but he was acquitted. Soon after the trial, Hepburn proposed marriage, but Mary refused. He then kidnapped the Queen and she married him, leading many to think that was the plan all along. The Scottish nobles demanded she turn the throne over to her infant son. Mary fought them, but in the end, she lost. She abdicated (gave up) her throne, and James, her 13-month-old son, became King.

1. **Who was accused of killing Henry Stuart?**
2. **Why do you think Hepburn kidnapped Mary?**
3. **Why might Mary have wed the man who had kidnapped her?**
4. **Why do you think the Scottish nobles rose up against Mary?**
5. **What do you think happened next?**

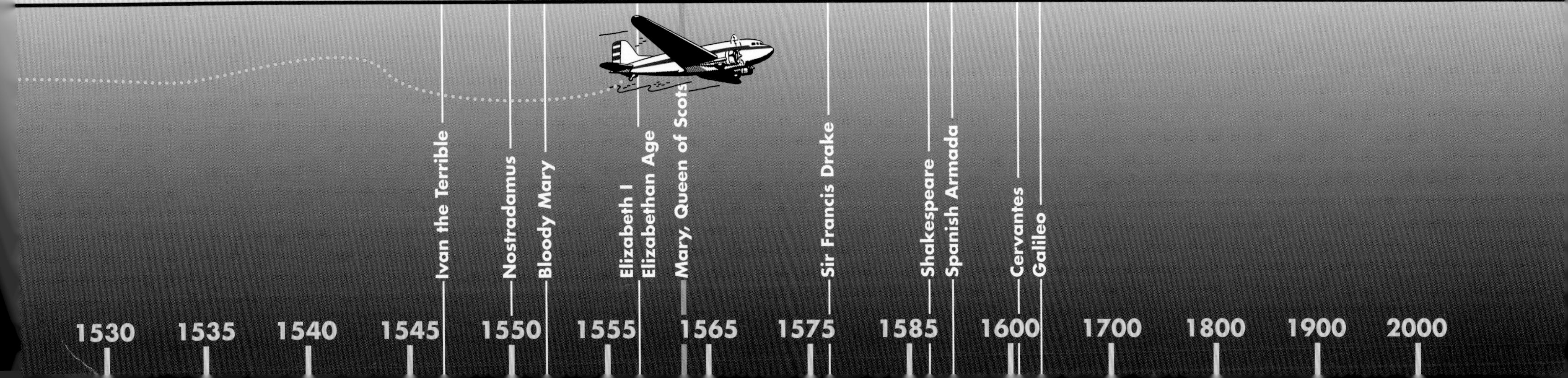
Ivan the Terrible
Nostradamus
Bloody Mary
Elizabeth I
Elizabethan Age
Mary, Queen of Scots
Sir Francis Drake
Shakespeare
Spanish Armada
Cervantes
Galileo
1530
1535
1540
1545
1550
1555
1565
1575
1585
1600
1700
1800
1900
2000

A portrait of Mary, Queen of Scots, from a miniature made while she was in mourning *(left)*; a drawing of Mary and Henry Stuart, her husband *(right)*

1566

Mary escaped the country and raised an army to win back her crown, but she lost. She then fled to England to ask her cousin, Queen Elizabeth I, for protection. But Elizabeth and her advisors saw Mary as a threat to her own crown. Mary was arrested and spent 19 years under guard. From prison, Mary and a group of her supporters set up a plot to overthrow Elizabeth. Through her spies, the Queen learned of their plan. In 1587, 45-year-old Mary was convicted of treason and beheaded on her cousin's orders.

1. **Where did Mary go when she fled Scotland?**
2. **Why do you think Mary tried to win back her crown?**
3. **Why might Mary have believed Elizabeth would help her?**
4. **Why do you think Elizabeth kept Mary under guard for 19 years?**
5. **What do you think of Mary?**

Mary's rosary and prayer book, with her at her execution on February 8, 1587 *(left)*; Mary's home, Holyrood Castle, Edinburgh, Scotland *(right)*

Ivan says—

Can you believe that Queen Elizabeth, Mary's cousin, had Mary arrested after she came to her for help? Can you believe Mary, Elizabeth's cousin, plotted against her? Those cousins were something, but let's read on, there's more. Look what Elizabeth's older sister, Mary, the Queen of England before her, did to her poor cousin, Jane. Lady Jane Grey was only 17 when a group of the noblemen wanted to put her on the throne. She lasted nine days before Mary and her supporters rousted and beheaded her for treason. Don't confuse that Mary with our Mary, Queen of Scots. Who am I kidding, the whole thing is confusing. They kept calling everyone Mary.

Oh, well. Let's move on to a great age in the Renaissance. England under Queen Elizabeth prospered and became the center of all arts and culture. Well, this glorious period of good writing and good theater was known as the Golden Age, or the Elizabethan Age, because Elizabeth I of England was a great ruler. Life was good.

Let's go. Rather, you go and I'll shed this kilt.

Flight 30

Elizabethan Age

1558-1603

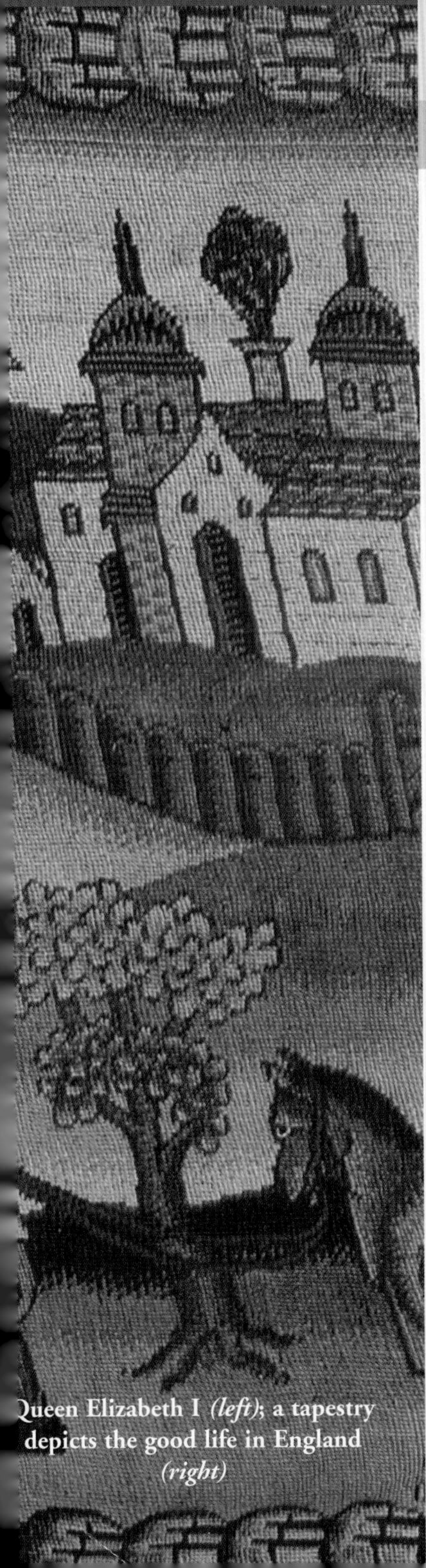

Queen Elizabeth I *(left)*; a tapestry depicts the good life in England *(right)*

Get set to smile, we have landed in a whole era: the Elizabethan Age. For the 45 years that Elizabeth I was the queen, England thrived. Before Good Queen Bess, as she was called, the country was in trouble. There were religious turmoils and expensive wars with France and Scotland. But the strong and determined Queen cracked the whip. She had no fear when it came to changing things to suit herself, and so she helped make London the most important city in Europe and the center of all high society. London exploded in size as people came to England. Buildings went up at a record pace. New bridges and better roads were put in place.

During this time, Elizabeth was thinking about the future of her people as well. She wanted to grab some of the new territory that was being discovered across the ocean to the west. She was the first of the English rulers to see the value in the New World. Adventurers like Sir Francis Drake used royal funding to conquer new lands. Except for the nagging voices of her advisors, all telling the poor girl to get married and have children, Elizabeth was doing great, and so were her people.

Even cats had it pretty good in the Elizabethan Age. Plenty of mice and straw to sleep in. Towns had festivals all the time, and one festival was described by a preacher as "a day of great gluttony...!" Yeah.

1

Few monarchs have ruled as long as Queen Elizabeth I of England. Her 45-year reign was a time marked by peace. She loved the arts, and her great influence helped bring the Renaissance to England. England grew and flourished during the time she ruled. Her father, the powerful Henry VIII, would have been proud. It was also a time when England began to dominate the seas and the world. Elizabeth said, "I may not be a lion, but I am a lion's cub and I have a lion's heart." This period of growth and change came to be known as the Elizabethan Age.

1. How long did Queen Elizabeth I rule England?

2. Why might a long reign help keep a nation at peace?

3. Why do you think England grew and flourished during Elizabeth's rule?

4. What do you think Elizabeth meant by saying "I am a lion's cub and I have a lion's heart?"

5. Why do you think this period became known as the Elizabethan Age?

2

Elizabeth loved the arts, even dabbling at writing poetry herself. Her castles were often filled with artists, musicians, and writers. She loved to dance and sponsored dance troupes (traveling groups) that would stay and perform in her palace. Elizabeth also enjoyed literature. She inspired many writers to create works, some of which became famous. These include the entire works of Shakespeare. She was also physically strong, riding horses almost daily with no thought for her own safety. She could hunt hawk and deer as well as any man could, and enjoyed watching sports like tennis and shooting matches.

1. Who often came to Elizabeth's castles?

2. Why do you think Elizabeth sponsored dance troupes?

3. Why do you think some of the most famous works in English were created during this period?

4. Why do you think Elizabeth was able to inspire so many different types of artists?

5. Why might it have been important to Elizabeth that she could ride or hunt as well as any man could?

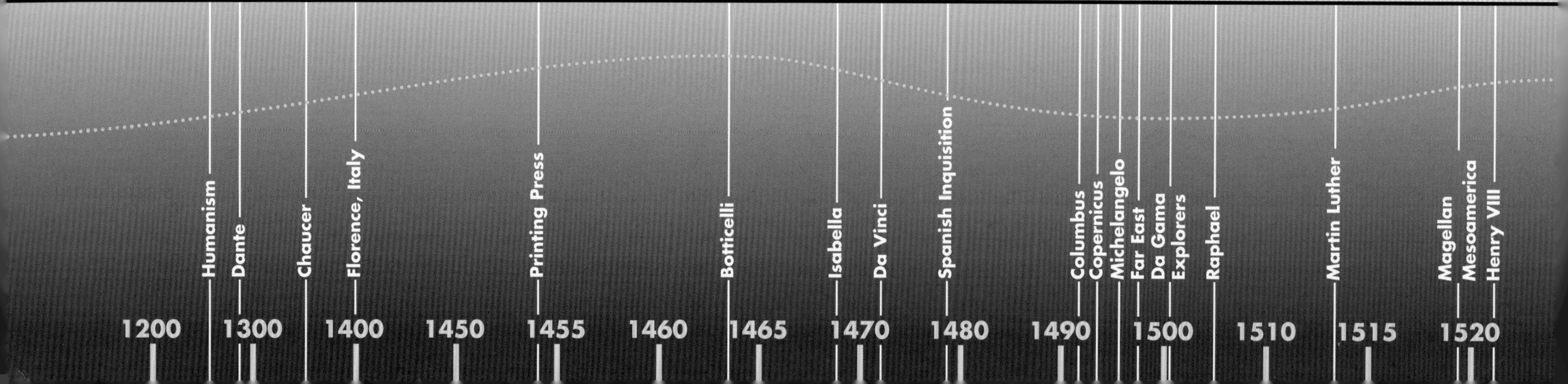
Humanism
Dante
Chaucer
Florence, Italy
Printing Press
Botticelli
Isabella
Da Vinci
Spanish Inquisition
Columbus
Copernicus
Michelangelo
Far East
Da Gama
Explorers
Raphael
Martin Luther
Magellan
Mesoamerica
Henry VIII
1200
1300
1400
1450
1455
1460
1465
1470
1480
1490
1500
1510
1515
1520

3

In the average home, great changes were happening also. The expanding trade brought new goods and spices into the lives of almost everyone. Cloves, cinnamon, and other spices helped flavor and hide the taste of salt-preserved meat and foods when they would begin to spoil. Women still could not go to school, but were now often educated at home. In addition, people from all walks of life attended plays at the theater. But women were not allowed to have a role in plays (even the female parts were played only by men). They could watch, although proper ladies in the audience had to wear veils or even masks. There was a different play every day, with many plays presented each season.

1. What were two of the spices that were introduced at this time?

2. Do you think people were glad to have the spices? Explain.

3. Why might the people of this time have eaten foods that had begun to spoil?

4. Why do you think women were not allowed to have roles in plays?

5. Why do you think the plays were changed so often?

4

The Elizabethan Age was a time of great growth for England as a world power. In the early 16th century, Spain was the only threat to England's shores. Spain was more powerful than England, mainly because of the gold and silver it took from the New World. However, the defeat of the Spanish Armada by the English Navy in 1588 left England in power. Then Elizabeth made a peaceful truce with England's other old enemy, France. Now English ships were free to sail across the globe, many with funding from Queen Elizabeth. They set up trading systems and imported products from the New World. Brave men and women developed colonies in North America, carving a prosperous new life out of the wilderness. Thanks to Elizabeth, England became the most powerful country in the world.

1. When did the English defeat the Spanish Armada?

2. Why might the battle have left England in power?

3. Why do you think Elizabeth funded voyages across the globe?

4. Why do you think men and women went to North America?

5. Why do you think England was able to become the most powerful country in the world?

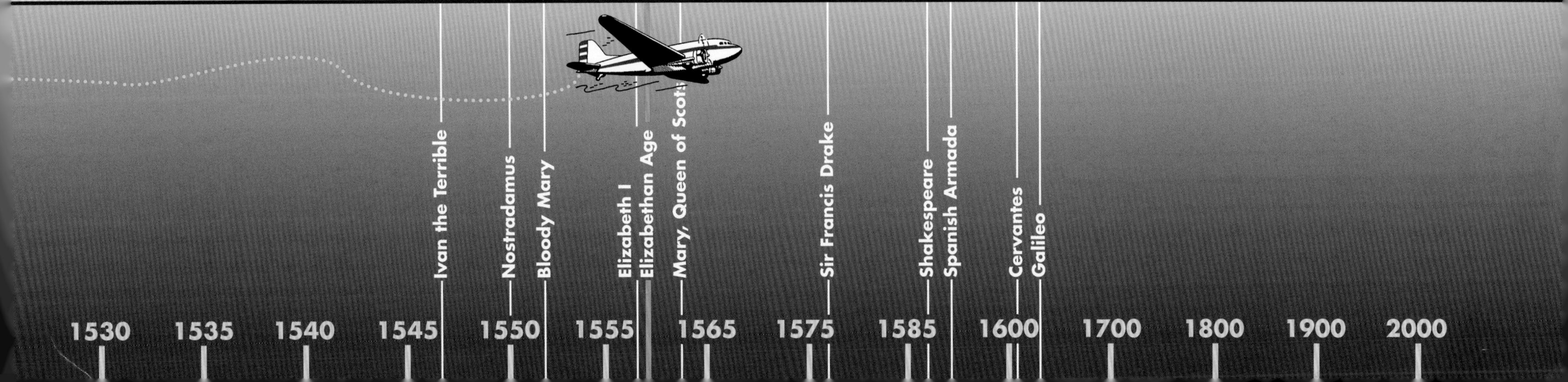
Ivan the Terrible
Nostradamus
Bloody Mary
Elizabeth I
Elizabethan Age
Mary, Queen of Scots
Sir Francis Drake
Shakespeare
Spanish Armada
Cervantes
Galileo
1530
1535
1540
1545
1550
1555
1565
1575
1585
1600
1700
1800
1900
2000

GLOBE . SOUTHWARKE.

The Tower of London, from an engraving by Thomas Homser Shepherd *(left)*; The Globe Theater, built in 1598, was the home for Shakespeare's acting troupe "Lord Chamberlain's Men," and a favorite theater of the Queen *(right)*

5 There were still problems for Elizabeth to deal with, like the endless struggle for power between Protestants and Catholics. Elizabeth tried to be fair and worked hard to be a perfect diplomat. Another problem was disease, made worse by the overcrowding of London. During this era, the plague struck several times. Tens of thousands died in London alone. But for the most part, life in England was getting much better. The people of England began to prosper, and there was peace for the 45 years she ruled. Until Elizabeth died, England enjoyed a golden age they later named after their Queen: the Elizabethan Age.

1. **Which two religious groups struggled for power?**
2. **Why do you think Elizabeth worked hard to be a diplomat?**
3. **Why might the plague have affected England's prosperity?**
4. **Why might the people of England have been so fond of their Queen?**
5. **Why do you think this time was called a golden age?**

The Chariott drawne by foure Horses upon which Charret stood the Coffin covered wth purple Velvett and upon that the representation, The Canapy borne by six Knights.
footemen.

The funeral procession for beloved Good Queen Bess

Ivan says—

So there they were, all happy as bedbugs in England. And they had a lot of bedbugs, let me tell you! Everyone in London used the Thames River that ran through the city as a water highway. People and goods were carried up and down the river in boat-taxis. The boatmen called out their direction, "Eastward-ho!" or "Westward-ho!" Sometimes passengers would see prisoners chained to the banks of the river, suffering when high tide rolled in. Other times, a golden barge carrying some important person would float by.

London Bridge might be draped with the severed heads of criminals. Once the taxi docked, the rider walked on narrow crowded streets of cobblestone among houses jammed together. They had to be wary of getting the contents of chamber pots dumped on their heads from windows above, as there was no sewage system in London. Eeeww! Just thinking about that gives me the shakes. Speaking of shakes...

TAXI

Your next Flight involves a human by the name of Shakespeare. He was one of the world's most famous writers. If I had opposable thumbs, I could be a great writer. Wait…I'll just use my claw to etch the words on the fridge door…how many O's are there in TUNA?

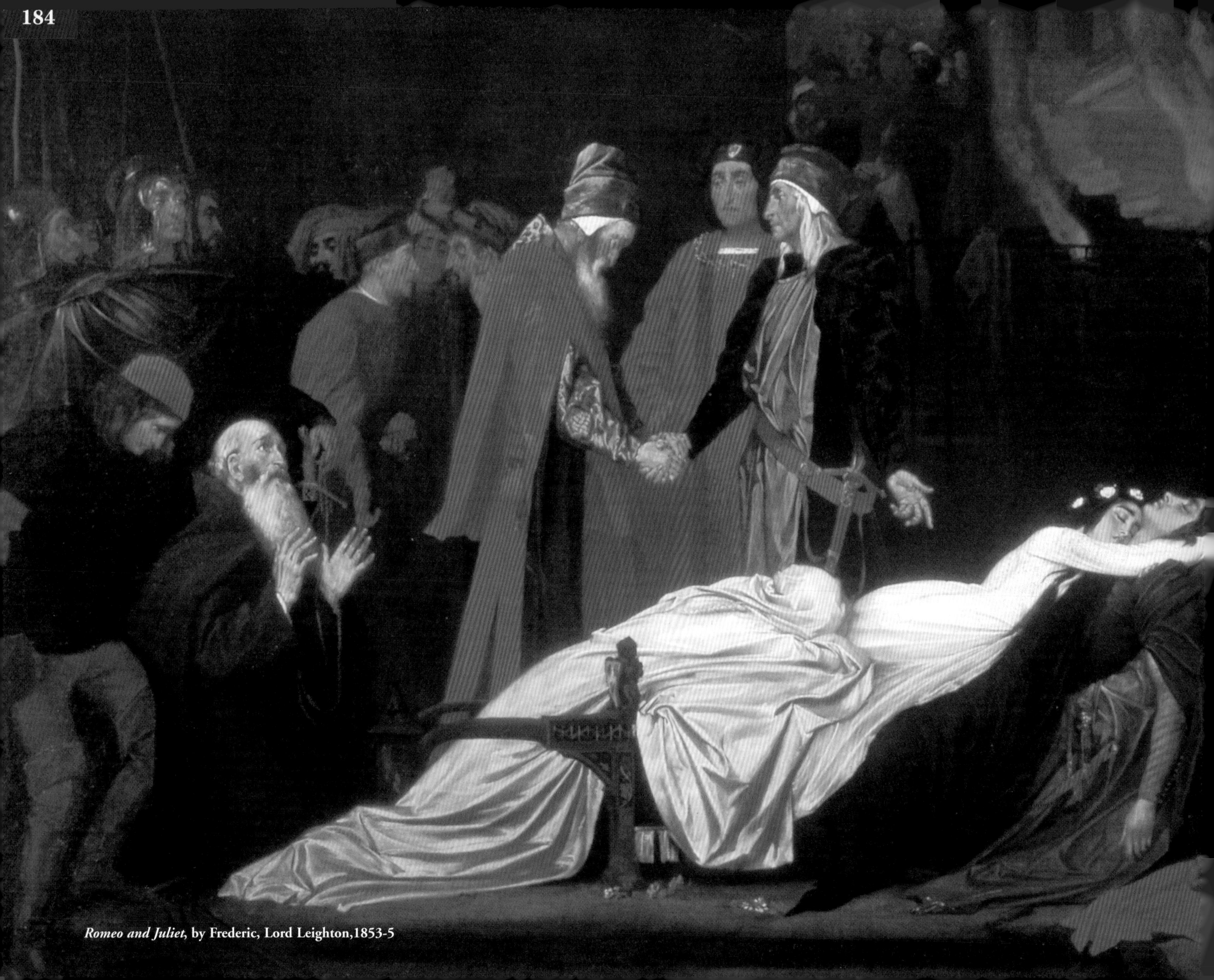

Romeo and Juliet, by Frederic, Lord Leighton,1853-5

Flight 31

Shakespeare

1564-1616

To eat, or not to eat? That is a *question*?

Your next Flight is about William Shakespeare, one of the greatest writers ever. Shakespeare was an actor and a playwright who lived in the late 1500's. He died when he was only 52, but he still managed to write an amazing number of plays and sonnets. I'm not even sure what a sonnet is, but I'm impressed nonetheless. Some of his plays were *Romeo & Juliet, Othello*, and *Hamlet*.

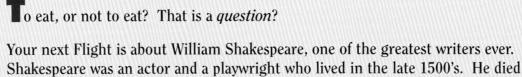

Shakespeare had the words to write just about anything. His vocabulary was huge. Most people of this time knew around 10,000 words, but Shakespeare had a vocabulary of over 29,000 words. And he had just an average education! Plus he added new words he made up to the English language, words like "bedroom" and "puke." Really.

Oh, and a sonnet is a 14-line poem. Bet you thought I didn't know that. Shakespeare is the man. I am the cat.

1

William Shakespeare was born in Stratford-upon-Avon, England, in 1564. He was one of eight children and attended one of the best grammar schools in England. When Shakespeare was 18, he married 26-year old Anne Hathaway and had a daughter. The six years of his life after the birth of his other kids, twins Hamnet and Judith, is a mystery. By 1588, when he was 24, he was in London working as an actor and playwright. Critics said the determined young man was brash and sure of himself, as an actor and a writer. Some criticized him for writing plays that he then put on and acted in himself.

1. **Where was Shakespeare born?**

2. **Why do you think it might have been important that Shakespeare attended one of the best grammar schools?**

3. **Why might critics have considered Shakespeare brash and sure of himself?**

4. **Why do you think Shakespeare acted in the plays he wrote?**

5. **What is the main idea of all this imagery?**

2

The plague, a deadly disease, swept across England in 1593. Over 15,000 people died in London. All theaters and public places where people gathered together were closed for over a year to slow the spread of disease. Shakespeare spent this time writing poems and plays, and investing money in a theater troupe called the Lord Chamberlain's Men. Then, when the theaters opened again, he went back to acting. For the next eighteen years, Shakespeare spent most of his time in London. The theater, known as the Globe, became very popular and even Queen Elizabeth often came to watch Shakespeare's plays being performed there.

1. **How many people died of the plague in London?**

2. **Why do you think Shakespeare invested in a theater troupe?**

3. **Why do you think Shakespeare went back to acting?**

4. **Why might the Globe have become popular?**

5. **How might it have helped Shakespeare to have Queen Elizabeth attend his plays?**

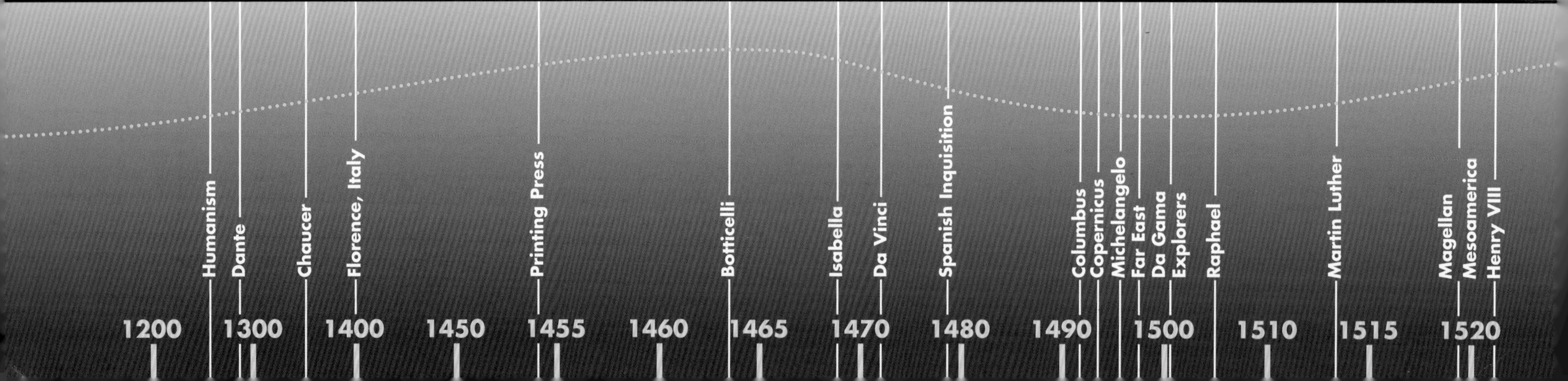
Humanism
Dante
Chaucer
Florence, Italy
Printing Press
Botticelli
Isabella
Da Vinci
Spanish Inquisition
Columbus
Copernicus
Michelangelo
Far East
Da Gama
Explorers
Raphael
Martin Luther
Magellan
Mesoamerica
Henry VIII
1200
1300
1400
1450
1455
1460
1465
1470
1480
1490
1500
1510
1515
1520

3

Shakespeare wrote many plays about recent history that was still somewhat fresh in the minds of Englishmen, stories of brave kings like Henry V and notorious villains like King Richard III. The playwright's versions of these men were so good that many assumed the plays were strictly factual instead of Shakespeare's clever imagination mixed with some truth. He also wrote side-splitting comedies like *Twelfth Night*, in which love mixes with mistaken identity. In this play, while Duke Orsino loves Olivia, she rejects him. He stubbornly hires Cesario to woo her for him. But Cesario is really a girl named Viola, posing as a man. Viola/Cesario then falls in love with the Duke, while Olivia falls for Cesario, unaware that "he" is really a "she" in disguise.

1. What was the name of Shakespeare's play about mistaken identity?

2. Why do you think it might have been important for Shakespeare to have a clever imagination?

3. Why might Shakespeare have written comedies?

4. Why might *Twelfth Night* be hard to understand?

5. Do you think Shakespeare was a good playwright? Explain.

4

One of Shakespeare's most famous plays is *Romeo and Juliet*. In this play, a young man and woman from feuding Italian families fall in love after seeing each other at a masquerade ball. The couple marries in secret, but before they can tell their families, tragedy strikes. While trying to break up a fight, Romeo kills Juliet's cousin and is banished for his crime. At the same time, Juliet has a plan for them to run away, the only way they can be together. She takes a potion to appear dead so that she won't have to go through with an arranged marriage set up by her parents. Romeo does not learn of the plan in time. He finds her body and, believing her lost to him forever, he kills himself just before she wakes up. Then Juliet sees her dead Romeo and throws herself on his knife, leaving their grieving families to find them entwined in death.

1. What is the name of one of Shakespeare's most famous plays?

2. Why do you think Romeo and Juliet married in secret?

3. Do you think Romeo meant to kill Juliet's cousin? Why or why not?

4. Why do you think Romeo killed himself?

5. Why do you think Juliet killed herself?

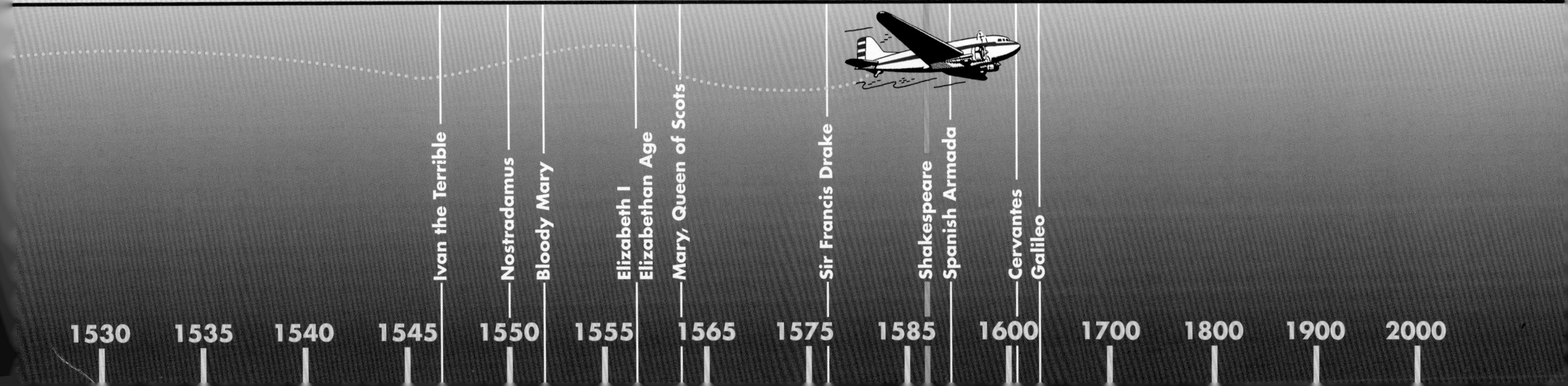

Ivan the Terrible
Nostradamus
Bloody Mary
Elizabeth I
Elizabethan Age
Mary, Queen of Scots
Sir Francis Drake
Shakespeare
Spanish Armada
Cervantes
Galileo
1530
1535
1540
1545
1550
1555
1565
1575
1585
1600
1700
1800
1900
2000

The house in Stratford-upon-Avon where Shakespeare was born *(left)*; a miniature from 1588 believed to be Shakespeare, painted by his friend, Nicholas Hilliard *(right)*

5

In 1611, Shakespeare retired and returned home to his family, done with writing and acting. There he lived a quiet and wealthy life until he died in 1616, at age 47. Shakespeare had been very successful, one of few writers whose works were published in his lifetime. He wrote 37 plays and 154 sonnets. His plays include *Julius Caesar*, *A Midsummer Night's Dream*, *Antony and Cleopatra*, *Hamlet*, *Macbeth*, and *King Lear*. His favorite themes were the comic results of mistaken identity and dramas with a flawed hero. Today, Shakespeare is regarded as the greatest playwright the world has known. His plays are more popular now than ever. They are seen on the stage and in movies all over the world.

1. What is the name of one of Shakespeare's plays?

2. Why do you think Shakespeare was able to live a wealthy life?

3. Do you think many people bought his plays? Why or why not?

4. Why do you think he is regarded as the greatest playwright the world has ever known?

5. What do you think of Shakespeare?

Twelfth Night*, by Walter Howell Deverell *(left)*; Shakespeare *(top)*; Ophelia, the doomed heroine from *Hamlet*, by J.W. Waterhouse *(right)

Ivan says—

Shakespeare was one of those rare artists whose work lived past him, and are as popular now as they ever were. King James I, son of Mary, Queen of Scots, who succeeded Elizabeth I to rule England, was a fan as well. In fact, Shakespeare changed the acting troupe's name to The King's Men in his honor. King James' favorite play by Shakespeare was *Macbeth*, a story of murder and betrayal set in James' native Scotland in medieval times. I like Hamlet...Ham-let. Get it?

Now on to another famous writer. Cervantes was a Spanish writer who wrote one of the best-loved books of all time. It involved windmills and donkeys and a beautiful maiden. Windmills, donkeys? I don't know.

Let's fly to sunny Spain and check it out. You read. I'll eat.

A tapestry depicts a scene from *Don Quixote.*

Cervantes

1547-1616

Put those tray tables up, spit out the peanuts, and let's meet Cervantes in Spain. Cervantes is Spain's most famous writer. He wrote the novel *Don Quixote* (*Kee-HO-tee*), which is about an old man who sees the world differently than everyone else. Let's practice that word. Quixote. Kee-HO-tee. Tongue back, lips round, tongue up. Got it? No *qu*. No *x*.

Cervantes wasn't really writing about a loony old man who imagines he's a knight, he was writing about knighthood and a way of life that was fast disappearing at the end of the Renaissance. The ideas of the Middle Ages and Renaissance in science, culture, and the arts, were being challenged, and new ways of looking at and doing things were emerging. Chivalry was one of the disappearing acts, and Cervantes wrote about a man who so loved the knightly ideal that he couldn't see the reality of his own life. Don Quixote really represented the end of the Renaissance.

And actually we're nearly to the end of the Renaissance too. I'm heading to the fish tank for one last time. You read and visualize. I eat and nap.

1

Miguel de Cervantes was born in Alcalá, Spain. Because his father was always looking for whatever work he could find, Cervantes spent most of his youth moving from place to place. Finally, his family settled in Madrid, where Cervantes began to study and write. His teacher was so impressed with Cervantes' writing that he published four of Cervantes' poems. But soon the young man's writing career was sidetracked. He joined the Spanish Army, was kidnapped by pirates during a battle, and spent years as a captive before finally getting home. However, the ransom paid for his release hung over his head as a large debt he needed to pay back, so he looked for a job.

1. **Where was Cervantes born?**
2. **How might living in so many places have helped Cervantes become a better writer?**
3. **Why do you think settling in Madrid might have helped him?**
4. **How do you think Cervantes' time in the army affected him? Explain.**
5. **Why might a ransom have been paid for Cervantes' release?**

2

Cervantes married and found work as a tax collector in Spain. Writing only in his spare time, he published several poems and plays. He was making a decent living, but he came up against the law. He was imprisoned twice. While in prison, he is believed to have started writing *Don Quixote*. *Don Quixote* is the story of an old man who lives in a dream world fed by reading stories of knights all the time. Don Quixote finds an old suit of armor that had belonged to his great grandfather. He believes he is a knight and then rides around the countryside fighting for justice. His fantasies cause him to confuse what he actually sees with fantastic visions like giants. His squire, a peasant named Sancho Panza, rides with him to try to be the voice of reality. But the old man always gets into trouble.

1. **What job did Cervantes find?**
2. **Why do you think Cervantes only wrote during his spare time?**
3. **Why might *Don Quixote* have been written while Cervantes was in jail?**
4. **Why do you think Don Quixote thinks he is a knight?**
5. **How might Sancho be important to Don Quixote?**

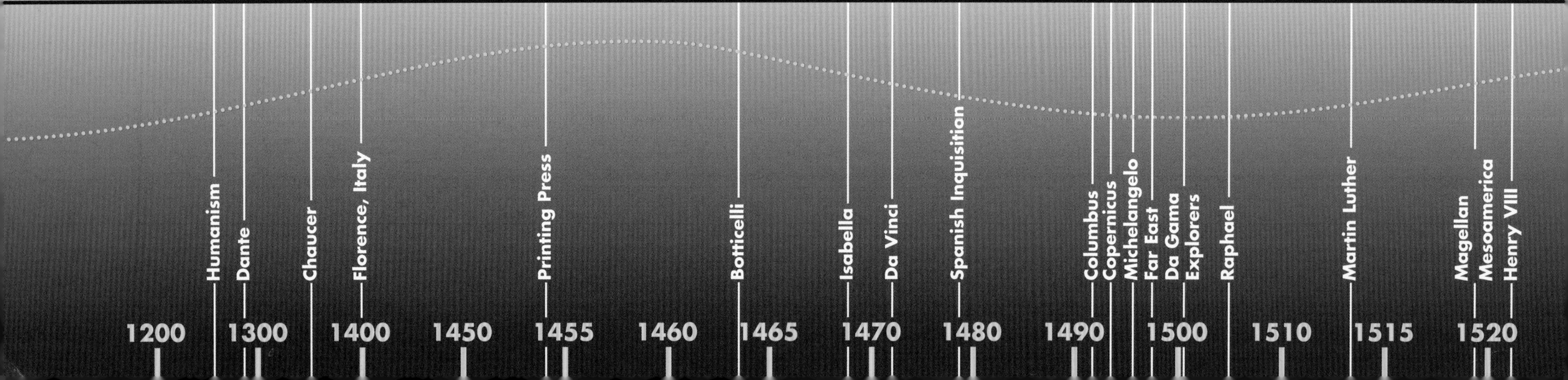
Humanism
Dante
Chaucer
Florence, Italy
Printing Press
Botticelli
Isabella
Da Vinci
Spanish Inquisition
Columbus
Copernicus
Michelangelo
Far East
Da Gama
Explorers
Raphael
Martin Luther
Magellan
Mesoamerica
Henry VIII
1200
1300
1400
1450
1455
1460
1465
1470
1480
1490
1500
1510
1515
1520

3 Don Quixote fills his head with tales of knighthood and chivalry, but he slips into madness at the same time. His squire, Sancho, cannot read or write, and has a weakness for food, but he is wise about the world. He feels that he must protect the old man, Don Quixote. As they travel together, they come upon windmills turning in the breeze, and Quixote exclaims that they are giants. Sancho points out that the arms of the "giants" are really the vanes of the windmill turning. Quixote simply replies, "It is easy to see that you are not used to this business of adventures. Those are giants."

1. **What does Don Quixote mistake for giants?**
2. **Why do you think Don Quixote needs protection?**
3. **Why might Don Quixote need Sancho?**
4. **Why do you think Sancho points out to Don Quixote that the windmills are not giants?**
5. **Why do you think Don Quixote does not believe what Sancho tells him?**

4 Don Quixote imagines himself as a knight, and as such, he needs a noble horse. He only has a weary old horse, but to Quixote it is a fine stallion. He finds a "lady" to serve in the form of a peasant girl he renames Dulcinea del Toboso. He insists he must do great deeds to impress her. His adventures include fighting an army that is really a herd of sheep, and mistaking a barber's metal bowl for the magical Helmet of Mambrino, a great prize. Sancho, his squire, helps save him from many bad situations with his quick mind and fast tongue. But in the end, Don Quixote's story has been told all over Spain, and he is welcomed home as a hero by his village.

1. **What does Don Quixote imagine the herd of sheep to be?**
2. **Why do you think Don Quixote wants to impress a peasant girl?**
3. **Why do you think Don Quixote goes on adventures?**
4. **How might Sancho's quick mind and fast tongue be helpful on their adventures?**
5. **Why do you think Don Quixote is welcomed home as a hero?**

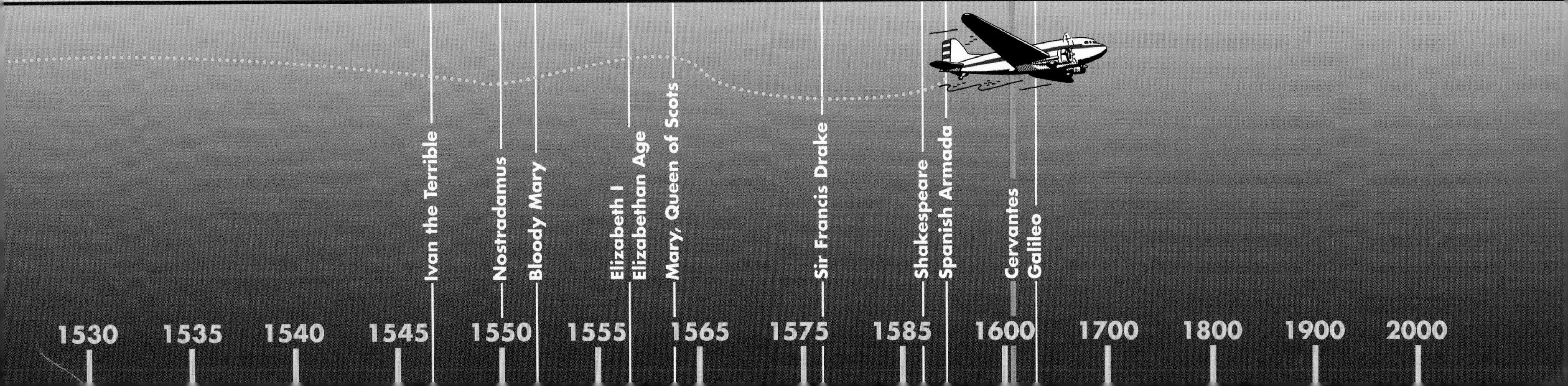
Ivan the Terrible
Nostradamus
Bloody Mary
Elizabeth I
Elizabethan Age
Mary, Queen of Scots
Sir Francis Drake
Shakespeare
Spanish Armada
Cervantes
Galileo
1530
1535
1540
1545
1550
1555
1565
1575
1585
1600
1700
1800
1900
2000

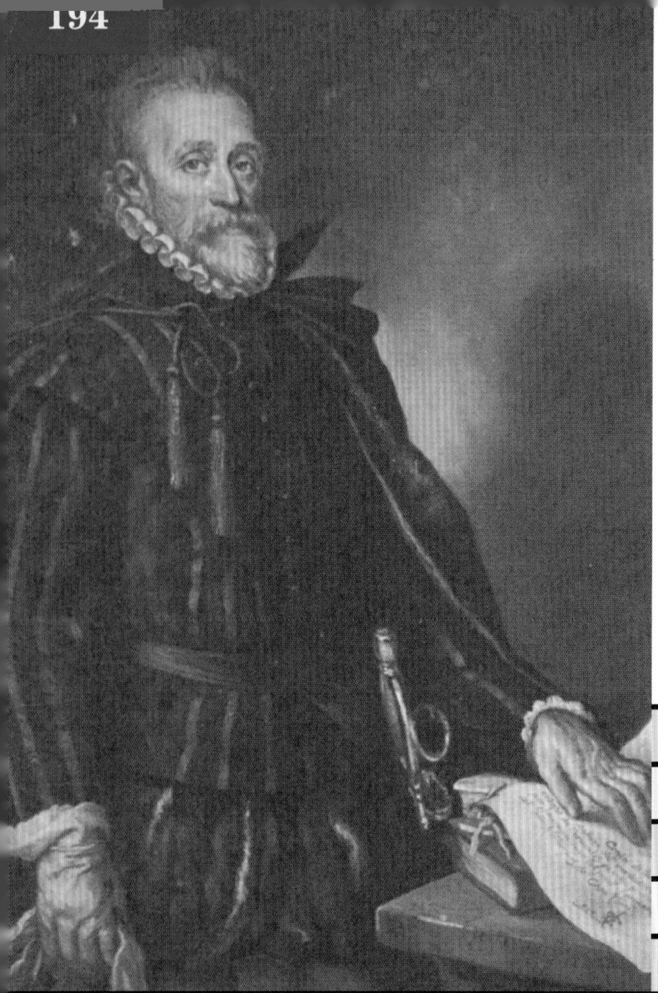

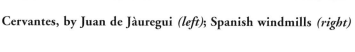

Cervantes, by Juan de Jàuregui *(left)*; Spanish windmills *(right)*

5 The popularity of *Don Quixote* grew in all of Europe. It is filled with funny scenes but also great drama and love. It brought Cervantes great fame, but little fortune. Cervantes continued to write books and poems until his death on April 23, 1616, at age 79. While most of his works have been lost, *Don Quixote* remains one of the most loved books ever written. In fact, it is the second most widely published book in the world today, after the Bible.

1. **How old was Cervantes when he died?**
2. **Why do you think *Don Quixote* became popular all over Europe?**
3. **Why might Cervantes have used both humor and drama in *Don Quixote*?**
4. **Why do you think Cervantes continued to write after *Don Quixote*?**
5. **Why might *Don Quixote* still be popular today?**

This may have been the very cell Cervantes lived in for months *(left)*;
Don Quixote, by Cèlestin-François Nanteuil *(right)*

Ivan says—

Quite a story, isn't it? Like Shakespeare, Cervantes contributed many phrases we still use today. From *Don Quixote,* he gave us the expressions "The sky's the limit," and "Thanks for nothing."

Ironically, Cervantes, the greatest writer in Spanish literature, died on the same date as William Shakespeare, the greatest writer in English literature. The dates were the same, but they actually died ten days apart. England and Spain were using different calendars back then.

You remember how we met Galileo waayyy back in the Spanish Inquisition? Well, next is his story. We're going back to where it all started; Italy. Galileo was a genius ahead of his time...which is a nice way of saying that he was making the kings and popes very uncomfortable. He was confined to house arrest for most of his life. I say, not bad.

Get set for our last Flight in the Renaissance. Enjoy! I'm off to you-know-where.

Flight 33

Galileo

1564-1642

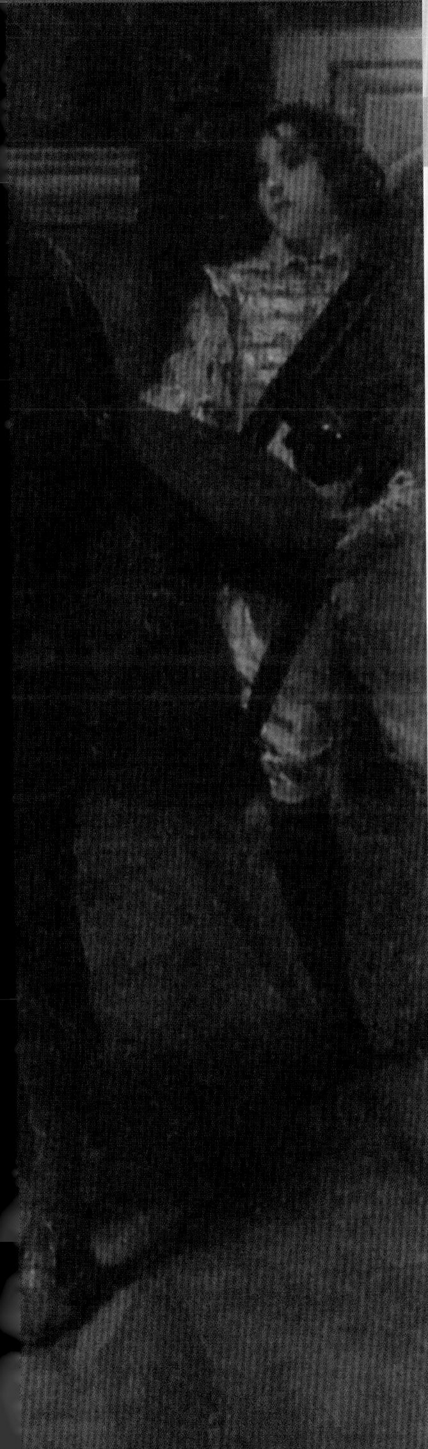

Galileo was often invited to dine with the wealthy and powerful, as shown in this painting

Last time to unbuckle. Spit out the peanuts for the last time. You are going to love Galileo (*Ga-li-LAY-o*). The Renaissance wasn't just about a love of the arts: Many of the new ideas were about science. Some people were learning about the human body, while others were attempting to understand nature, the Earth, or the stars. Some people even managed to find a destructive use for gunpowder, which had been brought from China. This resulted in guns and cannons that changed the way countries fought.

Some people were interested in the works of ancient scholars who were always looking up to the stars and trying to answer the question of why we don't fall right off this big ball called Earth. Each time one of these guys came up with a theory, another guy came along to test it. That's what Galileo did for Copernicus' theory that said the planets revolved around the sun.

I always thought science was really boring, but then I found out about Galileo. He was into pendulums (dangling weights on strings) and telescopes and experimenting with gravity by dropping objects off the Leaning Tower of Pisa (*PEE-za*). Okay, that last part is just a myth, but it sounds great, doesn't it?

Pizza. Pisa. Pizza. Pisa. No contest. Pizza.

1

Galileo Galilei is called the founder of modern science, although he is mostly remembered for his work in astronomy. But most important was his passion for challenging ideas and testing everything for himself. He helped people to better understand the world, the solar system, and the stars. He was born in Pisa, Italy. His father wanted Galileo to become a doctor and support his family. So the young man entered the University of Pisa to study medicine. But he did not want to become a doctor. During his studies, the intensely curious youth had come across Copernicus' and Ptolemy's (*TOE-luh-mee*) works on the universe. Now he wanted to study math and the stars.

1. What did Galileo study when he entered the University of Pisa?

2. Why do you think Galileo challenged ideas and carried out tests?

3. Why do you think Galileo wanted to help people understand the world, the solar system, and the stars?

4. How do you think Copernicus' and Ptolemy's works on the universe affected Galileo?

5. Why do you think it might have been important that Galileo was intensely curious?

2

In Galileo's spare time, he studied *geometry* (a type of math) and took great interest in trying to explain the world around him. He was never content to just believe what everyone else did. He took their beliefs and tested them, to see if they were right or not. Galileo would argue with anyone, loudly and with great passion, and some people avoided talking to him. He was known for tearing the arguments of others apart with no mercy, even making fun of them. Anything that caught his eye could become part of an experiment. Once, Galileo noticed a hanging lamp swinging in the breeze. He felt his heartbeat and used the beat to time the swing of the lamp. He found that long swings lasted the same amount of time as the short swings. This led to the invention of the pendulum clock.

1. What subject did Galileo study in his spare time?

2. Why do you think Galileo tried to explain the world around him?

3. Why do you think Galileo was not content with believing what everyone else did?

4. Why do you think some people avoided talking to Galileo?

5. Why do you think Galileo argued so much?

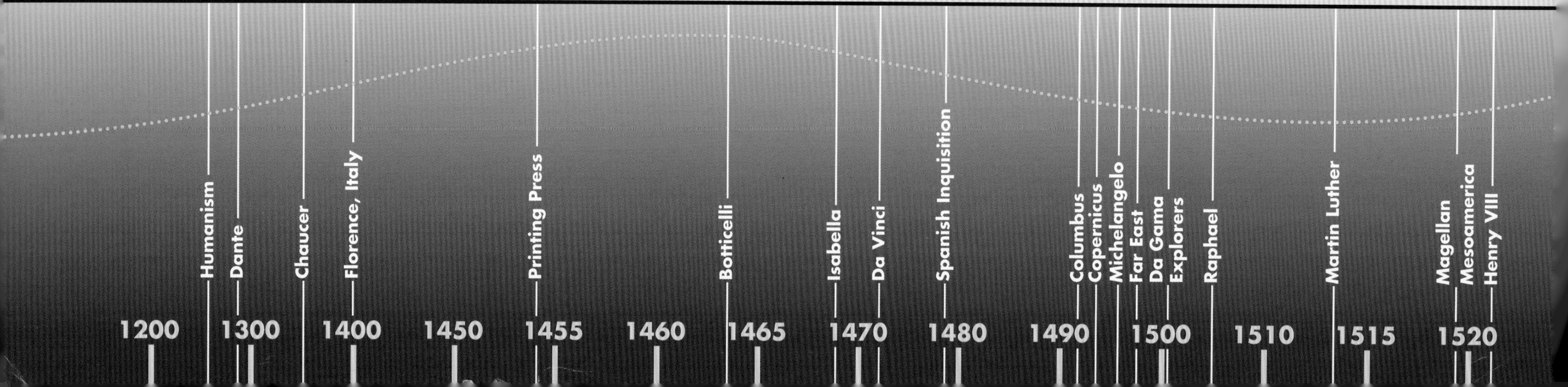

Humanism
Dante
Chaucer
Florence, Italy
Printing Press
Botticelli
Isabella
Da Vinci
Spanish Inquisition
Columbus
Copernicus
Michelangelo
Far East
Da Gama
Explorers
Raphael
Martin Luther
Magellan
Mesoamerica
Henry VIII
1200
1300
1400
1450
1455
1460
1465
1470
1480
1490
1500
1510
1515
1520

3

After four years, Galileo quit his classes in medicine and began to work as a private math tutor. A few years later, the University of Pisa hired him to teach math. Then Galileo began to devote all his free time to his experiments. He first set out to prove that Aristotle's theory of falling objects and gravity was wrong. Aristotle had believed that heavy objects fall faster than light ones. According to legend, Galileo climbed the tall Leaning Tower of Pisa and dropped balls of different weights and sizes off the top. But more than likely, Galileo proved his idea by rolling the balls down a ramp. They all rolled at the same speed, proving the force of gravity was the same for all. He was right, leading to more questions and more experiments.

1. **What subject did the University of Pisa hire Galileo to teach?**
2. **Why do you think Galileo wanted to prove Aristotle's theory to be wrong?**
3. **Why do you think Galileo used experiments to prove Aristotle's theory wrong?**
4. **Why do you think the Leaning Tower of Pisa would be a good place to test the speed of falling objects?**
5. **Why do you think Galileo proving an idea would lead to more questions and experiments?**

4

Next, Galileo turned his attention to the stars in the sky. He used the idea of a Dutch optician (eyeglass maker) who said that a lens could magnify far away objects. Soon Galileo had developed the telescope, which was able to make far-off things appear closer and bigger. Then he did something that had never been done. He used the telescope to observe the sun and discovered sun spots. He saw mountains on the moon, proving it was not a smooth ball, and he found four moons in orbit around Jupiter. He used his observations to prove the long-argued theory that the Earth revolved around the sun. His amazing findings made him very well known.

1. **What tool did Galileo develop and why?**
2. **Why do you think Galileo wanted to magnify far away objects?**
3. **Why do you think Galileo decided to look at the sun with his telescope?**
4. **Do you think Galileo was surprised at what he found as he looked at the moon? Why or why not?**
5. **Why do you think his findings made him well known?**

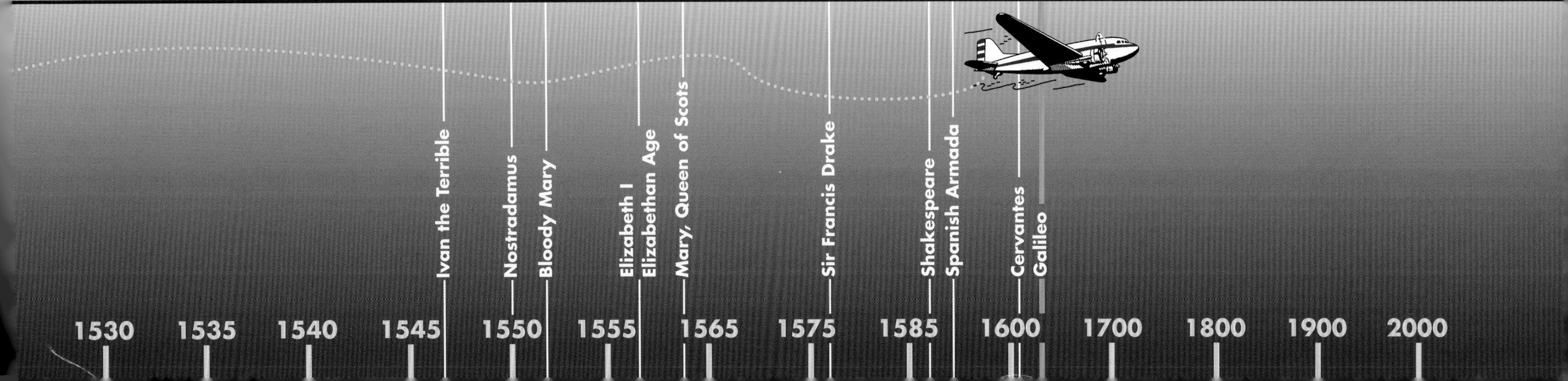
Ivan the Terrible
Nostradamus
Bloody Mary
Elizabeth I
Elizabethan Age
Mary, Queen of Scots
Sir Francis Drake
Shakespeare
Spanish Armada
Cervantes
Galileo
1530
1535
1540
1545
1550
1555
1565
1575
1585
1600
1700
1800
1900
2000

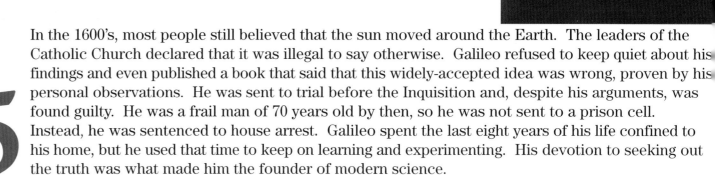

Galileo testifies before the Inquisition *(left)*; portrait of Galileo, 1636 *(right)*

5

In the 1600's, most people still believed that the sun moved around the Earth. The leaders of the Catholic Church declared that it was illegal to say otherwise. Galileo refused to keep quiet about his findings and even published a book that said that this widely-accepted idea was wrong, proven by his personal observations. He was sent to trial before the Inquisition and, despite his arguments, was found guilty. He was a frail man of 70 years old by then, so he was not sent to a prison cell. Instead, he was sentenced to house arrest. Galileo spent the last eight years of his life confined to his home, but he used that time to keep on learning and experimenting. His devotion to seeking out the truth was what made him the founder of modern science.

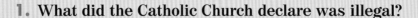

1. **What did the Catholic Church declare was illegal?**
2. **Why do you think Galileo refused to keep quiet?**
3. **Why do you think Galileo published his findings if he knew it was illegal?**
4. **Why do you think Galileo kept on learning and experimenting?**
5. **How might Galileo's devotion to seeking out the truth be important?**

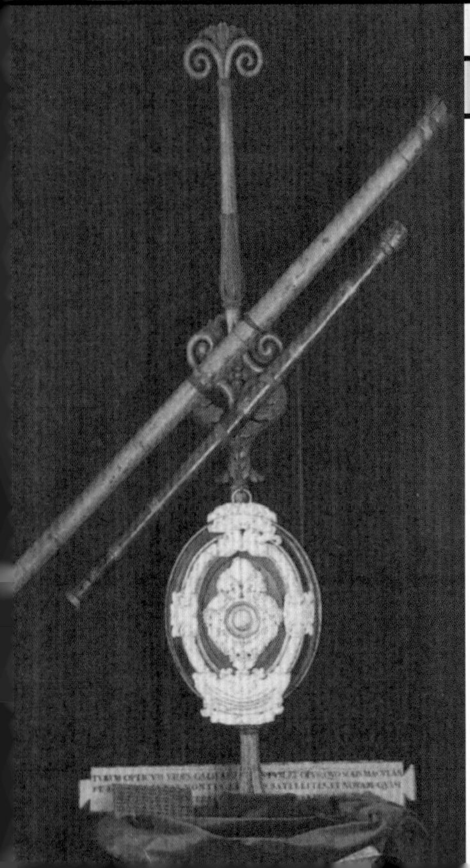

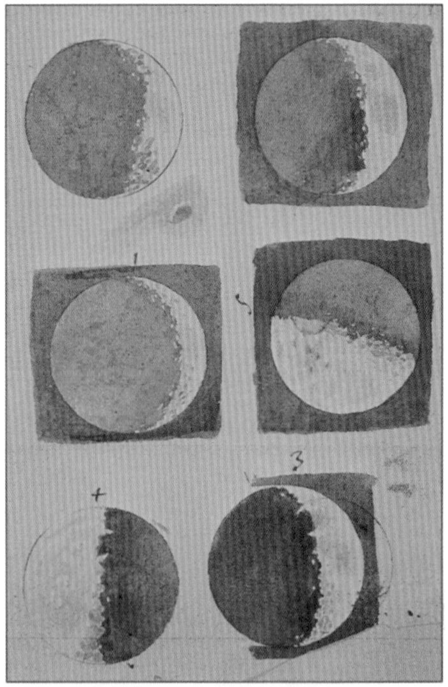

Galileo's telescope *(left)*; Galileo's own drawings of the phases of the moon *(right)*

Ivan says—

The man of science! Galileo opened the door for scientists everywhere. He held it open for them too. Such a polite fellow. In the next few centuries, the world changed dramatically, in part because of Galileo. He was in demand during his life, as the guest of many queens, kings, and important people, to explain his theories. Many young minds were exposed to Galileo's ideas and some of those minds went on to become scientists themselves, inspired by the old man.

Well, we've reached the end of the Renaissance. Now the world entered into an Age of Kings. The kings and queens of Europe raced around to gain control of all the new lands that had been discovered. They were getting richer than ever, and some of their kingdoms, like England, grew into empires. It was good to be King!

And now, you're done! I, being the king of this age—or at least this neighborhood—congratulate you on a job well done. Now enjoy a look at the best artists of the Renaissance as your Side Trip begins. I'd let these guys do a portrait of me any day...and they would all *want* to. Yes, they would.

The Side Trip

Here we go on our side trip! Yippee. No more airplanes. This is a cultural event, a real society party. These four men are the best artists that ever graced this planet, and they all developed their genius during the Renaissance. Without these guys, art would be in a sorry state. They're like a superhero team of artists. Take a tour with me in our *See Time Fly* museum of art. Each piece of art here is a masterpiece...one-of-a-kind...awe-inspiring...a little like me.

The Punishment of Korah, Dathan, and Abrham, 1481-82, fresco, Rome, Palazzi Vaticani, Sistine Chapel

Young Man, ca. 1490, Washington, D.C., National Portrait Gallery

Detail from *The Birth of Venus,* 1483-85, tempera on canvas, Florence, Galleria degli Uffizi

Botticelli (1445-1510)

A sketch that includes Botticelli's signature

Young Woman in Mythological Guise, 1480-85, tempera on panel, Frankfurt, Stadelsches Kuninstitut

Lamentation over the Dead Christ, 1490-92, tempera on wood, Munich, Alte Pinakothek

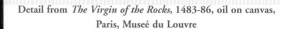

Detail from *The Virgin of the Rocks,* 1483-86, oil on canvas, Paris, Museé du Louvre

The Last Supper, 1495-98, wall painting, Milan, Santa Maria delle Grazie, Refectory

Young Woman Holding an Ermine, 1488-90, oil on canvas, Craców, Czartoryski Muzeum

Girl with a Unicorn, ca. 1478, pen and ink, Oxford, Ashmolean Museum

Leonardo da Vinci (1452-1519)

Sketch of the muscles of the right arm, pen and brown ink on paper

Leonardo's notes include the question, "What are the muscles that are united in men of extraordinary strength?"

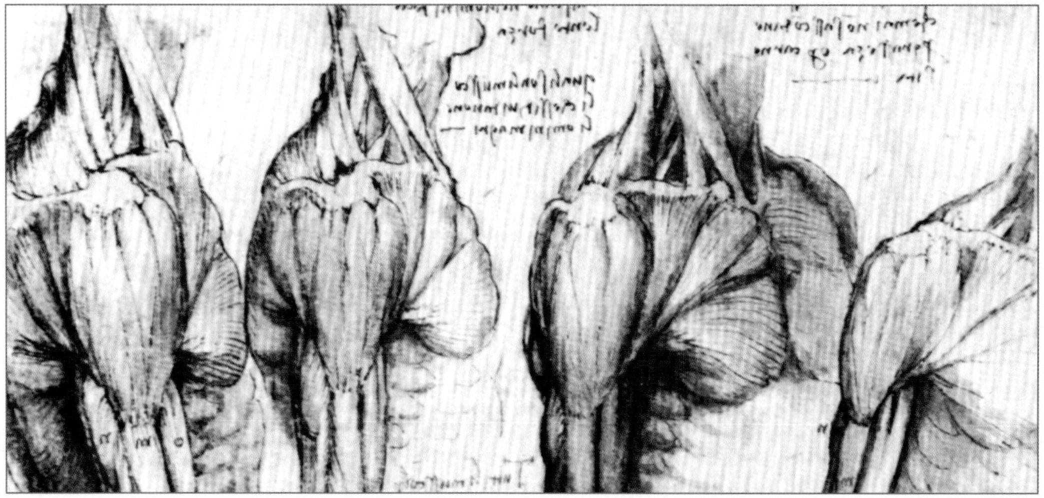

Sketch of a flower, 1483, pen and ink over metalpoint, Venice, Accademia Galleria

Vitruvian Man

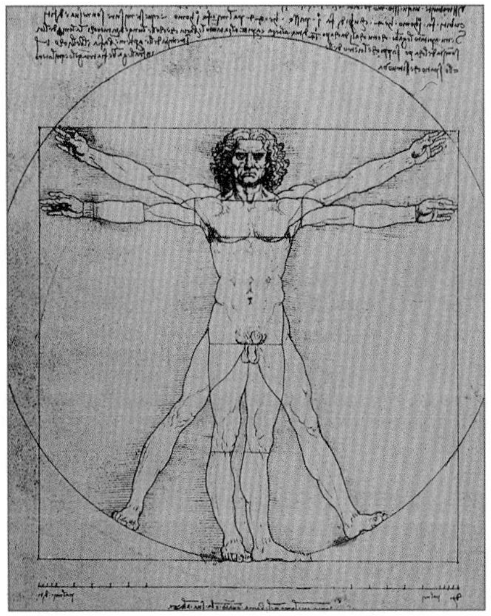

Michelangelo (1475-1564)

David, detail of statue, 1498-99, marble, 13' 5", Florence, Palazzo Vecchio

The Delphic Sibyl, 1508-12, fresco, Rome, Palazzi Vaticani, Sistine Chapel

Study for the Libyan Sibyl, 1508-12, red chalk, New York, Metropolitan Museum of Art

The Bound Slave, 1513-15, marble, Paris, Museé du Louvre

Self-portrait, painting the Sistine, 1508-12, Florence, Casa Buonarroti

Cleopatra, 1533-34, black chalk, Florence, Galleria degli Uffizi

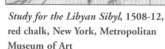

The Libyan Sibyl, 1508-12, fresco, Rome, Palazzi Vaticani, Sistine Chapel

Raphael (1483-1520)

Baldassare Castiglione, 1514-15, oil on canvas, Paris, Museé du Louvre

Study, 1517-20, black and white chalk, Amsterdam, Rijksmuseum

Vision of Ezekiel, 1518, oil on panel, Florence, Galleria Palatine, Palazzo Pitti

Study for St. Michael and the Dragon, ca. 1505, pen and ink, Venice, Accademia Galleria

St. Catherine of Alexandria, 1508, oil on canvas, London, National Gallery

The Triumph of Galatea, 1511, fresco, Rome, Villa Farnesina

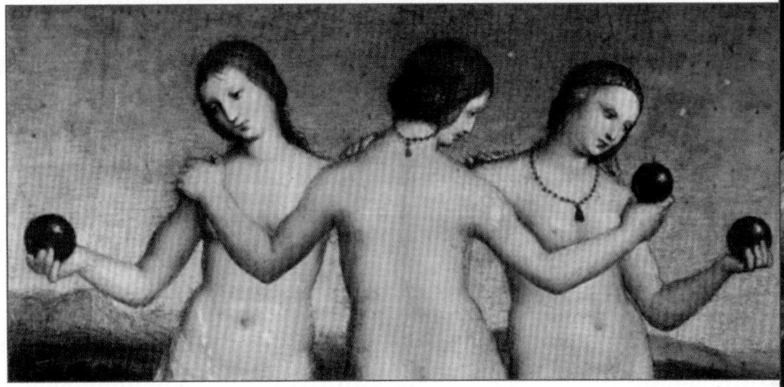

Detail from *The Three Graces*, 1504-05, oil on panel, Chantilly, Museé Condé

Joanna of Aragón, ca. 1505, oil on canvas, Private Collection

Ivan says—

Wasn't that an exciting tour? That artwork was amazing. Botticelli, da Vinci, Michelangelo, and Raphael—those guys really knew how to make jaws drop. The beauty of the paintings and sculptures made during the Renaissance still influences artists today.

I'm glad that you joined me on this journey through time. Some of the flights have been tough, but you made it. I knew you could do it. You can do anything!

I'll meet you again in *See Time Fly #3: The Age of Kings*. There, we'll visualize rich kings, daring explorers, fine artists and talented musicians. Sounds a lot like the Renaissance—except with more kings.

I'm a king, too, King of the Neighborhood. I'll fit right in!

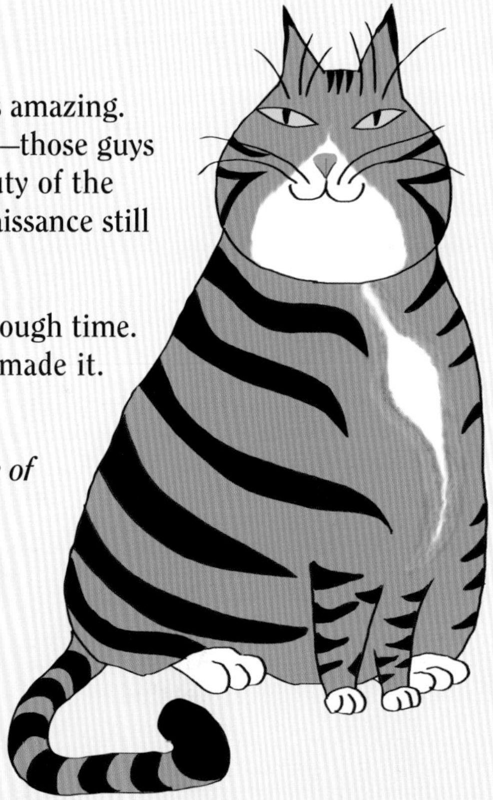

Glossary of People, Places & Events

Africa The second largest continent in the world (after Asia). Africa's terrain ranges from lush rain forests to the arid Sahara Desert.

America (New World) The continents of North, Central, and South America, where the modern United States, Canada, Mexico, and many other countries are located. Although populated, the New World was undiscovered by Europeans at the start of the Renaissance.

Ancient Greece The civilization of ancient Greece lasted many hundreds of years, but was at its height during 800-100 B.C. The Greeks created a culture so influential that it continues to affect the world today. The ancient Greeks made monumental strides in the arts, language, and philosophy, and their concept of the ideal human was adopted and spread by the Renaissance.

Anne of Cleves (1515-1557) Fourth queen to, and wife of, Henry VIII.

Aristotle (384–322 B.C.) Aristotle was one of the three most important Greek philosophers and teachers. He studied under Plato at the Academy, and wrote *Metaphysics*, *Rhetoric*, and *Poetica*, among many other works. He was the founder of biology, a leader in metaphysical thinking and modern physics, and the developer of logical thought, notably Aristotelian logic.

Armada, Spanish Fleet launched by Philip II of Spain for the invasion of England, in 1588; also called the Invincible Armada. The Armada consisted of 130 ships and about 30,000 men.

Asia The largest continent in the world. It includes such modern countries as China, India, Nepal, Mongolia, Pakistan, Russia, and more.

astrologer Someone who studies the positions of the stars in order to tell the future.

Atahuallpa (d. 1532) Ruler of the Incan Empire; son of Huayna Capac. He took the throne from Quito, in 1525, and invaded the lands of his brother, Huascar, in order to unite the Incan Empire under his name. He was killed by Pizarro, in 1532.

Atlantic Ocean Second largest sea on Earth that extends from Europe and Africa to the eastern side of North and South America.

Aztec Empire A large empire of American Indian people. They settled in the Valley of Mexico at the end of the 12th century. Their capital was Tenochtitlan. They defeated tribes from the north of Mexico to Guatemala to become a huge empire. The Aztec Empire was completely destroyed by Spanish conquistadors by 1525.

Bible The book of the sacred writings of of the religions of Christianity and Judaism. The first part is the Old Testament, which contains the sacred writings of the Jews, originally in Hebrew. The second part is the New Testament, originally composed in Greek, which relates the life of Christ and the growth of Christianity.

Black Death In the mid-14th century, the bubonic plague ravaged most of Europe, killing nearly a third of the population. Spread by fleas and rats, the plague was nicknamed the Black Death because of the black spots that appeared on the bodies of the victims. The Black Death raged for six years.

Boccaccio, Giovanni (1313-1375) Italian poet and writer; author of the *Decameron*. He was born in Paris and educated in Naples. He was a scholar of Latin and Greek works. His works include *Teseida*, *Ninfale d'Ameto*, and *Corbaccio*.

Boleyn, Anne (1507?-1536) Second queen to, and wife of, Henry VIII. Mother of Elizabeth I.

Borgia, Lucrezia (1480-1519) An Italian noblewoman, she was the daughter of Pope Alexander VI. She was married three times by her family, the last to Alfonso d'Este, Duke of Ferran. She supported the arts and was a patron to many artists and writers.

Botticelli (1445-1510) Born Alessandro di Mariano Filipepi, in Florence, and called Sandro, he was a famous painter and a favorite of the powerful Medici family. He painted frescoes at the Vatican. His most important works include *Spring*, *Birth of*

Venus, *Magnificat*, and the *Madonna of the Pomegranate*.

boyar A member of the nobility, or privileged class, of Russia prior to Peter the Great; able to have a role in government.

Cabot, John (1450-1498) An English explorer who relocated to Venice, in 1476, and sailed the trade routes. In the 1480's, he returned to England and then sailed from there to discover the North American coast, in 1497. A second expedition that sailed in 1498, led to his disappearance with his son.

cacao A tropical tree native to the Americas, where it was prized by the Aztecs for its fruit. The fruit is a pod containing a sweetish pulp and rows of seeds (beans). The pods were fermented and the seeds removed, cured, and roasted. Then the kernels are made into several things, one of which is a powder (cocoa) that is the prime ingredient in chocolate.

Canada A modern country on the continent of North America, north of the United States, made up of provinces and territories, including Quebec and Montreal.

Catherine of Aragón (1485-1536) First queen to, and wife of, Henry VIII. Catherine was the daughter of Ferdinand II of Aragón and Isabella of Castile. She was married in 1501, to Arthur, the older brother of Henry VIII, and upon his death, was married to Henry. She was the mother of Mary I.

Catholic, Roman see Christianity.

Central America Land that sits between Mexico and South America. It consists of seven small modern nations: Belize, Guatemala, El Salvador, Honduras, Nicaragua, Costa Rica, and Panama. It was home to the Maya and Aztecs.

Cervantes (1547-1616) Born in Alcalá de Henares, Spain, Miguel de Cervantes Saavedra went to Italy, in 1569, to study under a cardinal. In 1570, he enlisted in the army and fought in the naval battle of Lepanto (1571). He was captured by Barbary pirates and sold as a slave. He was ransomed, in 1580, and went on to write *Don Quixote*, as well as *La Galatea* and *Novelas Ejemplares*.

Charles V (1500-1558) Known as Charles I, ruler of Spain, and as Charles V, Holy Roman Emperor. He was the son of Philip I and Joanna of Castile, and was the grandson of Ferdinand II and Isabella, and Holy Roman Emperor Maximilian I.

Charles IX (1550-1574) Successor to his brother, Francis II, under the regency of his mother, Catherine de Medici. He was succeeded by his brother Henry III, upon his death.

Chaucer, Geoffrey (1340?-1400) Chaucer was born in England and served as a page in the household of Prince Lionel, later the Duke of Clarence. He served in the army of Edward III and later married Philippa Roet, a lady-in-waiting to the queen of England. He served as a diplomat for many years, and was known for his poetry. His works include *The Canterbury Tales*, *Troilus and Criseyde*, and *The Parliament of Fowls*.

China Located in Asia, China is the third largest modern country in the world. Its main religions are Buddhism and Confucianism. Throughout its history, China has mostly been ruled by family dynasties of emperors. Genghis Khan and Kublai Khan, Mongol warlords, ruled for a time. China is currently a Communist country and is the home of the Great Wall of China.

Christianity The largest worldwide religion. Christianity is based on the life and teachings of Jesus Christ. He preached of a kind, gentle, and Holy God, whom he said was his father. After his crucifixion, Christ's followers continued his teachings of love and fellowship, and developed the Bible, a sacred book. Major branches of Christianity include the Roman Catholic Church, the Lutheran Church, and the Protestant Church of England.

Church, Roman Catholic The Roman Catholic Church, (often just called, "The Church") is the largest and oldest of all Christian churches. Its central authority is the bishop of Rome, known as the Pope, based in the Vatican, in Vatican City, Italy. It was formed between 60 and 70 A.D. and gained great power from the 6th to 16th centuries.

cleric A person who works for the church and can read and write. They kept records and made copies of books and important church documents.

Columbus, Christopher (1451-1506) An explorer, born in Italy. Columbus spent many years in Portugal as a master mariner in the merchant service. He developed a plan he called "Enterprise of the Indies," and tried to get financing. After failing in Portugal, he made

his way to Spain and got the funding from the king and queen there. He sailed west, in 1492, but due to an error in his calculations, he landed on San Salvador, in the Bahamas, then Hispaniola. He made a second voyage, in 1493, again reaching the islands. Columbus never reached the Far East, but he is credited with discovering the New World (including North, South, and Central America).

conquistador A Spanish soldier sent to explore in the New World.

Copernicus, Nikolaus (1473-1543) A Polish astronomer. He studied medicine, astronomy, law, and mathematics at the University of Kraków. He later settled in Prussia where he researched and wrote *De Revolutionibus Orbium Coelestrium*, in which he detailed his heliocentric (sun-centered) view of the solar system. Though finished in 1530, it was not published until shortly before his death.

Coronado, Francisco (1510?-1554) A Spanish explorer, he led an expedition from 1540-1542 to the American Southwest in search of the fabled El Dorado, the Seven Cities of Gold. He nearly destroyed the American Indian Pueblo civilization.

Cortés, Hernán (1485-1547) A Spanish conquistador, he went to the New World in 1504, and again with Velázquez, in 1511. In 1519, he got his own expedition started, and went on to conquer Mexico. He first negotiated with, then killed Montezuma, emperor of the Aztecs. His army wiped out the Aztec Empire.

court (royal) The main meeting area of the king and/or queen and their advisors and courtiers. The term also refers to the members allowed to meet or socialize in court, usually nobles and advisors.

Da Gama, Vasco (1469-1524) A Portuguese sailor and navigator who sailed with orders from King Manuel I, to set up trade with India and the Far East. He found a new sea route to the Indies. With a fleet of 20 ships, on his second voyage, he established Portugal's hold over Indian waters and was honored as Count of Vidigueria and Admiral of the Sea of India.

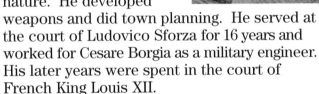

Da Vinci, Leonardo (1452-1519) Born in Tuscany, Italy, he moved to Florence at 14 years of age to work under Verrocchio in a workshop. In 1472, he was registered into the painters' guild and soon became a musician, scientist, artist, and engineer. In addition to his incredible artwork, da Vinci studied anatomy, biology, and nature. He developed weapons and did town planning. He served at the court of Ludovico Sforza for 16 years and worked for Cesare Borgia as a military engineer. His later years were spent in the court of French King Louis XII.

Dante (1265-1321) A poet and writer; author of *The Divine Comedy*. Dante Alighieri was born in Florence, where he served in the cavalry. Dante married Gemma Donati and had three children. He served as councilman, elector, and other political positions. Some of his other works include *La Vita Nuova*, *Convivo*, and *De Monarchia*.

Dias, Bartolomeu (1450?-1500) A sea captain and explorer born in Portugal, he found the passage around the southern tip of Africa.

Drake, Sir Francis (1540?-1596) English navigator and admiral. He is credited with being the first Englishman to circumnavigate the world. He was a pirate and an explorer, and a favorite of Queen Elizabeth's, who knighted

him on board his ship, the *Golden Hind*. He served as Vice Admiral in the fleet that defeated the Spanish Armada, in 1588.

Edward VI (1537-1553) Son and third child of Henry VIII and Jane Seymour. Edward Tudor succeeded his father to the throne of England when he was nine. His reign was short, and the sickly boy died of tuberculosis at 15. He was survived by his half-sisters, Mary I and Elizabeth I.

Elizabeth I (1533-1603) Queen of England from 1558-1603. Elizabeth Tudor was the daughter of Henry VIII and Anne Boleyn, the second of Henry's children. She assumed the throne after the death of her sister, Mary I. She was a patron of the arts and a lover of theater. She ruled over a period that is now referred to as the Golden Age, or the Elizabethan Age. Never married, she was succeeded by James I, the son of Mary, Queen of Scots.

England The largest country in Great Britain,

also called the United Kingdom. England sits on the southern part of the English Island, below Scotland. England lies directly across the English Channel from France. The two countries of England and France fought wars with each other for centuries.

Europe Europe is the sixth largest continent and includes the modern countries of United Kingdom, France, Germany, Austria, Spain, Portugal, Scandinavia, Denmark, Italy, Switzerland, and Greece among others.

Far East A area of countries that included the Spice Islands and the modern countries of China, Japan, and India, among others.

Ferdinand II (1452-1516) King of Aragón, Sicily, Naples, and León. He married Isabella I and united and ruled Spain with her. Their daughter Catherine later married Henry VIII.

Fra Filippo Lippi (1406-1469) An artist in Florence, he was one of the most famed fresco painters of his time. He served as a teacher to Botticelli, among others.

France A country in the continent of Europe. France lies directly across the English Channel from England, and was for many centuries its main rival.

fresco The technique of painting on a moist plaster surface with colors ground up in water. The paint must be applied while the plaster is still wet or it will not stick.

Galileo (1564-1642) Galileo Galilei was an Italian mathematician, astronomist, scientist, and physicist. He developed new telescopes, a microscope, and several other breakthroughs. He served as a professor at the University of Pisa and discovered the four largest moons of Jupiter. He was denounced by the Inquisition and spent the last years of his life under house arrest. His most famous work is *Dialogues Concerning Two New Sciences.*

Genghis Khan (1162?-1227) A title meaning, "universal leader," given to Temujin of Mongolia. By 1206, he had united the Mongol tribes and earned this title, which is now used in place of his name. By 1220, he had seized all of China and most of Asia. His army, the Mongol Horde, was one of the largest armies ever assembled.

Gentileschi, Artemisia (1597-1652) Born in Tuscany, she was the daughter of painter Orazio Gentileschi and became an artist herself. In 1616, she became the first woman ever admitted to the Academy of Design in Florence, and was in great demand for her talent.

geometry The area of mathematics dealing with the relationships and measurements of lines, planes, and solids.

Germany A large country in central Europe, once known as part of the Holy Roman Empire.

Greece A country in southeastern Europe that was home to one of the last of the ancient civilizations. Many of the greatest philosophers and writers came from Greece.

Grey, Lady Jane (1537-1554) A niece of Henry VII, she was the pawn in a plot to take the throne away from Mary I, but the plot was foiled and her rule lasted only nine days. She was executed.

Guam An island in the western Pacific Ocean that currently belongs to the United States. Europeans first discovered it when Magellan and his ships landed there, in 1521, on his voyage around the world.

Gutenberg, Johannes (1395?-1468) A German inventor, goldsmith, and printer. He is credited with the invention of the printing press.

Hebrew see Jewish.

Henry (Henry the Navigator) (1394-1460) Prince of Portugal, he was fascinated with exploration, and sent out many expeditions. He served in the army and was named Duke of Viseu by his father John I, King of Portugal. He financed many trips around Africa and to the Indies. The successful voyages brought in riches and advanced navigational science.

Henry VII (1457-1509) King of England from 1485-1509. He was of the Tudor family and his crowning was the beginning of the Tudor reign.

Henry VIII (1491-1547) King of England from 1509-1547. Henry Tudor was born the second son to Henry VII, but his brother's death left him on the throne in 1509. He married Catherine of Aragón, and then separated England from the Roman Catholic Church to obtain a divorce. He formed the Church of

England with himself as its head, and married five more times. He was succeeded by his young son, Edward VI, and by his daughters Mary I and Elizabeth I.

heresy Beliefs or views held by a member of a church that contradict its central beliefs. If a churchgoer was convicted of heresy, they could face any of a number of punishments, from exile to death.

heretic One who speaks or writes anything that contradicts the central beliefs of a church.

Howard, Catherine (1521?-1542) Fifth queen to, and wife of, Henry VIII. She was the daughter of Lord Edmund Howard.

Hudson, Henry (d. 1611) An English navigator and explorer who tried on several voyages to find the Northwest Passage, a fabled water route through North America, from the Atlantic Ocean to the Pacific Ocean. On his fourth trip, his crew, starving and trapped in ice, mutinied and set him and his son adrift in a boat.

Humanism A philosophical and literary movement of the Renaissance in which man and his abilities are the sole concern, rather than outside or supernatural forces. Humanism reflects a return to the ideals of human behavior as defined by the Greeks.

Inca The Inca lived in parts of South America that included present-day Peru, Argentina, and Bolivia, until the arrival of the Spaniards, in 1532. The Incan Empire was the largest in the Americas, numbering about 12 million people before its downfall, in the 1500's.

India A country in the southern part of Asia. It was a major trading center for textiles, spices, and other goods. Bordered by the Indian Ocean to the south and the Himalayas to the north, its capital is New Delhi. Calicut was a major trade city during the Renaissance.

Indian Ocean The large body of water found between the continents of Africa and Australia and below India.

inventor Someone who makes something for the first time.

Ireland An island in the Atlantic Ocean, west of Great Britain, that is currently divided into Northern Ireland and the Republic of Ireland. Northern Ireland is part of the United Kingdom.

Isabella I (1451-1504) Queen of Castile and later Spain, she married Ferdinand of Aragón to unite the kingdoms of Spain. Together, they conquered Granada, drove the Moors out of Spain, and implemented the Spanish Inquisition. Their daughter, Catherine, later married Henry VIII, of England.

Islam Islam is the second of the three largest religions of the world. Muslims exist in every part of the world. The Prophet Muhammad founded the religion in the 7th century in Arabia. Adherents read and follow the sacred words of the Koran.

Israelites see Jewish

Italy Italy is a country on the continent of Europe that includes the cities of Rome, Venice, and Genoa. Rome is the legendary home of Vatican City, the separate state of the Vatican, and the Pope of the Roman Catholic Church. It was also the center of the Roman Empire.

Ivan IV (1530-1584) Also known as Ivan the Terrible. Ivan the IV (Vasilyevich) assumed the rule of Russia when he was only three years old, and his mother served as his regent. In 1547, he was crowned and married a noble named Anastasia soon after.

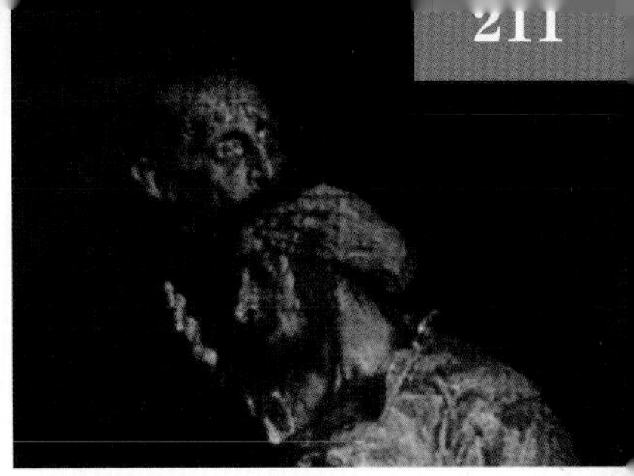

He increased Russia's power and territory, but also created a secret police and terrorized any who opposed him. He was the first Russian ruler to assume the title of Czar (also Tsar). He was succeeded by sons, Feodor I and Dmitri.

James I (1566-1625) King of England from 1603 to 1625. Also known as James VI, King of Scotland. James Stuart was the son of Mary, Queen of Scots and succeeded Elizabeth I. He sent men to colonize the New World. He was succeeded by his son, Charles I.

Jewish (Hebrew, Israelites) A religious group, the Jewish people trace their ancestry to Abraham and Isaac (3000-2000 B.C.) and follow Judaism. Their spiritual center is Jerusalem, Israel. The country of Israel was created in 1948 on the site of ancient holy lands in the Middle East, where an Israelite kingdom once stood.

Latin The language of ancient Rome, used by scholars throughout the Middle Ages and Renaissance, and still considered the language of science and academia.

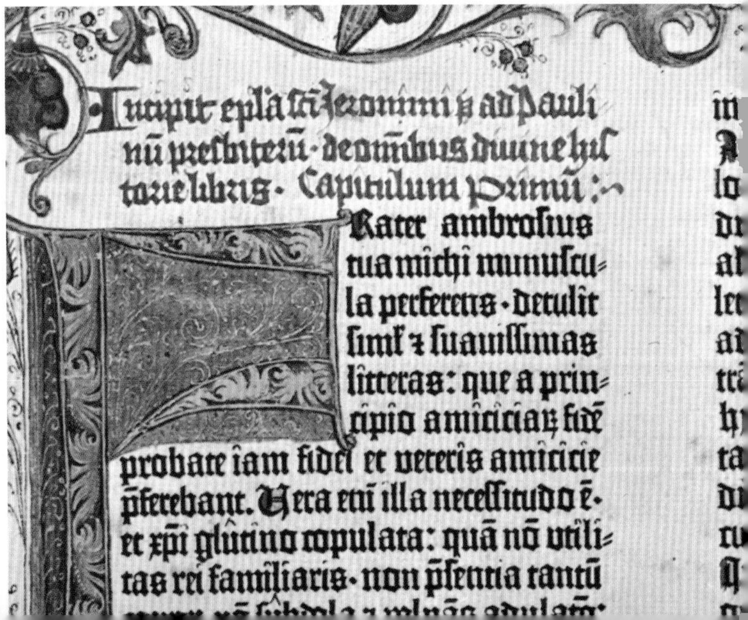

Magellan, Ferdinand (1480-1521) Portuguese navigator and explorer, he was born into a noble family and served in the navy. King Manuel turned down his request to fund an expedition, so he went to Spain, and Charles I approved it. He sailed in 1519, and is credited as the first man to circumnavigate the Earth.

Manuel I (1469-1521) King Manuel of Portugal succeeded his cousin, John II, in 1495, and funded the development of overseas trade with India, China, and the Spice Islands.

Martin Luther (1483-1546) A German monk who started the Reformation movement when he wrote and published the *Ninety-Five Theses*. His original intention in starting the Reformation was to reform the corrupt members and practices of the Church. But when the Church would not accept his changes, he broke away from it. He was later tried for heresy and excommunicated. Those who followed him in breaking away from the Roman Catholic Church called themselves Lutherans and/or Protestants.

Mary I (1516-1558) Mary Tudor was the Queen of England and Ireland, daughter of Henry VIII, and married Philip II, of Spain. She was a devout Catholic. She restored the Catholic Church to England and banned the Church of England and Protestantism during her reign (1553-1558).

Mary, Queen of Scots (1542-1587) Mary Stuart, also known as Mary, Queen of Scots, was the Catholic daughter of King James V of Scotland. She was married to the King of France until his early death in 1560. She also married Henry Stuart, the Lord of Darnley, and James Hepburn. She was the mother of James, who later became James I, King of England and James IV, King of Scotland. Mary made attempts to seize the English throne from Protestant Elizabeth I, for which treason she was arrested, tried, and executed.

Medici, Cosimo (1389-1464) The first of the Medici family to rule Florence. He was also called Cosimo the Elder. As a merchant and banker, he built up a large fortune and was a patron of the arts.

Medici, Lorenzo (1449-1492) Merchant prince and head of the Medici family, he was grandson of Cosimo and son of Pier. He was known as Lorenzo the Magnificent. He ruled Florence and was a patron of the arts. He spent a great deal of money buying Greek and Roman texts and had them translated.

Medicis, Catherine de (1519-1589) Daughter of Lorenzo de'Medici, the Duke of Urbino. She was married to the Duc d'Orléans, who later became the French king, Henry II. She served as regent for her underage, son Charles IX, until he took the throne, and then she served as his advisor.

Mediterranean Sea Known as *Mare Nostrum* (our sea) to the Romans, the Mediterranean is an inland sea, bordering Africa, Asia, and Europe. It is linked to the Atlantic Ocean by the Strait of Gibraltar. It has been a center of trading and exploration through the ages.

Mexico A country that connects North America with Central America. Mexico was home to the Maya and the Aztecs.

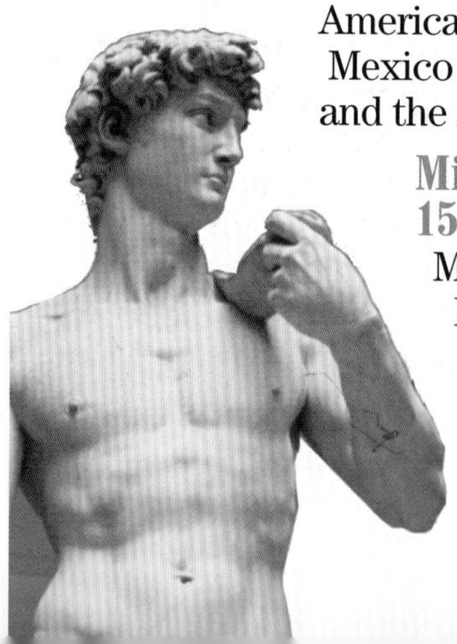

Michelangelo (1475-1564) Born Michelangelo Buonarroti, an Italian sculptor, painter, engineer, architect, and artist. He is widely considered to be one of the finest artists in history. He sculpted *David* and *La Pietá*, and he painted the ceiling of the Sistine Chapel in Rome, Italy.

Ming Dynasty (1368-1644) A family of rulers who grabbed control of China after the fall of the Mongols. They were the last native Chinese dynasty to rule the empire. Members of this family dynasty ruled China for more than 275 years. This period was one of China's most prosperous and peaceful times.

Mongols A united group of Mongol tribes and organized under leader Genghis Khan. By 1220, they had seized all of China and most of Asia. The Mongol Horde was one of the largest armies ever assembled.

Montezuma (d. 1520) Last Emperor of the Aztec Empire, he was killed by Spanish conquistadors.

Moors Once a nomadic people of North Africa, they migrated into Europe, settling mainly in Spain. Moors are mostly of Berber and Arab heritage, and the majority are Muslim.

Mughal India was unified by Mughal Emperor Akbar (1542-1605). India was then under the power of the ruling class, the Mughal. The Mughal held the country until 1707, when the empire fell apart. The Mughal were Muslim.

Muslim A person who follows the teachings of Muhammad. (see also, Islam)

mutiny An act of disobedience or betrayal by persons on a ship or in the military in which a group takes over command of the vessel or situation from the authority.

Netherlands A country in northern Europe. Much of the country lies below sea level and is kept dry by dikes that hold back the ocean. It is also called Holland, or the Low Countries. The capital city is Amsterdam.

New World see America

Nostradamus (1503-1566) A French astrologer and doctor, born Michel de Nostredame, who wrote rhymed prophecies under the title, *Centuries*.

oprichniki A secret elite police force established by Ivan the Terrible, Czar of Russia, to carry out his private orders.

Pacific Ocean The largest and deepest ocean in the world. This ocean covers about 1/3 of the Earth's surface. It extends from the western side of North and South America to the eastern side of Japan, Asia, and Australia.

Parr, Catherine (1512-1548) Sixth queen to, and wife of, Henry VIII. She was the daughter of Sir Thomas Parr, an officeholder at court, and was twice widowed before her marriage to Henry. She was responsible for educating Mary I and Elizabeth I. She married for a fourth time, after the death of Henry VIII, in 1547.

patron A person who finances an artist, writer, musician or other creative person, paying their bills so that he/she can focus on his/her art.

Perugino (1445-1523?) A famous painter from Umbria in Italy, who studied with da Vinci. Raphael was one of his students. His major works include *The Crucifixion* and *Madonna and Saints*.

Petrarch, Francesco (1304-1374) Italian poet and humanist whose style became a model for Italian literature for the next three centuries.

Philip II (1527-1598) King of Spain, Naples, and Sicily, and son of Holy Roman Emperor Charles V. He married England's Queen Mary I, and after her death, tried to marry her half-sister, Queen Elizabeth I. Sent the Spanish Armada to invade England, in 1588.

Philippines A collection of islands in the Southwestern Pacific. The Philippines were under Spanish control during the Renaissance.

Pizarro, Francisco (1476-1541) Spanish conquistador who conquered Peru and killed Atahuallpa, the leader of the Incan Empire.

plague A deadly disease that spreads quickly and easily. (see also, Black Death)

Plato (428-347 B.C.) One of the three most important Greek philosophers and teachers. He studied under, and preserved the teachings of, Socrates. He founded the first university, The Academy, in Athens, in 387 B.C. He wrote many important works of philosophy including, the *Dialogues* and the *Republic*. He developed the idea of Reason.

poet laureate The official poet of a country or kingdom; a high honor.

Ponce dé Leon, Juan (1460?-1521) A Spanish explorer, he fought in the war for Granada and went with Columbus on his second voyage to the New World. He conquered several areas of Mexico and was appointed governor. He went on many expeditions searching for treasures and claiming lands until he settled in Puerto Rico, in 1513. Then he sailed to the "island" of Florida. Florida, actually a part of North America, was filled with American Indians who attacked him and his men when they arrived.

Pope Julius II (1443-1513) A nephew of Pope Sixtus IV. His given name was Giuliano della Rovere. He served in the Roman Catholic Church as a Cardinal Priest, a head of the army, and later was a powerful advisor to Pope Sixtus IV and Innocent VIII. After the short reign of Pius III, he was elected as Pope Julius II. He was known as the soldier pope, and widened the Church's influence over Italy and Europe. He was also a patron of Michelangelo and Raphael.

Pope Leo X (1475-1521) First named Giovanni de'Medici, he was the second son of Lorenzo the Magnificent. He served the Roman Catholic Church in many positions, eventually as a cardinal. With the fall of the Medici family, he lived quietly until the death of Julius II, when he was elected as Pope Leo X. He lived a decadent life and was a patron of the arts (he funded both Raphael and Michelangelo, among others) and sciences.

Portugal A country that is bordered on the western and southern side by the Atlantic Ocean, and on the eastern and northern side by Spain. The capital is Lisbon.

privateer A term for a captain or crew member of a privately-owned ship that has been commissioned to fight in a war.

Protestant A western, Christian religion that split from the Roman Catholic Church during the Reformation.

Puerto Rico Currently a commonwealth of the United States, Puerto Rico is an island in the West Indies. Its capital is San Juan. It was a busy center of trade during the Renaissance.

Raphael (1483-1520) An artist considered to be one of the finest in history, known for his sensual and realistic paintings, such as *St. Anthony of Padua*, and many religious paintings, like the Madonnas.

Reformation The term for a religious revolution that took place in Western Europe in the 16th century. It was an effort to reform the Catholic Church to rid it of corrupt men. Part of the reason for this uprising was Martin Luther's *Ninety-Five Theses*. This was the

division that split Christianity into the Roman Catholic Church and the Protestant Church.

Renaissance A period of history marked by a resurgence of interest in the arts, sciences, technology, education, and exploration. Renaissance means "rebirth," and it was a rebirth of interest in the classical ideals of Greece and Rome.

Roman Empire This was a vast empire that extended from England to Babylon (present-day Iraq). The Romans ruled this empire from 27 B.C. to A.D. 476. The Roman Empire was known for its contributions to the arts, languages, and government. Under a series of emperors, Rome at one time influenced or controlled nearly every civilization in the world.

Rome Located in Italy, Rome was the center of the Roman Empire, and is the location of Vatican City and the Pope of the Roman Catholic Church. Legend says Rome was founded by brothers, Romulus and Remus. Rome has been the center of a kingdom, a republic, and an empire.

Russia A country bordered by China, Mongolia, and the Balkans. Russia was an empire united and ruled by czars (tsars), until 1917. Moscow is the capital city. Russia makes up 1/6th of the Earth's land surface.

Scotland Scotland is a political division of Great Britain, and takes up the northern end of the island. The capital city is Edinburgh. Scotland, England, Northern Ireland, and Wales have been united since 1707, under the name of "The United Kingdom."

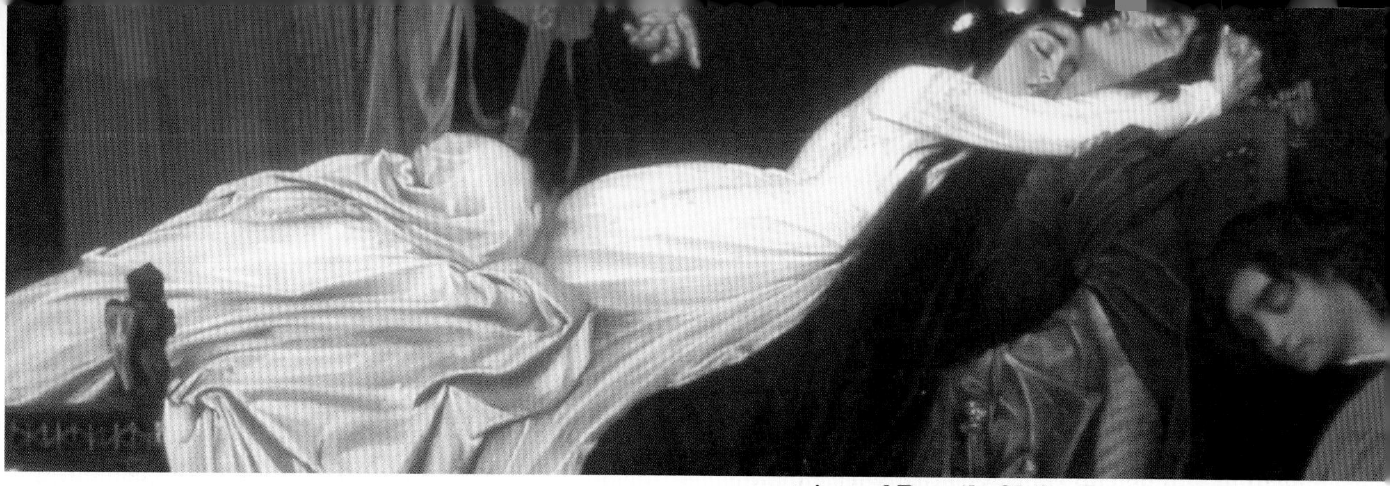

scurvy A disease caused by the severe lack of Vitamin C in the body. It can cause internal hemorrhages, bleeding of the gums, anemia, and weakness. It was especially common among sailors.

Seymour, Jane (1509?-1537) Third queen of, and wife to, Henry VIII. She served as a lady-in-waiting to Henry's two earlier wives. She had a son, Edward VI, but died after childbirth.

Sforza, Francesco (1401-1466) As Duke of Milan, he gained power and took over Genoa. He was a patron of the arts.

Sforza, Ludovico (1451-1508) Youngest son of Francesco Sforza, he took over as Duke of Milan in 1480. He was a patron of the arts, and supported Leonardo da Vinci for over 15 years.

Shakespeare, William (1564-1616) English dramatist, actor, and poet. He is considered the greatest playwright who ever lived. He was born in Stratford-upon-Avon and later lived in London, where he wrote and acted in plays, and managed the Globe theater.

Silk Road A series of long and difficult trade routes, over land, that started in China and led to the Caspian Sea. There, ships transported the goods throughout Europe and the Mediterranean. It was in use approximately from c. 140 BC to the 1500's.

South America South America is the fourth largest continent. It is made up of the modern countries of Brazil, Chile, Peru, and others.

Spain Europe's fourth largest country. For many years, Spain was home to tribes and was, once a part of the Roman Empire. Later, the country was under a monarchy aligned with the Roman Catholic Church. During the Middle Ages, Spain was under Muslim control.

Spanish Inquisition A separate offshoot of the Medieval Inquisition, the Spanish Inquisition lasted from 1478-1834. Its goal was to find and punish Jews and Muslims who practiced their outlawed religion in secret. It was highly organized, effective, and dangerous.

Spice Islands A group of Indonesian islands in the Pacific. The Spice Islands were the original source of nutmeg and cloves, as well as other

...e Seymour Queen.

spices. They were first colonized by Portugal, then the Dutch, in the 17th century.

tapestries Hand-woven fabric hanging rugs featuring designs or pictures. Tapestries have existed for thousands of years, and reached a high level of artistic beauty by the 15th century.

Torquemada, Tomás de (1420-1498) A Spanish churchman and personal priest to Queen Isabella I. He was appointed Inquisitor General and was the highest authority in the Spanish Inquisition.

Tower of London Built as a royal residence in London, England, in the Middle Ages. It later became a jail. The Tower is surrounded by a dry moat and features three sets of strong thick walls. The Tower was the site of nearly all royal imprisonments and executions. It now serves as a museum and houses a vault where the Crown Jewels of England are kept.

vegetarian Someone who does not eat the meat, blood, milk, eggs, or flesh of animals.

Verrocchio, Andrea del (1435-1488) An Italian sculptor and painter. From Florence, he may have studied with Botticelli under Lippi, and he taught Leonardo da Vinci.

Vespucci, Amerigo (1451?-1512) An Italian navigator who explored and mapped South America's coastline. America is named after him.

Virgil (70-19 B.C.) Born Publius Vergilius Maro, he was a Roman poet and literary figure, considered to have mastered and perfected the art of poetry. His work includes the *Aeneid.*

Art Information and Picture Credits

The sources for the images in this book are set forth below.

FLIGHT 1: p. 1-Courtesy of the Museo dell'Opera del Duomo, Florence. p. 4-Courtesy of the Rijksmuseum, Amsterdam (*left*); courtesy of the Museo Nazionale, Florence (*bottom center*); courtesy of the Galleria degli Uffizi, Florence (*bottom right*).

FLIGHT 2: p. 6-7-Courtesy of the Lady Lever Art Gallery, Birkenhead. p. 10-Courtesy of the Galleria Nazionale delle Marche, Urbino (*top left*); courtesy of the Thyssen Collection, Madrid (*top right*); courtesy of the National Gallery, London (*bottom right*); courtesy of the Musée des Beaux-Arts, Nîmes (*bottom left*).

FLIGHT 3: p. 12-13-Courtesy of the British Rail Pension Trustee Company. p. 16-Courtesy of the Palazzi Vaticani (*top left*).

FLIGHT 4: p. 18-19-Courtesy of the Biblioteca Nazionale Marciana, Venice. p. 22-Courtesy of the Musée des Arts Décoratifs, Paris (*top left*); courtesy of Corpus Christi College, Cambridge (*top right*); courtesy of the National Portrait Gallery, London (*bottom right*).

FLIGHT 5: p. 24-25-Courtesy of the British Museum (*left, right*). p. 28-Courtesy of the Gutenberg Museum, Mainz (*left*).

FLIGHT 6: p. 30-31-Courtesy of the Galleria degli Uffizi, Florence. p. 34-Courtesy of the Galleria degli Uffizi, Florence (*left, top right, bottom right*).

FLIGHT 7: p. 36-37-Courtesy of the Musée Bargoin, Clermont-Ferrand. p. 40-By permission of her Majesty the Queen Elizabeth II, Royal Collection, London (*top left*); courtesy of the Wolverhampton Art Gallery, Westmidlands (*bottom left*).

FLIGHT 8: p. 42-43-Courtesy of the Museo del Prado, Madrid. p. 46-Courtesy of the Musée Conde, Chantilly (*left*); courtesy of the Nuremberg Chronicle, British Library (*top right*); courtesy of the National Library of Austria, Vienna (*bottom left*).

FLIGHT 9: p. 48-49-Courtesy of the Metropolitan Museum of Art, New York (*left*); courtesy of the Museo Civico, Como (*right*). p. 52-Courtesy of the Library of Congress (*top right*); courtesy of the National Museum of American Art, Washington D.C. (*bottom right*).

FLIGHT 10: p. 54-55-Courtesy of the Musée du Louvre, Paris (*left*); courtesy of the Biblioteca Reale, Turin (*top right*); Courtesy of the British Museum (*bottom right*); Courtesy of the Galleria Nazionale, Parma (*bottom, left of center*). p. 58-Courtesy of the Musée du Louvre, Paris (left); courtesy of the Windsor Castle Royal Library (*upper right*); courtesy of the Galleria degli Uffizi, Florence (*lower right*).

FLIGHT 11: p. 60-61-Courtesy of the Biblioteca Ambrosiana, Milan (*center*). p. 64-Courtesy of the Windsor Castle Royal Library (*top right*).

FLIGHT 12: p. 68-69-Courtesy of the V & A Picture Library, London (*left*); courtesy of the Metropolitan Museum of Art, New York (*right*). p. 72-Courtesy of J.C. Revy and P. H. Bourseiller (*top left*); courtesy of the Cleveland Museum of Art (*top right*); courtesy of the British Library, London (*bottom left*).

FLIGHT 13: p. 74-75-Courtesy of the Metropolitan Museum of Art, New York. p. 78-Courtesy of the Musëum für Kunst und Gewerbe, Hamburg (*top left*); courtesy of the British Museum (*top right*).

FLIGHT 14: p. 84-85-Courtesy of the National Archives of Canada (*top left*); courtesy of the Library of Congress Rare Book and Special Collections Division (*top right*); courtesy of the Musée du Louvre, Paris (*bottom right*); courtesy of the Gold Museum, Bogotá (*bottom left*).

FLIGHT 15: p. 86-87-Courtesy of St. John's Basilica, Torun (*left*). p. 90-Courtesy of the Copernicus Society, Washington D.C. (*top right*); courtesy of the Science and Society Picture Library, Science Museum (*bottom right*).

FLIGHT 16: p. 92-93-Courtesy of the Palazzi Vaticani, Rome; p. 96-Courtesy of the Metropolitan Museum of Art, New York (*top left*); courtesy of the Palazzi Vaticani, Rome (*top right, bottom right*); courtesy of the Galleria degli Uffizi, Florence (*left*).

FLIGHT 17: p. 98-99-Courtesy of the Medici Chapel (*right*). p. 102-Courtesy of the Palazzi Vaticani, Rome (*top right*); courtesy of the Medici Chapel (*bottom right*).

FLIGHT 18: p. 104-105-Courtesy of the Duke of Alba; courtesy of the Northwest Picture Archives (*inset*). p.108-Courtesy of the British Museum, London (*top left*); courtesy of the Uffizi Gallery (*top right*); courtesy of the American Geographical Society Collection (*bottom right*).

FLIGHT 19: p. 110-111-Courtesy of the Pinacoteca Vaticana (*top left*); courtesy of the Gemäldegalerie, Dresden (*top right*); courtesy of the Palazzi Vaticani, Rome (*bottom right*); courtesy of the Washington National Gallery (*bottom right*); courtesy of the Palazzo Pitti, Florence (*center*). p. 114-Courtesy of the Palazzo Pitti, Florence (*left*); courtesy of the Palazzi Vaticani, Rome (*bottom right*); courtesy of the Musée du Louvre, Paris (*bottom left*).

Art Information and Picture Credits

Flight 20: p. 116-117-Courtesy of the Kurpfatzisches Museum, Heidelberg (*left*); courtesy of the Galleria degli Uffizi, Florence (*right*); courtesy of the National Portrait Gallery, London (*top left*); courtesy of the Staatsbibliothek, Berlin (*bottom left*); courtesy of the Museo del Prado, Madrid (*bottom right*).

Flight 21: p. 122-123-Courtesy of the Kunsthistorisches Museum, Vienne (*top left*); by gracious permission of Her Majesty, the Queen (*top center*); courtesy of the Bibliothéque Nationale, Paris (*top right*); courtesy of the Museé du Louvre, Paris (*bottom left*); by gracious permission of Her Majesty, the Queen (*bottom center*); courtesy of the National Portrait Gallery, London (*bottom right*); courtesy of the Thyssen Collection, Madrid (*far right*). p. 126-Courtesy of the Galleria Nazionale d'Arte Antica, Rome (*top right*); courtesy of the Mansell Collection (*bottom left*).

Flight 22: p. 132—Courtesy of the Bodleian Library, England *(upper left)*; courtesy of the New York Public Library, New York *(near right)*; courtesy of the British Museu, London *(lower center)*; courtesy of the Museo del Ejército, Madrid *(lower left)*.

Flight 23: p. 140-141-Courtesy of the Museo del Prado, Madrid (*left*); courtesy of the National Maritime Museum, Greenwich (*bottom right*).

Flight 24: p. 146-147-Courtesy of the Bodleian Library (*top left*); courtesy of the New York Public Library (*top center*); courtesy of the British Museum (*bottom right, bottom center*); courtesy of the Museo del Ejército, Madrid (*bottom left*).

Flight 25: p. 152-Courtesy of the Galleria Statale Tret Jakov, Moscow (*top left*).

Flight 26: p. 154-155-Courtesy of the National Trust Photographic Library, London; courtesy of the National Portrait Gallery, London; courtesy of the Marquess of Tavistock and the Trustees of the Bedford Estates; courtesy of the Duke of Portland; courtesy of the Royal Collection; courtesy of the Marquess of Salisbury (*clockwise from far left*).

Flight 27: p. 164-Courtesy of the Plymouth Museum (*top left*); courtesy of the National Maritime Museum (*top right*); courtesy of Northwest Picture Archives (*bottom right*).

Flight 28: p. 166-167-Courtesy of the National Maritime Museum, Greenwich. p. 170-Courtesy of the National Maritime Museum, Greenwich (*left, bottom right*); courtesy of the British Library (*top right*).

Flight 29: p. 172-173-Courtesy of the Galleria d'Arte Moderna, Florence. p. 176-Courtesy of the Scottish National Portrait Gallery, Edinburgh (*top left*); courtesy of the National Library of Scotland (*top right*); courtesy of the His Grace the Duke of Norfolk (*bottom left*).

Flight 30: p.178-179-Courtesy of the Hatfield House (*left*); courtesy of the Victoria & Albert Museum (*right*). p. 182-Courtesy of the British Museum, London (*top right, bottom*).

Flight 31: p. 184-185-Courtesy of Agnes Scott College, Decatur; p. 188-Courtesy of the Victoria & Albert Museum, London (*top right*); courtesy of private collection (*bottom right*); courtesy of the Forbes Magazine Collection, New York (*bottom left*).

Flight 32: p. 194-195-Courtesy of the Inst. Valencia D. Juan (*top left*); courtesy of the Musée des Beaux Arts, Dijon (*bottom right*).

Mary I (Bloody Mary); an illustration from Chaucer's *The Canterbury Tales*

Flight 33: p. 196-197-Courtesy of private collection. p. 200-Courtesy of the Musée du Louvre (*top left*); courtesy of the Gelleria degli Uffinzi, Florence (*top right*); courtesy of the Biblioteca Nazionale, Florence (*bottom right*); courtesy of the Museo di Storia della Scienza, Florence (*bottom left*).

Flight 29: p. 172-173-Courtesy of the Galleria d'Arte Moderna, Florence. p. 176-Courtesy of the Scottish National Portrait Gallery, Edinburgh (*top left*); courtesy of the National Library of Scotland (*top right*); courtesy of the His Grace the Duke of Norfolk (*bottom left*).

Flight 30: p.178-179-Courtesy of the Hatfield House (*left*); courtesy of the Victoria & Albert Museum (*right*). p. 182-Courtesy of the British Museum, London (*top right, bottom*).

Flight 31: p. 184-185-Courtesy of Agnes Scott College, Decatur; p. 188-Courtesy of the Victoria & Albert Museum, London (*top right*); courtesy of private collection (*bottom right*); courtesy of the Forbes Magazine Collection, New York (*bottom left*).

Flight 32: p. 194-195-Courtesy of the Inst. Valencia D. Juan (*top left*); courtesy of the Musée des Beaux Arts, Dijon (*bottom right*).

Flight 33: p. 196-197-Courtesy of private collection. p. 200-Courtesy of the Musée du Louvre (*top left*); courtesy of the Gelleria degli Uffinzi, Florence (*top right*); courtesy of the Biblioteca Nazionale, Florence (*bottom right*); courtesy of the Museo di Storia della Scienza, Florence (*bottom left*).

Above: p. 216-Courtesy of Fitzwilliam Museum, Cambridge (*top left*); courtesy of private collection (*top right*).

Design Information

Type set throughout this book includes Century Book (general text), Clearface (Ivan text), and Futura (timeline text and some headings).

Series Book Design by:
Pierre Rademaker Design

Book Design by:
Valarie Jones

Ivan Illustrations by:
Henry Santos

Original Art Concept of Ivan by:
Phyllis Lindamood